T0347399

Contemporary Minority Nationalism

Minority nationalism is a significant not to say potent force in the modern world. In many countries, not least among the richer developed ones, West or East, new problems of and for minority nationalism have recently surfaced. This book presents a wide-ranging examination of the state of minority nationalism in the 1970s and 1980s. It considers many different cases in detail: Britain, Ireland, the Soviet Union, Canada, France, Spain and South Africa. It explores the political and socio-economic circumstances surrounding minority nationalism, analyses its successes and failures in recent times and looks at an exhaustive range of issues: structures and policies of minority nationalist movements, relations with government, ideology, attitude to human rights, and so on. Interestingly, it views Afrikaners in South Africa and Protestants in Northern Ireland as cases of minority nationalists in dominant positions now having to pay for the 'success' of their particular, xenophobic brand of nationalism. Finally, it charts a possible way forward for minority nationalism in advanced democratic, or democratising, systems.

The editor

Michael Watson is Senior Lecturer in Politics in the Department of International Politics, University College of Wales at Aberystwyth. He is the author of *Regional Dev lopment Policy and Administration in Italy*; co-editor (with J.E.S. Hayward) of *Planning, Politics and Public Policy*; and author of a variety of articles for journals and chapters in edited books on the politics of planning, regional development and regionalism.

Contemporary Minority Nationalism

Edited by

Michael Watson

London and New York

First published 1990
by Routledge
2 Park Square, Milton Park, Abingdon, Oxon, OX14 4RN

Simultaneously published in the USA and Canada
by Routledge
270 Madison Ave, New York NY 10016
Routledge is an imprint of the Taylor & Francis Group
Reprinted 1992, 2001, 2002

Transferred to Digital Printing 2007

© 1990 Michael Watson

Laserset by LaserScript Limited, Mitcham, Surrey

British Library Cataloguing in Publication Data

Contemporary minority nationalism.
   1. Nationalism
   I. Watson, Michael
   320.54

   ISBN 0-415-00065-3

Library of Congress Cataloging in Publication Data

Contemporary minority nationalism / edited by Michael Watson.
     p. cm.
   Includes bibliographical references.
   ISBN 0-415-00065-3
   1. Nationalism. 2. Ethnic groups—Political activity.
   3. Minorities—Political activity. I. Watson, Michael, 1983–
   JC311.C647 1990
   320.5'4—dc20   90-8248
                                                            CIP

Publisher's Note
The publisher has gone to great lengths to ensure the quality of this
reprint but points out that some imperfections in the original
may be apparent

Contents

Contents

Tables

Contributors

Dr Michael Watson is Senior Lecturer in the Department of International Politics, University College of Wales where he teaches Comparative Politics. He obtained his Ph.D. (Wales) for a study of French regional policy, planning and institutions. He has previously published in the field of national planning and regional development in Western Europe, including (ed. with J.E.S. Hayward) *Planning, Politics and Public Policy* and most recently in *Regionalisation in France, Spain and Italy* (eds. Hebbert and Machin).

Dr Denis Balsom is Senior Research Associate in the Department of International Politics, University College of Wales, Aberystwyth. He is a graduate of the University of Wales, is a former Director of the Welsh Election Study and has published widely on Welsh politics and electoral behaviour.

Dr George Boyce graduated from the Queen's University, Belfast. He worked for three years in the Department of Western Manuscripts, Bodleian Library, Oxford. He is now Reader in the Department of Political Theory and Government, University College, Swansea. His books include *Englishmen and Irish Troubles : British Public Opinion and the Making of Irish Policy, 1918–1922*, *Nationalism in Ireland*, and *The Revolution in Ireland, 1879–1923*.

Dr Jack Brand was born and brought up in Scotland, but has worked in Sweden and the United States. He is currently Senior Lecturer in Politics in the University of Strathclyde and his main interests are nationalism and the distribution of power and political parties. He has also been involved with the study of Spanish politics and especially the politics of Catalonia.

Dr John Dreijmanis holds the degrees of B.A., Suffolk University, M.A., Boston College, and D.Phil., Potchefstroom. He has taught at several American and Canadian universities and recently has been a visiting researcher attached to the Division for Political Science research at the Human Sciences Research Council in Pretoria. His publications include *Government Coalitions in Western Democracies*, and *The Role of the South African Government in Tertiary Education* plus over twenty articles and conference papers. His main research interests are coalitions, South African politics and tertiary education policy.

Dr Peter J.S. Duncan is Lecturer in Contemporary Soviet Economic and Social Policy at the School of Slavonic and East European Studies, University of London. Previously he taught at the University of Glasgow and the University College of Wales, Aberystwyth, and worked on the Soviet Foreign Policy Programme at the Royal Institute of International Affairs. He is the author of *The Soviet Union and India* (Routledge, 1989) and co-editor of *Soviet–British Relations* since the 1970s (C.U.P., 1990).

Dr Jean Grugel is a Lecturer in Politics at York University. She received a Ph.D. from the Department of Political Theory and Institutions, Liverpool University in 1986 with a thesis on nationalism and populism in Chile, and has published articles on Spanish, Chilean and Argentine politics. She has carried out research into Spanish foreign policy at the Universidad Complutense de Madrid and is currently working on right-wing movements in Latin America.

Dr Michael Keating, M.A. (Oxon), Ph.D. (CNAA) is Professor of Political Science at the University of Western Ontario. His previous appointments were at the Universities of Strathclyde and Essex, and North Staffordshire Polytechnic. He is author or co-author of nine books and numerous articles on urban and regional politics. His most recent book is *Nations, Regions and the State: Territorial Politics in the United Kingdom, France, Italy and Spain*.

Dr Michael Macmillan is Associate Professor of Political Studies at Mount Saint Vincent University in Halifax, Nova Scotia, Canada. He was born in Parrsboro, Nova Scotia in 1950. He obtained his B.A. at the University of New Brunswick and completed his M.A. and Ph.D. at the University of Minnesota. He has published several articles on language rights and language conflict in the Quebec and Canadian settings. He is currently preparing a book on the theory and practice of language rights in Canada.

Dr Simon Murphy obtained his Ph.D. at University College of Wales in 1986 on Conflict and Conflict Regulation in Northern Ireland. He gave a paper to the International Conference on Peace Studies and Conflict Resolution at the University of the South Pacific, Fiji, in January, 1986. He has published 'The Northern Ireland Conflict 1968–1982: British and Irish Perspectives' in *Conflict*, Vol.7. no.3. He now works as Political Assistant to the MEP for the West Midlands.

Dr Peter Savigear is Senior Lecturer in the Department of Politics at Leicester University. His research interests include European politics, particularly France, and international relations. He has written several articles on French history and politics in British and continental journals. His most recent publication is a book entitled, *Cold War or Détente in the 1980's: the international politics of American-Soviet relations.*

Vaughan Rogers is a graduate of Stirling University and taught at Loughborough for two years in European Studies before being appointed in 1983 to develop the study of contemporary French society and politics in the Department of French at Edinburgh. He has written on theoretical models of centre-periphery relations, French regionalisation, and Breton nationalism; publications dealing with the last two are in *Politics*, April 1984, and in *Inequality and Inequalities in France*, ed. P. Morris.

Dr Howard Williams is a graduate of the University of London and obtained his Ph.D. at Durham in Political Theory in 1975. He has lectured at University College, Bangor, and since 1979 at University College of Wales, Aberystwyth, being promoted to Senior Lecturer in 1988. He has written *Marx, Kant's Political Philosophy, Heraclitus, Hegel and Marx's Dialectic* and *Concepts of Ideology*. Research interests: political theory, German idealism, Marxism and methods of political science.

Acknowledgements

I would like to thank the Nuffield Foundation for a grant of £1,000 for the conference, held in November 1986 at Gregynog Hall, which initially brought the contributors to this book together to discuss the 1980s experience of minority nationalism. I also wish to thank Mrs Susan Davies for her sterling work in typing and preparing the manuscript, and also my wife for assistance in proof-reading.

Introduction

Michael Watson

This book has arisen from a proposal, launched at a University of Wales conference at Gregynog in November 1986, to bring together the contributions of a number of specialists interested in reviewing and reappraising minority nationalism as the decade of the 1980s moved towards its close. It was felt that thee 1980s were proving a significant decade for minority nationalism, though probably in a differet way from the 1960s and 1970s, when it had erupted on the political scene and strongly impressed academic, political and public opinion. It was time to examine what had been happening in the 1980s and in particular how minority nationalism had responded to changing circumstances and conditions. Had developments shed new light on its political and ideological nature, role and significance? There was a feeling that the 1960s and 1970s view of it, which generally stressed its importance and positive character, was in need of revision or at least reconsideration. The undeniable success of the 1960s and 1970s, which had shaken not only fashionable political integration theories but existing political structures, had given way to a decade of questioning, not to say doubt, about minority nationalism's future; it seemed to have fallen out of favour in public, and academic, opinion. How far was this really so? And why should it be?

In seeking answers to the sorts of questions and issues identified above, it was thought worthwhile to cast the net rather wider than the principal 1970s focus on Western Europe and Quebec, itself justified by minority nationalism's phoenix-like resurgence there. A certain similarity of context is maintained by drawing on cases from economically advanced, industrialised countries with well-established state systems (rather than comparatively new states of the developing world). Moreover, we are dealing with a 'European-type' nationalism even when we go further afield, and certainly with Western nationalism in Plamenatz's categorisation.[1] All the nationalisms studied have deep historical roots in respect of distinctive cultural[2], institutional, not to say (at some period) political embodiments of the minority in question; they

1

are thus differentiated from those concerned with 'nation-building' in new states[3], even if sometimes preoccupied with national reawakening. In considering these minority nationalisms, we have not been concerned with whether such political movements are 'really' nationalist or 'really' regionalist; or whether these undoubted minorities, in their respective states, are 'authentic' nations. The movements certainly see themselves as nationalist and are generally regarded as such (with the Northern Irish Unionists it is not now so clear whether this is in the sense of 'British' nationalism or of Ulster nationalism, a question with which Chapter 3 deals).

A range of cases is presented in which the term 'minority nationalism' can be justifiably and significantly applied to a political movement, according to widespread designation. Minority nationalism can, as in Scotland or Wales, be very largely identified with a single party; equally, as other chapters reveal, it can encompass a number of parties; and it may also find significant expression in cultural, socio-economic or para-military groups. Our focus is on parties as the prime political expression of minority nationalism (the USSR is, evidently, an exception to this). We recognise that not all parts of every movement, such as individual parties or groups, consider themselves out-and-out nationalists, in the sense of demanding an independent state. There is clearly in practice a continuum between those who will not accept anything less than independence and full political sovereignty and those ready to settle for autonomy within the existing state; these may, indeed, be regarded as regionalists. However, the basic meaning of autonomy is complete 'home-rule', that is political power in the full range of domestic or internal governmental functions, while leaving external political and economic relations, and defence, to the existing central authorities. If this is regionalism, it is thus a maximalist one. Indeed, both ends of the continuum are pursuing self-determination or self-government for the territorial minority, but in one case completely and in the other in respect of most, but not all, governmental powers. Gellner has put it as wanting, in their turn, to have their own political roof.[4] In terms of constitutional arrangements, autonomy points to some form of federalism, most likely of a 'classical' sort[5] in which the legislative and judicial powers of both government levels are co-ordinate – but maybe even points to confederalism, with the central authority derived from and responsible to the component state governments.

Autonomists thus have much in common with separatists in the ends they defend. But in reality the continuum is wider, in that a minority nationalist movement, or at any rate a significant part of it, may in its practical politics adopt a stance of pursuing, or at least working with, less than full autonomy (such as the Basque Nationalist Party). Of course, any particular movement is for the most part only concerned with the political status of its own nation; however, in practice it will very likely be in a situation in which there are others in the state seeking varying degrees of political power for their territories, if only as regions on a local-government model, and still others, notably parties, advocating a generalised devolution of power of that sort or on a federal basis. Thus the minority nationalist movement will be pushed to take cognisance of the range of constitutional and political options available and probably to dealing with other political forces, not to say government, in these terms. How circumstances have evolved in these respects in the 1980s, how movements have been affected by them and the direction they have moved in, are clearly of major interest.

The country chapters elucidate a variety of cases of minority nationalism, which show its different faces and the different situations – political, cultural and social – in which it finds itself. The specific focus is the 'ism', rather than the minorities as such, and its contemporary political embodiment and expression(s) in each instance. The spectrum of ideological and political options portrayed is wide and the 1980s have seen a number of significant developments in this respect, affecting most movements studied. While we hope that the range covered has major interest in its own right, on an *à la carte* basis if so desired, it also enables the phenomenon to be seen in a wider and more revealing perspective (beyond the rather cosy, generally liberal if not progressive, view taken of it in the 1970s, based largely on the Scottish and Welsh, Basque and Catalan, Quebec and Breton cases).

The minority nationalisms studied are to be found occupying different political, governmental and strategic circumstances. Notably, some have never achieved any political power in the sense of governmental office (namely those in Britain and France); while others have experienced major governmental responsibility, either (the Québécois and Basques) at an intermediate level in a federal or devolved system, or (the Afrikaners) in wielding full state power (effectively so too, for many years, for the Unionists in running Northern Ireland – so that Dr Boyce can refer to the Northern Irish state and its essential Unionist nature); and yet another case is that of the USSR where minority nationalism is not normally manifested, but is implicitly recognised in the respective Republics' provisions, constitutionally backed, for the national minority's culture (not to say in the practical exercise of a Republic's government) and can also erupt from time to time on a populist basis in a given instance or instances. These different circumstances in relation to political power contribute to the variety of minority nationalisms considered. We can see how their recent development, and the problems in which they are involved, are related in certain respects at least to these circumstances, and see what the 'latest twist of the dialectic' is in respect of the interplay with political power; further light is thereby thrown on their respective political and ideological natures, and thus of minority nationalism's potentialities in general in this sense. We think that a more complete picture emerges of 'advanced' minority nationalism and its recent impact and evolution (which indeed confirms a wide spread of political and ideological options and adaptations to changing situations, the latter affected in part at least by minority nationalism's greater salience whether as power wielder or challenger).

By bringing in South Africa and the USSR, and including both Northern Irish communities, particularly significant aspects of the minority nationalist experience are encompassed, giving, we believe, a completeness to our portrayal of the 'ism's' contemporary manifestation in well-established economically advanced states (this may be interpreted as being so, to an important extent, because they are not politically 'advanced' systems). In any case, South Africa, with the Afrikaners' domination of political power under increased challenge, has spotlighted media and public attention on another, less agreeable 'face' of minority nationalism. To get behind this 'face' and analyse the complexities of the situation and evolution of Afrikaner nationalism is thus all the more important; not least, it is, presumptively, a cautionary tale of when a minority nationalism achieves striking political 'success'. Recent developments in the USSR point to its different yet still important role where political domination is in other hands, ones which are, however, seeking to introduce some life, into what is viewed as a sclerotic system. Other qualities of minority nationalism have been brought home by the intractability of the Northern Ireland 'problem' in respect of any agreed solution (or indeed any solution other than the current military holding operation under direct British rule). But even there another possibility, in which minority nationalism is not for nothing, may be on the cards, if only as yet rather faintly inscribed (as Chapter 3, Section 2 suggests); in this, Ulster would largely go its own way, though one could only envisage it with safeguards for the way of life of both minority peoples constitutionally enshrined and within the context of a wider British Isles and/or European political structure of a confederal or federal nature.

This variety of cases does clearly indicate the problematical, not to say paradoxical, side of minority nationalism. In its resurgence in Europe (including the USSR) and North America it has proclaimed itself (and is largely viewed) as a progressive force, notably in the assertion of political and civil, not to say human, rights, of democracy and of cultural expression and pluralism. Nevertheless it can, in so-called 'advanced' countries, harbour dangers for these very values, exhibiting the 'negative' nationalist traits of authoritarianism, intolerance, repression, xenophobia, even recidivism; and these seem to come to the fore when political domination is acquired – and then threatened – and to be all the worse for the domination being wielded by what is a minority in the state. Of course, the role of ideology is not to be minimised in this; for some minority nationalists at least it is clearly central to their behaviour and action (including – the opposite case – when they are outside the established political process). On the other hand, minority nationalist ideology cannot be regarded as inherently fated to be extremist, whether reactionary or revolutionary, or necessarily the determining factor in nationalist politics. Elucidation of such matters is justification for our basic concern with the ideological tendencies and their recent evolution in the difficult times of the 1980s for all the minority nationalisms under consideration (Afrikaner nationalism, as a limiting case, appears to be becoming less monolithic). Some 'loosening' – if not in some cases such as the Afrikaners or Unionists some 'cracking' – of the movement in its beliefs and attitudes, may well be a condition of a progressive development of the ideology, away from its most archaic forms. Minority nationalist ideology, as the Conclusion argues, also needs development (which is not to say simply the adoption of pragmatism). Isolation of extremists certainly has its costs, but ultimately it paves the way for a full and effective insertion of minority nationalism in democratic politics (the Basque movement, for example, provides some evidence of this).

In the treatment of the various nationalisms there has been no attempt to lay down a detailed, rigid framework of themes or issues; it would be too reductionist of a complex phenomenon. This is so, notably, in respect of the attention devoted to historical explanation, which occupies a larger place in some accounts where authors have judged it necessary because of its bearing on the contemporary situation; in other instances, consideration of contemporary developments needed, it was felt, much less supporting by a historical backdrop (in part, though only in part, because these may be considered more familiar in the light of accounts of the 1970s). However, in all cases the basic purpose is to take the 'story' forward and to explain and account for what has happened in the 1980s, set in particular against the 1960s/1970s picture (which is generally examined in the first part of the Conclusion). The sea change in nationalist fortunes and circumstances is thus central to the book's agenda. This leads to a number of broad concerns, which can receive different emphases according to the particular case. There are the new conditions and challenges faced in the 1980s, including the political shift to the right in many countries, the preoccupation with economic problems and their solution by market methods, the retrenchment in social provision and public spending, the growth of violence, and in general a radical confrontation with the political, economic and ideological status quo of the post-1945 era (including in the USSR). What has been minority nationalism's role in these developments, how has it been affected by them, how has it responded?

The changed environment – political, economic, ideological – for minority nationalism in the 1980s has posed distinct problems in relation to its strategy, policy programmes, electoral tactics, not to say ideology. What has been the reaction or outcome? A number of (over-lapping) possibilities seem to present themselves which can be clarified in each case: political and ideological reorientation or retrenchment? pragmatism or dogmatism? a growth in extremism or ascendancy of moderates? greater conflict, division, not to say fragmentation or regrouping and reforging of unity? loss or renewal of political direction, significance and potency? and so on. Of course, the answers may well not be clear-cut; developments may be contradictory, or a continuum rather than an either/or involved. There is undoubtedly a more diverse political picture than in the 1970s – and not simply due to the range of cases. Nevertheless, there is an underlying preoccupation with what has gone wrong. For in general the 1980s have seen a set-back for the minority nationalist cause, especially in its maximalist sense (in which state sovereignty, not to say control of society, is what matters). It is this and its decline as a viable, and worthy, political vehicle – from which its more moderate, devolutionist forms have not been spared – which in the first place attract attention. At the same time, new possibilities and potentialities of a positive sort, as reviewed in the Conclusion, have emerged (and not least under Soviet Communism). Its role remains, at bottom, to speak for and defend its respective national minority and thereby a certain sort of plural, democratic society. But what this means and requires certainly changes with the times. There is no particular reason, as Tarrow found,[6] to believe that central government in a multi-national state is ever likely to regard the interests, or for that matter the survival, of the various nationalities and their cultures within its borders (except, of course, the majority or dominant one) as of overriding importance *per se*, notably in the face of other demands, such as those relating to the economic performance of that state. In these circumstances, beyond the individual cases considered, the book works towards a reinterpretation and reconstitution (in the last three chapters), of minority nationalism's significance and importance, and where its positive contribution to political society lies, in the late twentieth century.

Notes

1. See ch.2 in E. Kamenska (ed.), *Nationalism: the Nature and Evolution of an Idea*, London, 1976.

2. Taken here to encompass language, religion, art, custom, myth and legend.
3. Some Afrikaners seem increasingly to favour a sort of 'nation-building' in South Africa, bringing together the white, and perhaps even the white and coloured, peoples.
4. E. Gellner, *Nations and Nationalism*, Oxford, 1983, pp.1–3.
5. See K.C. Wheare, *Federal Government*, Oxford, 1963.
6. S. Tarrow, P.J. Katzenstein and I. Graziano, *Territorial Politics in Industrial Nations*, New York, 1977, p.236.

Chapter one

Wales

Denis Balsom

In March 1979, the Secretary of State for Wales, Mr John Morris, reacted to the result of the referendum on modest plans for a Welsh assembly, by remarking 'when you see an elephant on your doorstep, you know that it is there'. The rejection of the devolution proposals in Wales was so unequivocal that the prospects for Welsh nationalism might also be inferred to be bleak. The wider impact upon British politics of the referendum result – the fall of the Callaghan government and the subsequent election of Mrs Thatcher – created further circumstances in which the very future of Plaid Cymru might appear extremely problematic.

Although the nationalists could rightly deny paternity of the devolution proposals embodied in the Wales Act 1978, the party had little choice but to campaign on their behalf. Purists within the party argued the case for their rejection, but it seems unlikely that the general public would have understood a boycott, or formal resolution to vote 'No' coming from Plaid Cymru.[1] The demand for greater self-determination for Wales and the future of Plaid Cymru appear inevitably locked together and thus to have sunk in unison. Yet Plaid Cymru displays a resilience and a character that was once described as akin to 'a sturdy dwarf plant'.[2] Even allowing for a somewhat contrived metaphor, this is an accurate analogy of Welsh nationalism and Plaid Cymru's current position in Wales. The roots of nationalism in Wales are strong and enduring, the party is productive and exhibits vitality but its potential for absolute growth remains strangely limited.

Wales in British politics 1925–79

Nationalism in Wales is a pervasive phenomenon. A crowd of 50,000 can spontaneously harmonise and sing *Hen Gwlad Fy Nhadau* to intimidate a visiting English rugby team. An outcry can accompany the appointment of an English MP as the Secretary of State for Wales. The Permanent Secretary of the Welsh Office, the leaders of most public bodies, those appointed as college principals and school headmasters will inevitably be of Welsh origin. The tendency to promote people and things Welsh is so entrenched in most institutions in Wales as to be unremarkable. Yet this penchant for national advancement, or rather 'soft' nationalism, has never been fully transformed into a successful political movement. Formal political nationalism has been articulated in Wales by Plaid Cymru, since its creation in 1925. Plaid Cymru has contested Parliamentary elections and local-government elections largely without widespread success. There have been, however, some spectacular by-elections and other momentary victories. Plaid Cymru has become well entrenched in certain parts of Wales, but across much of the remainder has merely a token presence. Welsh nationalism, defined more broadly, also reveals itself involved in a range of conventional and unconventional political activities but neither Welsh nationalism, nor Plaid Cymru, appear to have fully come to fruition.[3]

Nationalism is not an ideologically rigid doctrine. Plaid Cymru, at the outset, was 'essentially intellectual and moral in outlook and socially conservative. Its principal concerns were the Welsh language, the Welsh identity and Christianity in Wales'.[4] More recently Plaid Cymru's predominant ideological stance has been described as modernist,[5] a mixture of cultural conservatism and innovative social democracy. The evolution of Plaid Cymru's philosophy has owed much to its leadership. The early intellectual leader was Saunders Lewis, an academic and later a distinguished playwright, whilst between 1945 and 1981 the party was led by Gwynfor Evans, a non-conformist, pacifist, lawyer of almost classic Welsh stereotype, save that he acquired the Welsh language as an adult, rather than from birth, and was from a South Wales commercial family. Although Plaid Cymru's ideological stance has recently become more explicitly socialist, its broad outlook has inevitably, at times, been tempered by political expediency and electoral opportunities.

Plaid Cymru has contested elections since 1929, but has only fought every Welsh constituency simultaneously at general elections since 1970. The party has also acted, and campaigned, on a wider political canvas such as resorting to direct action in the burning of the Penyberth R.A.F. bombing school in 1936 and in non-partisan campaigns, such as the Campaign for a Welsh Parliament in the 1950s. Throughout this period, however, Plaid Cymru might be considered to be acting largely as a broad linguistic and cultural pressure group.[6] A more determined party political realism seems to have imbued Plaid Cymru after the 1959 general election and the two decades up to 1979 show considerable advancement and development. Table 1.1 charts Plaid Cymru's electoral record over this period and whilst the total number of votes gained increases dramatically, this remains largely dependent upon the number of candidatures. The high number of lost deposits, where the candidate failed to secure 12.5 per cent of the vote cast, demonstrates that the party remains pitifully weak in many areas of Wales.

Table 1.1 Plaid Cymru's electoral record 1959–79

Year	Cands.	Deposits lost	Votes	% of the vote	MPs elected
1959	20	14	77,571	5.2	0
1964	23	21	69,507	4.8	0
1966	20	18	61,071	4.3	0
1970	36	25	175,016	11.5	0
1974F	36	26	171,364	10.7	2
1974O	36	27	166,321	10.8	3
1979	36	29	132,544	8.1	2

Plaid Cymru's growing political professionalism, and indeed electoral success, also led to an ideological shift away from narrowly defined nationalism, which usually expressed itself through linguistic or cultural concerns, to a broader economic and social philosophy.[7] In this transformation they were undoubtedly aided by the creation, in 1962, of Cymdeithas yr Iaith, the Welsh Language Society.[8] Cymdeithas yr Iaith was able to pursue a far less inhibited campaign regarding the politics of the Welsh language and numerous legal and illegal activities have been undertaken. These have been largely obstructive and, whilst retaining a strict code of personal non-violence, often destructive of private property. As a result many members of the Society have received prison sentences. This division of labour, within the nationalist community, did not absolve Plaid Cymru of concern for the Welsh language; it did however facilitate a public debate concerning cultural affairs in Wales for which Plaid Cymru, for once, was not the sole protagonist. Cymdeithas yr Iaith's greatest achievement, perhaps, was to raise general consciousness regarding the Welsh language and, through being formally non-partisan, respective administrations in the Welsh Office were able to respond to demands outside of the normal conventions of adversarial party politics. Considerable advances have been made in the provision of Welsh-medium services throughout Wales in the period under review.

Plaid Cymru's greatest breakthrough came with the victory of Gwynfor Evans at the Carmarthen by-election, 14th July 1966. Although it has been argued that the essential transformation within Plaid Cymru pre-dates this election,[9] the public impact of Plaid's success at Carmarthen was immense. Since that date, Plaid Cymru has maintained a presence in Welsh politics far in excess of that warranted by their real electoral strength. Further spectacular by-elections were fought in Rhondda West, Caerphilly and Merthyr Tydfil; in each case very substantial Labour majorities were slashed, without being overturned. Furthermore at subsequent elections the Plaid presence appeared to have become established and electoral success followed at local level, for example, in both Merthyr Tydfil and Caerphilly (Table 1.2). Welsh by-elections have not been frequent, however, and Plaid Cymru's ability to maximise these opportunities when they arise appeared to have dissipated by the time of the Gower by-election in 1982 and the Cynon Valley election in 1984. Both these seats had considerable potential for Plaid Cymru, but this was not mobilised. At Brecon and Radnor in 1985, although an unpromising seat, the party's showing was minimal.

Table 1.2 Plaid Cymru's by-election record 1966–85

Constituency	Date	% poll at previous general election	% poll at by-election	% poll at next gen. election
Carmarthen	7/66	16.1	39.0	30.1
Rhondda W.	3/67	8.7	39.9	14.0
Caerphilly	7/68	11.1	40.4	29.5
M. Tydfil	4/72	9.6	37.0	22.9
Gower	9/82	7.2	8.7	3.2
C. Valley	3/84	9.3	10.9	6.7
Brecon and Radnor	7/85	1.7	1.1	1.4

The surge of nationalist support in Wales, and more importantly, in Scotland, created a delicate Parliamentary balance at the 1974 elections. Initially two Welsh and seven Scottish Nationalists were returned to a House without an overall majority. Subsequently three Welsh and eleven Scottish Nationalists were returned in October to a House of Commons with a barely sustainable majority. Indeed, Labour were only able to continue in office after 1978 courtesy of the Lib–Lab pact. In this Parliamentary impasse attention came to focus upon the introspective issue of devolution for Scotland and Wales rather than upon the more usual diet of inter-party conflict. The background to, and Parliamentary progress of, the devolution proposals contained in the Wales Act 1978 are well known.[10] Of note here, however, is that poor party discipline and the delicate party balance at Westminster denied Wales, and Scotland, an administrative and political reform which, under the normal political conventions of the British constitution, they might have expected. For indeed not only did the manifesto of the victorious party at the October 1974 election contain such a pledge, but all parties campaigned on a promise of some such reform. Instead the electorate of Wales and Scotland were granted direct participation in the implementation of this policy via a referendum.

The referendum was defeated, a general election ensued and Britain embarked on what was to become a sustained period of government from a Conservative Party noticeably more ideological and doctrinaire than seen in Britain for many generations. In such a context the future for the distinctiveness of Welsh politics, let alone Welsh nationalism now, with hindsight, looked bleak and yet:

> Welsh politics retain all their complexity and charm, appropriate for a nation most dedicated to radical change yet most hidebound by immemorial tradition.[11]

The changing face of Welsh politics

Far from being the high point of an era of nationalism anticipated by K.O. Morgan,[12] the defeat of the referendum in March 1979 provided a cruel anti-climax. Indeed for some 'Welsh Politics had ceased to exist'.[13] Even from such a set-back, Plaid Cymru might have salvaged some consolation had the detailed pattern of results revealed pockets of support. They did not: neither geographically nor within significant social groups. For although the proportion supporting devolution was markedly higher in Gwynedd than in Gwent, to lose the referendum by a margin of 2:1 in the heartland of Welsh speaking Wales, and in Plaid Cymru's Parliamentary constituencies, still offered little prospect for building future success. Sociologically, devolution did not enjoy the majority support of any group within the population when classified by either sex, age, socio-economic status, language or party affiliation, save for the overwhelming proportion of Plaid Cymru's own supporters.[14]

Thus, to the extent that the debate over devolution can be seen as a surrogate for the nationalist quest, the outcome from 1979 appeared bleak. Furthermore, due to divisions within the Labour Party, ostensible public leadership of the anti-devolutionists had fallen to the Conservatives. This opportunity was well taken, giving the party a status and relevance to Wales that had not been enjoyed for many years. The referendum results also showed that the Conservatives had clearly 'won' this electoral battle and were much closer to the prevalent mood of the Welsh public. Clearly such an analysis is flawed and the role of the rebel Labour MPs in the anti-devolution campaign should not be underestimated, but even so, the Conservatives were able to seize a valuable initiative which was soon to bear fruit.

As a direct consequence of the referendum, the Callaghan administration was forced to a confidence motion in the House of Commons, which it lost and a general election was called. The Conservatives increased their support in Wales at this election by 25 per cent and returned eleven Members to Parliament. Plaid Cymru lost one of their MPs, Gwynfor Evans at Carmarthen, saw their total vote decline by 30,000 and slip to a mere 8 per cent of the total vote cast. Labour's support held up well in aggregate, in contrast to other parts of Britain, although they lost Brecon and Radnor in the face of, not only a strong Conservative candidate, but also long-term structural socio-economic change and minor boundary revisions. Flushed with this success, a Junior Minister at the Welsh Office was able to boast of being able to drive from the Severn Bridge to Holyhead without leaving Tory-held territory.[15] A more measured analyst, Ivor Crewe, writing in *The Times House of Commons*, was able to conclude '...Class appears to have replaced chapel and language as the main source of partisan allegiance in rural Wales...'.[16] If this were to be so, a fundamental challenge was being mounted to the conventional explanation of support for Plaid Cymru. A challenge, however, which might enable the party to throw off the yoke of having mere cultural salience and grasp at issues closer to the prevailing concerns of British electoral politics.

The 1979 election brought Mrs Thatcher to power in Britain on a programme likely to have an especially significant impact upon Wales. It has been estimated that, in 1979, Wales had the highest proportion of its workforce employed in the public sector of any economy west of the Iron Curtain. Although the period since the Second World War had already seen major transformation of the economy, especially that based upon coal in South Wales, the arrival in office of a government committed to reducing public expenditure, the privatisation of public assets and to nurturing the enterprise culture, was likely to be of great consequence for Wales.

Following the election, Michael Foot replaced Mr Callaghan as leader of the Labour Party. But the party, rather than attend to its recent electoral rebuff, seemed more concerned with internal strife, out of which, in the end, was born the Social Democratic Party (SDP). Three Labour MPs in Wales transferred their loyalties to the new party but, in contrast to some other parts of the country, the Labour Party in Wales seemed relatively untroubled by either the infiltration of extremists and the Militant Tendency or by the defection of long-standing MPs to the fledgling new party. The overwhelming impact upon Wales during the 1979–83 period, however, was one of economic turmoil: massive redundancies in steelmaking, the retraction of manufacturing industry,

13

further reductions in coal-mining and the very slow process of job creation in newer, technologically more sophisticated sectors. Such jobs as were created have also tended to employ a higher proportion of women than hitherto, have weaker trade-union structures and consequently depart radically from the traditional stereotyped view of the Welsh working-class community. Such root and branch socio-economic change was bound to have further political consequences.

A related implication of this economic and social upheaval was the degree of population movement. Traditional communities were in decline, the developing locations were in the major cities and in sites adjacent to better communications, such as North-east Wales and the M4 corridor. The review of parliamentary boundaries undertaken at this time reflected this shift, as well as allocating two new constituencies to Wales. Thirty-eight seats now represented Wales at Westminster with a much higher proportion of them being politically competitive rather than being expected to return large safe majorities.

Although Mrs Thatcher went to the country in 1983, flushed with victory in the Falklands engagement, there was little to suggest that her image as a firm leader would prove especially electorally advantageous in Wales. Yet the Conservatives won fourteen seats, their highest total this century, whilst the Labour Party slipped to 20 MPs and 47.5 per cent of the poll, their lowest since the First World War (Table 1.3). Plaid Cymru support remained largely static in aggregate, but showed signs of becoming increasingly concentrated in Gwynedd. In the course of the campaign, the newly founded Alliance picked up support everywhere; not enough to win many seats, but enough to undermine the conventional balance of the parties substantially.

Table 1.3 General election results for Wales 1983 and 1987

| | 1983 | | 1987 | |
	% of vote	*MPs elected*	*% of vote*	*MPs elected*
Conservative	31.0	14	29.5	8
Labour	37.5	20	45.1	24
Alliance	23.2	2	17.9	3
P. Cymru	7.8	2	7.3	3
Others	0.4	–	0.2	–

Labour's disappointing performance in Wales was repeated, but magnified, across Britain. The blame for this débâcle was quickly laid at the door of Michael Foot and within a few weeks he had resigned to be replaced by Neil Kinnock, yet another South Wales leader of the Labour Party. One of the most significant tasks facing Mr Kinnock in the early period of his leadership was his, and the Labour Party's, attitude to a national strike by the National Union of Mineworkers (NUM). The NUM's leader, Arthur Scargill, in many ways embodied the strident militancy that Labour felt obliged to reject if they were ever to campaign effectively again. And yet the cause of the miners also served as a cameo for the struggle of the entire working class, attempting to retain its traditional industrial position against the incursions of Thatcherism. Kinnock's own view was widely interpreted as ambivalent, critical of the government, but not wholly supportive of the NUM. In Wales the solidarity of the mining communities was absolute, networks of relationships were forged linking rural with industrial Wales in mutual support and a good deal of the political initiative at this time was seized by Dafydd Ellis Thomas, the new President of Plaid Cymru. Although the strike caused great hardship and threatened the integrity of the NUM itself, in South Wales it proved a remarkable, if perhaps anachronistic, affirmation of traditional values and collective action. Coming so soon after an election which suggested that social change may be undermining these traditional communities and loyalties, perhaps Labour could still regroup.

A test of Labour's revitalisation was offered by the Brecon and Radnor by-election. The death of Tom Hooson had vacated the seat, only won by the Tories in 1979 and previously a Labour monopoly. Minor boundary changes, however, and the decline of the industrial villages at the fringe of the constituency did not now, perhaps, make this, largely agricultural, seat a natural Labour target. However, as is often the case, the British national party political battle can descend upon any constituency, however seemingly inappropriate. Called at a time when the government appeared to be floundering a little in the polls, Labour ran a very close second to the victorious Liberal/Alliance candidate Richard Livesey. A very worthwhile Tory candidate, Chris Butler, was forced into the humiliation of running third in a seat the government was defending, a situation not seen for over thirty years. As previously noted, Welsh by-elections have often produced unlikely results, and very often the prime mover of such change has been Plaid Cymru. In Brecon and Radnor, however, Plaid Cymru polled pitifully; when taken together with dismal performances at Gower and in the Cynon Valley, Plaid Cymru's claim to be an effective by-election force appeared thoroughly spent.

The paucity of Labour's performance in 1983 and their revival at Brecon, all suggested the 1987 election might re-establish an electoral pattern in Wales more recognisable from past experience. As Table 1.3 demonstrates there was a sizeable shift of both seats and votes. But these changes do not necessarily complement each other. In aggregate votes, a good deal of the former support for the Alliance returned to the Labour Party but this shift tended to be in areas where the Labour Party was already dominant. Large majorities were thus made larger. Where seats changed hands tended to be in the newer constituencies of the developing parts of Wales where more balanced communities and economies nurtured more marginal and responsive politics. Again, absent from this pen portrait of the election is Plaid Cymru. Although undoubtedly bolstered by their success in Ynys Mon, elsewhere the party largely stagnated. The return of Mrs Thatcher for a third term, and still retaining a vote of nearly 30 per cent in Wales, did not appear to augur well for those who promote the particular causes of Wales, Welsh politics or Welsh nationalism.

The changing nature of Welsh nationalism

The numbing anti-climax of the St David's Day referendum defeat was compounded, for Plaid Cymru, by the success of the Conservative Party at the subsequent election and the personal defeat of Gwynfor Evans at Carmarthen. The synchronisation of the 1979 general election with local elections also placed the party at a considerable disadvantage and many local government seats were also lost. Further, it became clear that Gwynfor Evans' tenure of the party presidency could not continue indefinitely. Having been in post since 1945 change was inevitable and, taken together with these other omens, 1979 offered Plaid Cymru the opportunity, and the motivation, seriously to reconsider its role and direction for the future. The party immediately established a commission of enquiry

> ... to consider and report back on the position of Plaid Cymru following the referendum and the elections of 1979, and on the steps that need to be taken to facilitate the attainment of Plaid Cymru's goals of securing self-government for Wales, safeguarding the culture, language and traditions and economic life of Wales and securing the right to become a member of the United Nations.[17]

Published early in 1981, the report contained detailed proposals for many aspects of reform and reorganisation. Of particular importance, however, were the conclusions regarding tactics and strategies and the major differences which were exposed between those who signed the majority report, broadly the mainstream party establishment, and the minority report submitted by Dr Phil Williams. The majority report saw as its objective: '... [to] bring together the forces of nationalism, radicalism and socialism by espousing a decentralised, community based form of socialism not to be confused with the state centralism and

British imperialism of the Labour Party ...'.[18] The path required to secure this objective was left rather unclear, leaving the recommendations open to the criticism that what is offered was not new, but merely a continuation of previous strategy, but now requiring better organisation and even more brilliant opportunism.[19] As ever, broad philosophical stances were being used to mask specific differences in perceived objectives. The majority view, whilst claiming that the party had suffered from playing too respectable a role in politics, remained committed to a strategy where success at Westminster remained paramount. The minority, secure in the moral authority of having advocated rejection of the devolution proposals prior to 1979, proposed a more vigorous commitment to local government elections as providing the opportunity to put Plaid Cymru policy actually into practice and to maximise other opportunities when the party could promote single-issue politics relevant to Wales.

Inevitably, perhaps, the party has adopted aspects of both strategy proposals. Westminster elections remain important but other tactics have also been put into practice, even though the success enjoyed by the party in local government in the late 1960s and earlier 1970s has not been repeated. This internal debate raises a general question for all aspirant nationalist parties: to what extent should they co-operate with a political system, the overthrow of which remains their ultimate objective and *raison d'être*? The attractions of success in conventional democratic electoral politics are obvious, yet the dangers of institutionalisation are high and political impotence, especially under a constitution such as Britain's, almost assured.

Whilst such philosophical questions of nationalism were pursued behind closed doors, in public great attention was being attracted by the question of a Welsh-medium television channel. The campaign to secure such a channel had been hard fought by many nationalists, conventionally by Plaid Cymru, but also through a variety of unorthodox political campaigns, both legal and illegal, by such groups as Cymdeithas yr Iaith. It is a measure of the success of such broad-based pressure politics that all major parties contested the 1979 election with manifestos containing a commitment to a Welsh-medium channel. There was a considerable outcry therefore, when within a few weeks of coming to power, the new Conservative Home Secretary, William Whitelaw, revoked the pledge. Gwynfor Evans issued an ultimatum that he would commence a fast to death unless the policy was not implemented. Tension mounted as the date for the commencement of the fast drew closer and various bodies pressed their case on the government. The breadth of support mobilised on behalf of the Welsh channel, culminating in a final delegation to the Secretary of State for Wales, of the Archbishop of Wales, Sir Goronwy Daniel, a former

Permanent Secretary at the Welsh Office, and Lord Cledwyn, former Secretary of State for Wales and Shadow Leader of the House of Lords, enabled the government to back down in the face of 'moderate' opinion rather than concede to Plaid Cymru pressure. Nevertheless, the incident left no one in any doubt that nationalism in Wales, if not Plaid Cymru alone, had secured a notable victory. Sianel Pedwar Cymru (S4C) began broadcasting in November 1982.

The politics of cultural nationalism in Wales received a great fillip from the creation of S4C yet, ironically, this also created difficulties for Plaid Cymru. As the minority report had noted:

> Unfortunately, there was no similar fight for the non-Welsh speakers, who were also facing a deep social and cultural crisis'.[20]

The fundamental question remains as to whether Plaid Cymru can effectively bridge the linguistic divide in Wales and whether nationalism, although a comprehensive political ideology, can achieve, and perhaps more importantly, be accredited with, successes beyond the narrow field of promotion of the Welsh language and other cultural concerns. In an effort to combat such questions, the 1981 conference saw several changes to the traditional party stance. Constitutionally the party's commitment to socialism was defined much more specifically, support for 'left' issues such as unilateralism was again re-emphasised and feminism, another fashionable 'left' concern, was formally recognised through an amendment to the constitution giving a special place on the Party Executive to women. 1981 also saw Dafydd Wigley replace Gwynfor Evans as Party President and although this victory was seen as a success for the 'moderates' within the party, the accession of Wigley also symbolised an immediate modernisation in the party's public image to set beside the new emerging policy changes. The first test of this new approach was the 1983 general election. The election was fought on new constituency boundaries and, whilst the initial proposals of the Boundary Commission had been bitterly opposed by Plaid Cymru, those finally adopted by Parliament did not appear to threaten unduly the party's current seats or best prospects. The election outcome in Wales was dominated by the impact of the Alliance, particularly upon Labour seats, and Plaid Cymru's support and representation remained largely static (Table 1.3).

The dominant event in Welsh politics during 1984/5 was the miners' strike. As has been noted above, this industrial conflict posed particular problems for Mr Kinnock and the Labour Party, whilst also allowing Wales to display rare unity of purpose. Such an opportunity was irresistible for Plaid Cymru. With Dafydd Ellis Thomas having assumed the Presidency of the party in October 1984, following Dafydd Wigley's resignation for family reasons, and Plaid's analysis of current politics appearing evermore left orientated, the miners' strike provided a perfect focus for a campaign based upon the future of Welsh communities, the fight against unemployment and the need to expand industry in Wales. Plaid Cymru was also well placed to participate in the Welsh Congress in Support of Mining Communities, a non-party agency created to facilitate assistance from rural Wales for the mining villages. Plaid Cymru was able to achieve great publicity during the dispute, but would this necessarily translate into political capital? The one test offered in the summer of 1985, the Brecon and Radnor by-election, albeit not the most conducive of constituencies for Plaid Cymru, suggested very little direct return from such an obvious demonstration of being the party of Wales. A later bitter industrial dispute in North Wales, involving the slate quarrymen of Blaenau Ffestiniog in Dafydd Ellis Thomas's own constituency was well supported by the party but received, in comparison with the miners' strike, minimal publicity even within Wales.

In the autumn of 1985 Dafydd Ellis Thomas was returned unopposed to the Presidency of the party and considerable factional infighting regarding party ideology appeared to have been resolved following the adoption of revised party aims. These were accepted with an overwhelming majority effectively crushing the so-called 'right' associated with the Hydro Group and others. Such factionalism had become an important element of Plaid Cymru with the National Left emerging in 1981, initially as a ginger group, but quickly capturing the key policy positions to become, in effect, the prevailing mainstream ethos of the party. Hydro, on the other hand, created at, and named after, an hotel in Llandudno, became increasingly more isolated even though their policy tried to incorporate some of the more obvious populist aspects of public policy being deployed to such good electoral effect by the Conservative Party. Thus support for small businesses, encouragement of the entrepreneur, the sale of council houses were not to be dismissed solely because of their association with the politics of Thatcherism. Hydro wished to evoke a populist, rather than a socialist, nationalism. Between these ideological poles there existed, of course, a broad spectrum of opinion often described, disparagingly by either side, as 'traditionalist', where cultural concerns were perhaps still predominant. But cultural nationalism is also often inseparable from economic issues and especially important and relevant in those areas where Plaid Cymru had actually achieved electoral and political success.

September 1st 1985 recorded the death of Saunders Lewis, one of the founding fathers of the party and its outstanding intellectual figure. In an obituary published in *Welsh Nation*, the party's English-language newspaper, Gwynfor Evans notes, rather bitterly:

... his fate was to be born a Welshman, among a people without loyalty to their nation or the will to live as a nation, but content to decay, without national freedom or dignity, as a peripheral region of England.[21]

In their quest to prevent their previous sixty years being dismissed so depressingly, the new party aims now stated:

To secure self government and a democratic Welsh state based on socialist principles. To safeguard and promote the culture, language, traditions, environment and economic life of Wales through decentralist socialist policies. To secure for Wales the right to become a member of the United Nations Organisation.

Conscious of the forthcoming election, Plaid Cymru also pursued two other issues of significant popular interest: revised proposals for a Welsh Assembly, now renamed Y Senedd, or Senate; and an electoral pact with the Scottish National Party (SNP) designed to exploit their joint position in the House of Commons in the event of there being a hung Parliament. The Senedd proposals envisaged a forum of 100 members elected by proportional representation. It would assume responsibility for the current powers of the Welsh Office, the Welsh Joint Education Committee, the University Grants Committee in Wales, the Research Councils and those powers of the Home Office concerned with broadcasting. The proposals also envisaged the abolition and transfer of powers from the numerous quangos that operate in Wales. The Senedd would also have powers of legislation and taxation in certain areas of tourism and the environment.

Although greeted with limited enthusiasm, Plaid Cymru's Senedd proposals did appear to be striking a balance between their ultimate goals and recognition of the magnitude of the 1979 referendum defeat. The logic of the plan clearly built upon the *de facto* administrative devolution that existed within Wales already, set out to secure political control of this structure, especially from the hands of the Conservatives and allow further developments as and when feasible.

The pact with the SNP, signed 12th April 1986, pledged mutual support of each other's objectives, listed demands for support of a minority government, whilst confirming that such support would be denied to any potential Conservative government. In the event of a hung Parliament, support was dependent upon the establishment of a Scottish Convention, to propose a suitable model for the future government of Scotland, within six months. For Wales, a pledge was required from the government to review the structure of government in Wales. The very realism of the Senedd proposals and of the pact with the SNP suggests that Plaid Cymru continues to be torn between the demands of respectable conventional politics and its seemingly unachievable goal. The size and totality of Mrs Thatcher's victory in the 1987 election at least ensured that the appropriateness of this strategy need not yet be put to the test.

Conclusion: whither Welsh nationalism?

Nationalism in Wales remains a pervasive phenomenon. It is sustained by the high proportion of people who chose to identify themselves as being Welsh, rather than chosing to identify with some wider sense of Britishness. Nationalism and Welshness are undermined, however, by the weakness of political mobilisation attributable to this identity in the past two decades. An emotional attachment to Wales does not necessarily bring with it a political commitment to Wales.

The basic reality of contemporary Wales poses several fundamental problems for Plaid Cymru. Do they maintain their commitment to independence, knowing their immediate support base to be small; or do they compromise to become the party for Wales, rather than of Wales, a posture which gives them a role but may well deny them power? For Plaid Cymru is widely respected as being the party with the best policies for Wales and as the most committed to protect Welsh interests. The party is widely disparaged, however, for adopting policies and tactics that appear extremist or overly ideological.[22] A dilemma is thus posed whereby patriotism is acceptable but nationalism is not – Plaid Cymru cannot monopolise patriotism in the political debate, whilst their opponents will happily allow them to monopolise the commitment to nationalism.

Modern Wales, however, is a far from homogeneous society and such a dilemma exists, perhaps, only at the aggregate, artificial, level of political interaction. The cross cutting cleavages of language and national identity enable Wales to be defined into rather more uniform areas of political interest, where the outlook and range of concerns are likely to be either much more, or much less, conducive to Plaid Cymru's ambitions.[23] The party's challenge is to compete effectively in Welsh Wales, that part of the country which, although not Welsh speaking, is guardian of a distinct Welsh industrial culture, and in Y For Gymraeg, the Welsh-speaking heartland, where in electoral terms Plaid Cymru is already *primus inter pares*. In British Wales, the highly integrated section of the community where a distinct Welsh identity is weakest, Plaid Cymru can only hope to build upon discontent and the growing administrative relevance of the distinct territorial integrity of Wales.

The political agenda across this landscape differs, economic regeneration remaining paramount but carrying a differing weight of cultural and linguistic consequences in various communities. The recent 'boom' in South-east England has had a spill-over effect into Wales, part economic, but seen primarily through the in-migration of a relatively wealthy middle class seeking recreation, retirement or a retreat. The reaction to such an inflow, and the corresponding outflow of young local people, is also primarily economic but popular attention is more often focused upon the more immediate cultural consequences. Extreme reactions to these trends have also been observed in the systematic campaign of burning holiday homes in many parts of rural Wales and, as yet, the police have been remarkably unsuccessful in apprehending the perpetrators of the attacks. In conventional political terms, however, it is extremely difficult for Plaid Cymru to address these issues: it is caught between constant cross-pressures of economic demands about which it can do little, and cultural demands, which to the extent that they are independent of economic matters, may be conceded by an indulgent central government confident in there being no fundamental readjustment in power relations.

A further dilemma entraps Plaid Cymru. Its broadly conventional political agenda, designed to attack mass electoral support, must have as a goal, if only as a first step, some form of Welsh assembly such as envisaged in the Wales Act 1978, the party's own current Senedd proposals or the all-Wales level of authority still anticipated by the Labour Party and the former Alliance parties. To secure such mass support Plaid Cymru must be the Party for Wales, the all-purpose protest party-cum-pressure group. Effective adoption of such a strategy prejudices the realistic adoption of nationalist, independentist, objectives. Should an autonomous Welsh assembly ever be established within Britain this will, of course, mark a great achievement for the forces of Welsh politics and, not least, Plaid Cymru. At this point however, all political parties in Wales will realign their electoral appeal on an all-Wales dimension and Plaid Cymru will lose their unique electoral advantage. A simpler commitment to political nationalism will remain Plaid Cymru's alone, but may well prove an electoral liability.

Hence the debate over the correct path to an independent Wales continues and will be keenly contested within the ranks of Plaid Cymru. The party must ensure, however, that the fight to resolve this issue within its ranks, does not become a surrogate for the real political battle beyond.

Notes

1. A full analysis of the referendum campaign is available in
   D. Foulkes, J.B. Jones and R. Wilford, *The Welsh Veto: The Wales Act 1978 and the Referendum*, University of Wales Press, Cardiff, 1983.

2. Denis Balsom, P.J. Madgwick and D. van Mechelen, 'The Red and the Green: Patterns of Partisan Choice in Wales', *British Journal of Political Science*, 13, 1983, p.323.
3. For a general discussion of the history and development of Plaid Cymru see D.H. Davies, *The Welsh Nationalist Party 1925–1945: A Call to Nationhood*, University of Wales Press, Cardiff, 1983; A. Butt-Philip, *The Welsh Question*, University of Wales Press, Cardiff, 1975; Denis Balsom, 'Plaid Cymru' in H.M. Drucker, *Multi-Party Britain*, Macmillan, London, 1979.
4. Butt-Philip, op. cit., p.15.
5. P.M. Rawkins 'An Approach to the Political Sociology of the Welsh Nationalist movement', *Political Studies*, 27, 1979.
6. D.H. Davies, op. cit., p.261.
7. Plaid Cymru, *Economic Plan for Wales*, 1970.
8. C.H. Williams, 'Non Violence and the development of the Welsh Language Society' *Welsh History Review*, 8, 1977; Cynog Davies 'Cymdeithas yr Iaith' in M. Stephens, *The Welsh Language Today*, Gomer Press, Llandyssul, 1973.
9. Phil Williams, 'Work for Wales', *Culture and Politics*, Plaid Cymru, 1975; Balsom, op. cit., p.134.
10. For example, D. Foulkes *et al.*, op. cit.
11. K.O. Morgan 'Welsh Politics' in R. Brinley Jones (ed.), *The Anatomy of Wales*, Gwerin Publications, Cardiff, 1972, p.119.
12. ibid., p.119.
13. G.A. Williams, *When Was Wales?*, Penguin, Harmondsworth, 1985, p.297.
14. Denis Balsom, 'Public Opinion and Welsh Devolution' in Foulkes *et al.*, op. cit., p.206.
15. Hansard H.C. Debs. v.967 c.1183.
16. *The Times House of Commons 1979*, Times Books, London, 1979, p.252.
17. Report of the Plaid Cymru Commission of Inquiry, Plaid Cymru, 1981, p.i.
18. ibid., p.iii.
19. ibid., p.94.
20. ibid., p.102.
21. *Welsh Nation*, October 1985.
22. Denis Balsom, P.J. Madgwick and D. van Mechelen, 'The Political Consequences of Welsh Identity', *Ethnic and Racial Studies*, 7, 1984.
23. Denis Balsom, 'The Three Wales Model' in J. Osmond (ed.), *The National Question Again*, Gomer Press, Llandyssul, 1985.

Chapter two

Scotland

Jack Brand

Since 1979, the Scottish National Party has moved to the left. As significantly, it has acknowledged its position there. By 'left' I do not mean that it has adopted a socialist programme. Rather, I am referring to a position which is overtly sympathetic to the needs of the working class. I am also referring to policies generally viewed as left wing: opposition to nuclear arms, to apartheid, support for Nicaragua and so forth. We are speaking about a family likeness rather than a strict definition.[1]

There was always a section of the party which was on the left. The years which we examine are special because this position has become the official basis of the party's ideology. This chapter will describe the process which has taken place and offers an explanation. As a background, it is necessary to speak about the 1979 general election, which followed on the referendum on a Scottish assembly earlier that year. It was, in part, the disaster of not securing devolution and, even more, of the ensuing electoral set-back which pushed the SNP on to its present path (which a decade later seems to be starting to bear fruit: see appendix p.35). We must look closely, therefore, at the reactions of the party to the 1979 defeats. I shall suggest that in the 1980s a process of party modernisation has taken place[2] and that the SNP has become more like the other parties.

The turning point of 1979

The depth of the 1979 disaster was emphasised by the heights which the party had scaled. In the October 1974 election they had taken eleven seats and 30 per cent of the vote; in 1979 they lost all but two seats and only 17 per cent of Scottish voters chose them. Even this is to under-estimate what happened. After 1974 several polls had shown a majority of Scottish preferences for the Nationalists and they had been the motor of Scottish politics.[3] Along with the economic situation, Scottish devolution had been a central question of British politics.[4] Now all that was gone. The reaction within the SNP was triggered by the referendum. The party was outraged when James Callaghan announced that the majority voting for devolution was not enough to satisfy the 'Forty per cent rule'.[5] A decision to end co-operation with Labour and effectively to bring down the government was taken by the National Council. Henceforth, the party would have nothing to do with promises of devolution. They would fight for 'independence, nothing less'. This was the first and overwhelming reaction. It was led by an 'Old Guard' made up of Nationalists who had been prominent in the movement for many years. 'Independence nothing less' rejected not just devolution but all policy-making on other aspects of Scottish life. This policy-making had been associated with the younger elites who had come into the party in the 1960s. The attitude of the 'Old Guard' came out clearly in an editorial in the *Scots Independent*: 'To be successful, we must be single-minded on the Scottish issue'.[6] But for what happened after 1979, the earlier policy-making was very important. The procession of documents started in 1975 with a statement on energy. Thirty more followed, covering every aspect of Scottish life. They were debated at Conference or National Council, often amended, but mostly they were accepted. To deny the validity of this exercise was to force the party back to the stance it had had in the 1950s. It was the approach of the 'true believer' for whom principle is more important than playing politics in the real world. 'Independence nothing less' in effect reversed the movement of the party towards a moderate left position.

There was another reaction. It affirmed that nationalism was about more than the ultimate goal of independence. Its source was a small group of young people which was not homogeneous in terms of ideas, but they were sympathetic to the left and, rather vaguely, described themselves as 'socialist'. Their first meeting set the aim of exploring a new strategy. One origin of their approach lay in the polls which had been done for the party before 1979. These showed that the profile of Nationalist voters was almost identical with that of Labour voters in Scotland. This was interpreted to mean that both parties depended heavily on the working-class vote. Furthermore, the Labour vote in Scotland was strengthening compared with the rise of the Conservative vote in the United Kingdom as a whole. Southern England grew more prosperous as a result of a series of economic factors including the benefits of the Common Market. Scotland did not enjoy these benefits or only enjoyed them to a reduced degree. The effect of this was that Labour would increase its vote in Scotland, but the Conservatives would remain supreme in England and thus in the United Kingdom as a whole. In two or three elections, Scottish Labour voters (already very similar to Nationalist voters) would realise that their party could never improve the condition of Scotland. Provided that the SNP became a party committed to the Scottish working class, it could hope to inherit these discouraged Labour voters until it, and not Labour, became the hegemonic Scottish party.

From a socialist perspective, as Maxwell points out, the 79 Group, as it called itself, was lacking in theory.[7] They produced a number of papers, but these either rehashed some of the party's policies or developed the above strategic argument.[8] Political scientists familiar with the theoretical literature on nationalism might expect references to Gramsci or an internal colonial argument or to 'dependencia' theory.[9] There is no substantial trace of any of this in their statements. Above all, the 79 Group denied the mainstream Nationalists' view of the situation. For the 'Old Guard' leaders, national self-determination was a natural right of the Scots. The voters might shift in their support for the SNP, but the Scottish people would claim their right. More than this, the struggle was for the whole of the Scottish people and not for sections. To this the 79 Group said: national victory will only come if we work out the correct strategy. This, they believed, meant targeting particular groups in the electorate. Since the working class seemed to the 79 Group the 'softer' target, it should be the primary aim of the party's efforts. The Group offended the established leaders because it denied the inevitability of national victory and because it differentiated among Scottish groups. In addition the leaders were bound to feel that an illegitimate challenge was being made by a party within a party. This interpretation was encouraged by the organised form taken by the group, with membership cards, badges, regular meetings, co-ordinated conference motions and slates for the election of delegates and officials. The Old Guard, after their 'independence nothing less' at the 1979 Conference mounted a campaign which led to the disbanding of the group in 1982. This was the end of open factional activity; but it did not stop the party's shift leftwards.

The SNP moves left

Even as the fight over the 79 Group raged, there were clear signs that new concerns were dominating the party. The economic decline of Scotland and the government policies of these years had a more devastating effect on Scottish society than anything under the Labour government. According to Buxton, 'After growing more rapidly than the UK economy over the late Sixties and early Seventies, the economy's advance slowed notably during the rest of the Seventies before absolute decline set in... from 1979'.[10] Thirlwall describes the nature of this decline: 'Scotland has experienced a run down of its manufacturing labour force which is without equal among advanced industrial nations including the UK itself'.[11] For the ordinary citizen and for the activists

of the SNP, the most easily understood indicator of the crisis was unemployment.

Table 2.1 Percentage unemployed in Scotland, 1974–86

(Second quarter in each year)												
'74	*'75*	*'76*	*'77*	*'78*	*'79*	*'80*	*'81*	*'82*	*'83*	*'84*	*'85*	*'86*
3.6	4.3	6.4	6.8	7.0	6.6	7.6	11.0	12.4	13.7	14.0	14.8	14.9

Source: Scottish Economic Bulletin, June 1986, p.46.

These figures provide the background to what then happened in the
SNP. In the introductory pages of the 1982 SNP diary, the party nailed
its colours to the mast. It described itself explicitly as 'a moderate, left
of centre party'. In a pamphlet, *Introducing the SNP*, published about
the same time and intended to recruit supporters, the same phrase is
used. It has remained in every issue of the diary up to the present. No
such identification of the position of the party exists in any previous
official document, especially not in a document as central as the
members' diary. The previous recruiting pamphlet, *The SNP and You*,
published in 1977, described the SNP as 'The Democratic Party' and a
'radical and democratic alternative'. The 1979 election manifesto,
Return to Nationhood, used the same phrase and said that everyone was
entitled to equal opportunity and consideration. 'The SNP has a deep
committment to Scotland's distinctive history and culture and to the
social and economic wellbeing of the Scottish people'.[12] All of these
official statements made before 1982 presented the SNP as a party
which cared for the future of the Scottish people and specifically about
its economic future, but this was a long way from identifying the party
as a party of the left; even of the centre left. This was the way in which
the party now presented itself to its own members and to all Scottish
electors.

It is this rather than the policy changes themselves which should be
noticed first, since the party issued many policy statements in the 1970s
which placed it on the left. Its land-use policy called for extensive public
control, for locally elected land commissions and firm measures to deal
with absentee landowners.[13] Transport policy was also characteristic of
a left-wing party with its emphasis on the integration of different forms
of transport.[14] Industrial policy was strongly in favour of public investment and supported a form of worker co-operatives as recommended by
Tony Benn but by no other prominent Labour leader.[15] The National
Party has supported the removal of nuclear weapons from Scotland

since 1961. The Labour Party did not become unilateralist for another twenty years. Opposition to apartheid dates from 1967. During all the period when these radical policies were being developed and approved by the party, great care was taken not to identify the SNP as an organisation standing on the left–right spectrum. To have done so would have been against the ruling myth of the party that it stood for the whole of Scotland. It was expressed very well at the 1975 Conference in a resolution coming from Glasgow Hillhead: 'This conference recognises that the political outlook of the SNP is new in that the British convention of being essentially left-wing, right-wing or centre has been broken in favour of a new style politics applicable to Scotland'.[16]

In the 1980s something happened to change the rules of the game. It became acceptable to say that the party was on the left. In 1985, there was a resolution by the Bannockburn branch, supported by the Old Guard, to turn the party back to the path of traditional nationalism and to abandon the prominent appeal to the working class. This resolution was remitted back.[17] It was not just a faction or the remains of a faction which identified with the left, but the majority of the party including most of its leaders.

This change in the self-image of the party has accompanied a shift in policy. Since 1979 many of the policies of the 1970s have been modified to become more radical. The 1981 Conference, after confirming the anti-nuclear stance, decided that an independent Scotland should leave NATO. In 1984, SNP CND was launched and became affiliated to the party. In 1985, Conference condemned the Star Wars strategy.[18] The same Conference, in the presence of a spokesman from the banned African National Congress, voted for sanctions and the disengagement of Scottish firms from South Africa.[19] At the 1986 Conference, there was a strong support for the Sandinista government in Nicaragua.[20] It is interesting to compare this with the debate on El Salvador in 1980, when it was argued that the party's policy to that country should be changed because it was hostile to the United States.

To this point, we have looked at policies which are not in the main thrust of SNP policy as it has changed since 1979. These policies and those of the 1970s might be thought of as 'cost-free radicalism'. The core of the change lies in the party's industrial policy. Since its foundation, the SNP has been aware of the problems of the Scottish economy.[21] We have seen that in the 1980s the decline speeded up. In view of this, the party had little option but to fight. In doing so, it identified with the workers whose jobs were at risk. Even before 1979 the party supported Scottish industry, but this was not done very consistently as was illustrated when one of the MPs, Hamish Watt, tore up telegrams from shipyard workers asking for support for Clyde yards during the parliamentary debate on the Shipbuilding Industry Bill.[22]

After 1979, the scale of the economic disaster was such that the party had to take sides. Thus it is that the 1980s have been characterised by a series of industrial campaigns. This concern has been shown by the numbers of Conference resolutions dealing with employment and the decline of industry, from under one a year in the 1960s and 1970s on average to 4.9 a year in the 1980s.

Giving time to campaign for industry shows a deeper level of commitment than passing resolutions. As early as September 1979, the party became involved in efforts to keep open the Robb Caledon shipyard in Dundee. Many members went to support the pickets. Thereafter, a large number of campaigns were mounted for a host of factories, mills and other enterprises which were threatened. It is possible to mention only the more important episodes. In August of 1981, the party put a great deal of effort into helping the women of the Lee Jeans factory in Greenock to stay in work. In 1982, a team of SNP lawyers fought for and won the right of the Plessey workers to occupy their factory. The closure of the stripmill at Gartcosh was, however, particularly important. It was the occasion of large demonstrations because the end of Gartcosh was seen as a threat to the last large unit of British Steel (Ravenscraig) still working in Scotland.

One final example of the Nationalists' industrial involvement illustrates an important point. It is their support for the National Union of Mineworkers during the miners' strike of 1984–5. The significance of this is that neither the Labour Party nor the TUC was ready to come out so clearly in support. In Scotland, the miners' leadership was particularly clearly identified with the left, including prominent Communists. Pits were closed in the 1970s and there were many industrial disputes. No doubt some Nationalists supported workers in these years, but there is no evidence that the majority of the party took this as a central policy. There have been rewards. The party has enjoyed publicity from its industrial campaigns. More than this, there has been more co-operation with the unions.

Other policy changes since 1979 indicate a new direction. In 1986 a pact was concluded with the Welsh nationalist party, Plaid Cymru, which was seen as clearly left wing. The greatest significance of this agreement is that it commits both parties to reject any alliance with the Conservative Party. Section 4 of the Agreement reads:

> Provided the constitutional objectives are secured, the Parties will be prepared to offer conditional Parliamentary support to one or more of the London Parties in order to achieve the agreed political programme. No support will be offered to the Conservative Party in view of its record in Scotland and Wales and its hostility to any form of self-government.[23]

This choosing between UK parties on the mainstream left–right spectrum would not have been possible in the 1970s.

Earlier in the article I discussed the SNP's proclamation that it would have no further truck with devolution. This was soon breached in spirit. In March 1980, the party chairman and MP for Dundee West, Gordon Wilson, introduced a ten-minute rule bill setting up a Scottish Convention to decide the future of Scotland rather than leaving it to the politics of the UK Parliament. This was important since, by definition, the Convention could vote for independence for Scotland, but equally it might opt for the status quo or devolution. Meanwhile, the party went on its rigorous separatist path until the 1983 Conference when a door was left open for devolution by officially accepting a Convention. At the March 1984 National Council it was agreed to start a dialogue with the Campaign for a Scottish assembly. This body works for co-operation among all parties to establish a Scottish assembly subject to the United Kingdom Parliament for decisions on such subjects as foreign affairs and defence. This is not evidence of a move to the left. It is a departure from fundamentalism.

One final example of a policy change since 1979 should be noticed. During the 1970s, the party had opposed entry to the EEC. At its Conference in 1983, the party declared that it had a 'positive' attitude to post-independence negotiations for membership of the Community. Scotland in Europe would make nonsense of the claim that independence would bring machine-gun nests at the border. Scotland would be a full member of a modern industrial and trading alliance with all that meant for the standard of living and for bringing the Scottish economy into the twentieth century. Scotland would enjoy close relations with England as with every other member of the Community.

These last three policy shifts – the alliance with Plaid Cymru, willingness to work for devolution and a positive attitude to membership of the EEC – are mentioned here because each one was supported by the majority of members of the left tendency and for the same reason. The Old Guard approach was to concentrate on the fight for independence and to regard everything else as a distraction. The new elites had a different set of arguments. They wanted the party to concentrate upon that section of the Scottish people which had lost most in the industrial collapse. The party should be alive to any cause or any method of making the SNP and independence acceptable to the majority of the Scottish people.

It has been demonstrated that the Scottish National Party has taken some new directions in the 1980s. At the outset the 79 Group liked to call itself 'socialist', but this was a very loose description. The left tendency in the party today cannot be seen as socialist either, let alone the party as a whole. Just as the 79 Group's pamphlets did not concern themselves with theory, so also it is striking that there is no contemporary debate in the party about any theoretical issues within left-wing nationalism. No one has taken part in the contemporary argument about municipal socialism or 'enterprise socialism'. The movement has been towards 'Labourism' rather than socialism. The Nationalists have shown their concern for the working classes in Scotland, but not in general principles which would reorganise Scottish society.

Some explanations

It is possible to explain the above sequence of events on several levels. In what follows I shall first tackle this at the level of certain factors in Scottish and British politics. I shall then look at the shift in terms of certain medium-range models of political parties.

Some of the explanations of the shift in the SNP are implicit in what has already been written. It has been pointed out that left-of-centre policies were accepted in the 1970s even if they were not acknowledged as such. What has happened more recently is the development of an existing trend. Why has this taken place and why has the party become prepared to acknowledge its position on the left–right spectrum? The SNP could not ignore Scotland's worsened economic position, with its closures and redundancies. It could have made purely symbolic protests, simply mentioning the problems in speeches or passed conference resolutions. As I have shown, it did more than this in the industrial campaign. Are there other reasons why it should have gone as far as it did? One relatively simple factor is that, in 1980, a charismatic and well-known ex-trade union leader and ex-Labour MP, Jim Sillars, joined the party. It was significant that, when he addressed a 79 Group meeting at his very first Conference, the large hall was packed out by people who never had been and would never become Group members. It is not surprising that he was elected a Vice Chairman at the very next Conference when he had been barely a year in the party. The views of one man or woman, however attractive, do not, on the other hand, have such an effect on a party unless there is a change in the composition and condition of the party.

The composition of the SNP leadership has changed to the extent that 1979 is a watershed. Some of the old leaders who were MPs left because they lost their parliamentary seats. Others became less active because they had given all their spare time to Nationalism in the previous ten or twenty years and they were exhausted and deeply disappointed by the results of the election. In a general way, one can divide the leadership into three generations. We have already referred to the Old Guard. For the most part, this was made up of people who had been active in the party since the 1940s or 1950s, when it appeared that there was

31

absolutely no chance that independence would ever come about. Such people have been described as 'true believers' and are a distinct type.[24] When the movement grows, the party must play politics, think about the best type of propaganda and so forth. The true believer finds it difficult to cope with the new situation. He may be offended by the type of leader who starts to take over. For the SNP, these new leaders began arriving in the 1960s. They had a broader idea of what the party should be doing. It was not fanciful to imagine that the party might win an election in Scotland and they wanted to prepare themselves by writing policies to be implemented when they became the government of Scotland. This was the group, let us call them the 'Young Guard', which was responsible for the policy statements of the 1970s. They dominated the party in the 1970s. The young men and women who joined the 79 Group mostly came into the party in that decade. By the 1980s their time had come to form a new leadership generation. By the same time, many of the first generation, the Old Guard, had left simply because of age. Those who remained put up a spirited rearguard action against the 79 Group, but youth had a massive advantage. The Young Guard were not so far removed from the 'Young Turks' of the 79 Group in terms of ideas. They were able to incorporate those who were only slightly further left.

In a study of Scottish Nationalism between 1960 and 1974, Robert Crawford uses the idea of 'core persistence'.[25] This concept allows us to view systematically the turnover of the leadership in our own period. By calculating how many of the members of the National Executive Committee in 1964 were also members in 1974, Crawford showed that the individuals who had run the party in the 1960s still largely ran it in the mid-1970s. In his ten year period, ten out of thirty who were on the NEC in 1974 had had continuous membership since 1964. The ten-year period 1976 to 1986 was taken for comparison. Of the twenty members in 1986, only three had been members continuously since 1976. Comparing the two periods, the 'core persistence' had gone down from 33 per cent to 15 per cent. It is also worth noticing that eight of the twenty members of the NEC in 1986 were either members of the 79 Group or were generally identified with the 'Young Turk' position.[26] Given the radicalism and the amount of controversy it caused, it is remarkable that it should have captured 40 per cent of the NEC seats by 1986.

In place of the Old Guard, then, came those who belonged to a generation whose ruling culture was radical and left wing. The opinion polls show clearly that, in Britain as a whole, there was a higher probability of the young supporting Labour even if they had Conservative-voting parents.[27] In the SNP, the effect of this was a generation with left-of-centre ideas. One further point may drive this home. In 1981 the party set up a youth wing: the Young Scottish Nationalists. From its very first conference, it was primarily concerned with questions of employment and industrial relations. Although it is not as far left as the Labour Party Young Socialists, it certainly expresses the frustrations of youth looking for work and their support for 'left' solutions. This is associated with a more general factor. The ideological gap between Labour and Conservative has widened, creating a polarising process in British politics. Given its generational make-up, it is difficult to think that the SNP could move right. In a country where unemployment is always at the top of the political agenda, there is a strong possibility that the party will move to the left and, in the contemporary climate of the United Kingdom, the move is likely to be further to the left than would have been the case in the 1960s or 1970s.

Earlier, the general election of 1979 was described as a watershed for the SNP. The 1983 general election was also important since, once again, events in the whole of the United Kingdom as well as Scotland forced changes in the party. A second win for Mrs Thatcher together with a continued erosion of the Conservative vote in Scotland put more pressure on the SNP to move left. It was not simply the continued opposition of the Conservatives to Scottish devolution, but what appeared their uncaring attitude to the disastrous economic situation in Scotland. It was the impetus for the Young Guard of the 1970s to co-operate more closely with the Young Turks. Thus the 1983 election like the 1979 one underlined the fact that the move of the SNP to the left was determined not only by new thinking among Nationalists, but by external events to which they had to respond.

These movements of opinion explain what has happened to force the SNP to the left in terms of the processes of British politics. We can use a parallel argument which derives from social theory. At the beginning of the chapter, it was suggested that, in the course of the 1970s and 1980s, the SNP had become more like other British parties. When it was founded in the 1920s, the SNP was organised on the model of the Independent Labour Party. In other ways, however, it was closer to the classical model of a social movement. In defining this, John Wilson admits that it is difficult to draw the line between a party and a social movement. It is more a distinction of emphasis, especially in the early stages of party development. Nevertheless, Wilson describes a social movement as 'a conscious, collective, organised attempt to bring about or resist a change in the social order by non-institutionalised means'. In comparing them with parties, Wilson says, 'They are more inclined, however, to step outside [conventional tactics] and use unconventional methods to make themselves heard'.[28] The SNP has certainly used methods which were not conventional among British political parties. The Bannockburn demonstration might be a case in point, in the sense that it is a political demonstration, but one based on the commemoration of an event from far-distant history and is accompanied by a cultural display. One might suggest that May Day was similar, but there is really no emphasis on far-distant history in this way. In terms of this move from a movement to a party, it is interesting that, at the 1982 Conference, for the first time in the history of the party, it was proposed that the Bannockburn Rally should be discontinued because it was archaic and not in sympathy with the new image. The proposal was defeated, but it is significant that it should have been made.

There is another characteristic which typifies a movement rather than a party. In its early stages at least, it is more concerned with developing and keeping pure its objectives than with thinking about how these ideas are to be realised. Parties, by contrast, 'live in a house of power'.[29] Their aim is to become the government or to take part in government and thus to exercise power. In so doing, they may have to compromise some of their ideals. In the 1970s, the SNP moved from being primarily a movement to being a party first and foremost. The new elite, the Young Guard, faced the possibility that they might run the country in the foreseeable future. As such, they became involved in politics in the sense that they had to develop policies and to recognise that development could only take place after compromise. Most of them also recognised that, if they came into power, they would have to go through the same process of compromise and politicking with other bodies in the nation: business organisations, trade unions and the whole paraphernalia of interests that exist in a modern state. The final clue to the growth of a party model is given in the 1986 Autumn Campaign document. This is largely reproduced in the 1987 general election manifesto and uses the same slogan: 'Play the Scottish Card'. It argues that British governments will pay attention to the needs of Scotland only when there is a strong SNP. It emphasises the role of the party in the fight to retain a steel industry, getting jobs for the young, securing the Cold Climate Allowance for the whole of Scotland and so on. Independence is mentioned, but, to a greater extent than ever before, the emphasis is upon the role of the Nationalists in forcing Westminster to recognise the needs of Scotland.

Why then, should the party modify its policies and take part in activities which seem closer to the left? Weber and Michels suggest that it should remain as a catch-all party, obviously of a different type from the 1950s, but nevertheless one which still tries to appeal to all. A more recent theorist of parties, Anthony Downs, predicts that an electorally successful party must move to the centre of the political spectrum. A move towards either end would alienate those who are situated towards the opposite end.[30] It is from this that we have a clue to the reason for the Nationalists' change of stance. Since 1955 the Scottish electorate has become less and less inclined to vote Conservative until today, as we have seen, Labour is the hegemonic party. In terms of voter identification, Scotland has moved to the left. Saying that the SNP is 'neither a party of the left or the right' would inevitably be interpreted as placing the party mid-way in a policy spectrum between the two main parties. The result would place the vast majority of the Scottish electorate on one side of the SNP's position while a tiny percentage of Conservatives stand on the other. It is not the central position which Downs talks about. To gain this central position, the SNP, as a pragmatic party, must identify itself as a party of the left. With more and more Scottish electors supporting Labour, to the point where a Tory government now finds it difficult to staff the Scottish Office with Ministers, the centre for Scotland as a whole lies towards the Labour end of the Downsian Main Street. In the last analysis, this is the reason for change in the SNP.

Appendix: Scottish election results, 1979–87

Table 2.2 Scottish election results, 1979–87

		CON	LAB	LIB/ALLIANCE	SNP
1979	% vote	31.4	41.5	8.7	17.33
	seats	22	44	3	2
1983	% vote	28.4	35.1	24.5	11.8
	seats	21	41	8	2
1987	% vote	24.0	42.4	19.2	14.0
	seats	10	50	9	3

The Govan by-election

The striking SNP victory at Govan in November 1988, overturning a Labour majority of 18,000, confirmed it in its left-wing orientation and its strategy to present itself as the party with the viable alternative for Scotland to continuing Conservative dominance of the UK government (while Conservatism continues to languish badly in Scotland). The new MP, Jim Sillars, who has contributed so much to leading the party on this path, immediately offered a welcome to members and supporters of other parties in Scotland and especially of Labour, to join in a broad-based movement to demand self-government within the European Community. In this way it is intended that the bogey of an isolationist separatism will be laid, in putting forward progressive policies for Scotland as a member of the Community in its own right, alongside other smaller nations, as this evolves towards greater union.

Notes

1. Ludwig Wittgenstein, *Philosophical Investigations*, Oxford, 1963, Section 67.
2. Myron Weiner, *Modernisation* (New York, 1966), pp.196–217.
3. See Jack Brand, *The National Movement in Scotland* (London, 1978).
4. M. Keating and D. Bleiman, *Labour and Scottish Nationalism* (London, 1979).
5. This required that, to become law, the provisions of the Scotland Act establishing an Assembly should be approved by 40 per cent of the Scottish electorate and not by a simple majority of those voting.
6. *Scots Independent*, May 1980, p.1.
7. 'The problematic issues of contemporary socialism – the decline of the working class vote, the barriers to socialism caused by the individualistic ethos of a consumer society, the relations between socialism, feminism and environmentalism ... received brief reference in Group publications and debate, but were not, in any sense, on the Group's agenda.' S. Maxwell, The 79 Group: A Critical Retrospect, *Cencrastus*, no.21, Summer 1984, p.12.
8. The 79 Group papers were as follows: 'The 79 Group: its principles and aims', 'Local Government Elections', 'Scotland and the British Crisis', 'Has the Scottish Private Sector a Future?', 'The Case for Left-wing Nationalism', 'Scotland's Industrial Resistance'.
9. See Michael Hechter, *Internal Colonialism* (London, 1979).
10. N.K. Buxton, A Position Paper, given at the Gleneagles Conference, Scottish Council for Development and Industry, 1986, p.21.
11. A.P. Thirlwall, 'Deindustrialisation in the United Kingdom' (*Lloyds Bank Review*, no.144, 1982).
12. *Return to Nationhood* (Edinburgh, SNP, 1979), p.4.
13. National Council, October 1977.
14. National Council, November 1976.
15. Annual Conference, 1976.
16. Annual Conference 1975, Resolution 16.
17. Annual Conference 1985, Resolution 28.
18. Annual Conference 1985, Resolution 30.
19. Annual Conference 1985, Resolution 31.
20. Annual Conference 1986, Resolution 34.
21. See J. Brand, op. cit., pp.230–2.
22. On 24 February 1977.
23. Communiqué of the joint meeting of the National Executive Committees of Plaid Cymru and the Scottish National Party, 5 November 1986, Para 5.

24. Eric Hoffer, *The True Believer: Thoughts on the Nature of Mass Movements* (New York, 1951).
25. Robert Crawford, 'The Scottish National Party 1960–74' (Glasgow University Ph.D. Thesis, 1982), p.211.
26. The Young Turks on the NEC in 1986 were D. Cameron, A. Currie, R. Gibson, K. MacAskill, A. Salmond, J. Sillars, R. Wyllie.
27. See Mark Franklin, *The Decline of Class Voting in Britain* (Oxford, 1985), pp.170–1.
28. John Wilson, *Introduction to Social Movements* (New York, Basic Books, 1973), p.9.
29. H.H. Gerth and C.W. Mills, *From Max Weber* (London, Routledge, 1948), p.194.
30. A. Downs, *An Economic Theory of Democracy* (New York, Harper, 1957).

Chapter three

Northern Ireland: The Nationalists

George Boyce

The northern nationalist tradition

George Bernard Shaw remarked that a man with a broken leg is likely to be unhealthily preoccupied with his leg. Ireland's 'broken nationality' would seem to bear out the truth of his contention. Modern Ireland is divided into two states, each containing majorities and minorities: in the Republic the population is overwhelmingly Roman Catholic in composition; in the north there is a Protestant majority. Religious and political terms are easily interchangeable: the south was the product of Irish nationalism which, in the first two decades of this century, demanded self-government, first in the form of home rule, then, after 1916, in a separatist mode; the state of Northern Ireland was created to meet Unionist objections to the separation from the United Kingdom. Both states were the product also of the British desire to find a settlement of the Irish Question that would satisfy the main groups in Ireland, and of their identification of 'two nations' which would be endowed with equal self-governing status. Above all, the 1920 settlement fulfilled Britain's wish to keep Ireland, politically speaking, at arm's length, at one remove from the centre of British politics.

Its realisation in constitutional form in the 1920 Government of Ireland Act, which established the state of Northern Ireland, and the 1921 Anglo-Irish Treaty, which gave dominion status to the south – a status which was subsequently eroded into that of a Republic in 1949 – left minorities on both sides of the border. In the south there remained a small, but socially influential Protestant or Unionist minority, which soon found that, while it escaped the worst fate of minorities, active persecution, nevertheless was taught that it was no longer the master in the new house, and must accept the majority culture. Northern Ireland retained within its boundaries a much larger Roman Catholic or Nationalist minority, some one-third of the population, but a minority that was poor, and regarded with deep suspicion by the Unionist people and government.

From the beginning, however, the iron law of Irish politics – that nothing is quite as it seems – began to operate in Northern Ireland. For the question was posed at the very inception of the state: was the Roman Catholic minority really a minority at all? It was after all Roman Catholic and therefore nationalist; and it could, and did, claim to be part of the majority of the whole island of Ireland. The early years of its existence in Northern Ireland witnessed the political impotence induced by this attitude of mind: nationalists in the north hardly troubled themselves to organise as any kind of political party, and were inclined to look to an (increasingly indifferent) Dublin government for assistance in their battle against this new, enforced minority status.

Yet there was a real sense in which it had always been a minority, or had experienced minority status, even before the partition of Ireland. Nationalism in the north was certainly part of the wider movement; but it was different in important respects from its southern counterpart. When Catholic nationalism was first mobilised as a mass political movement by Daniel O'Connell between the 1820s and the 1840s, the northern Catholic remained quiescent. When Charles Stewart Parnell organised his formidable home-rule party, Catholic Ulster played little or no part, save as voters. Northern Catholic political quiescence throughout the nineteenth century was attributed by one observer to the fact that Ulster Catholics felt the 'political ascendancy of the Protestants pressing more closely upon them'. This ascendancy meant that the 'Ulster Catholics ... born and bred in practical Helotism, though very Irish and patriotic at heart, and in mind, are very cautious and timid politicians'.[1]

This prudence made any central organisation of the Ulster Catholics a difficult task; it was only with the organisation of the Ancient Order of Hibernians that Catholic Ulster at last began to awaken. The AOH was a mixture of friendly society and defender of Catholic interests. But its sectarian character, giving expression to hatred of the Orangemen, was not universally welcomed by the broader nationalist movement, even if its ability to muster the Ulster Catholic vote was gratefully received.[2] Moreoever, it was soon found to be expendable; for when partition was first offered as a price for home rule in 1916, John Redmond was quick to abandon the Ulster nationalists to their fate. Ulster's nationalist people were not, then, quite like those in the rest of Ireland: a fact established electorally in 1918 when they were one of the few parts of Ireland to adhere to the old Home Rule Party and reject the rising power of Sinn Fein. And in a country where the priesthood had once been the *clercs* of Irish nationalism, but from the 1880s were a declining influence, the north remained the exception.

The *de facto* minority tradition of the Ulster Catholic was made *de jure* in 1921, and confirmed when the Boundary Commission failed to undermine the state of Northern Ireland in 1925. This status meant that the already different experience of the northern nationalist before partition from that of nationalists in the rest of Ireland, became even more divergent. As the south established its credentials as an independent state, it soon developed its own obsessions and political goals; and while these always formally included the reunification of Ireland, even de Valera, nationalist Ireland's greatest modern political figure, was unwilling to compromise the interests of the Ireland that he had got for the Ireland that he had not got.[3]

This Catholic minority had always experienced an inferior status in the Protestant-dominated north; now it had to come to terms with the formal, constitutional preservation of that status. This was not the product alone of Unionist fear of its large and discontented minority; it was a status that Roman Catholic political aspirations contributed to as well. The idea that the northern Catholic was part of the 'natural' majority of Ireland as a whole drove Catholic politics into a formal non-recognition of the state of Northern Ireland, expressed in the almost incoherent nature of Catholic politics between 1925 and the 1960s. The Nationalist party abstained from the Northern Ireland parliament between 1921 and 1925, and from 1934 until the late 1940s.[4] There was always the alternative to constitutional nationalist politics, which a minority firmly established in solid Catholic areas of the cities of Belfast and Derry, and with a border to escape over, might exploit: that of terrorism and guerrilla warfare, which indeed had looked as if it might jeopardise the new Northern Ireland state in 1920–2. But this action threatened also to jeopardise the safety of the minority itself, vulnerable as it was to Unionist reprisal.

Yet Catholics had to settle down in the northern state, however much they resented its existence; and the passage of time, and the needs of their society, meant that they had to deal in some respects with the Unionist government. Reasonable compromises were made on the issue of Roman Catholic primary and secondary schools; which amounted to a kind of informal recognition of the state.[5] Individual educated Roman Catholics might rise in the legal profession, or the medical profession. Some were willing to give the state the benefit of the doubt. In the early 1960s the Nationalist Party even accepted the formal position of Her Majesty's Opposition in Stormont. Moreover the failure of the IRA campaign of 1956–62 demonstrated that the minority were largely unmoved by an appeal to turn its grievances into political violence. And when Ulster seemed about to revert to street politics in the general election of October 1964, following the attempt by the Royal Ulster Constabulary to remove a republican flag from nationalist offices in West Belfast, the urgent calls by Catholic political and religious leaders for calm and responsible behaviour seemed to show that minority politics had come to rest finally on the constitutional path.

New directions

The passage of time had altered the minority perspective in Northern Ireland; indeed, it could be said – at least, in the 1960s – that it had finally established that perspective as a minority one. This acceptance partly explains the profound change in Catholic politics in the north when a new, articulate, and modern political movement first emerged in the form of the 'political study group', National Unity, founded in 1959, which arranged a convention of nationalist representatives to consider the idea of reunification by consent, and a new strategy of concentration on social and economic issues instead of the principle of the constitution. The nationalist party leader, Eddie McAteer, was hostile to the ambitions of the new movement, and when it constituted itself the National Democratic Party in 1965 it made no impression on the electorate. But it had put forward the idea of a secular progressive party, based on Catholics but not on exclusive Catholic political traditions. In 1964 a campaign for social justice was launched and this idea was taken up more effectively by the Northern Ireland Civil Rights Association in 1967, which signified that Northern Catholics had, for the time being at least, abandoned their old-style nationalist goals for a concentration on minority grievances: discrimination in housing, work, local government and the like.

The NICRA tacitly, and in a few cases more openly, recognised the constitutional position of Northern Ireland; and they seemed almost to be more Unionist, in that they looked to London and especially to sympathisers in the Labour government, rather than to Dublin, for support. But their emergence was not attributable to the sterility of old nationalism, or to their rejection of IRA violence, alone. Nor was it merely the creation of the middle-class educated generation created by the Education Act of 1947 (modelled on the Butler Act of 1944), now bearing fruit. Social and economic change, the prosperity of the newly educated Catholics growing to manhood might have provided the material for the new Catholic political style.[6] But this was not enough. What mattered finally was that, even in Northern Ireland, the 1960s had arrived: the questioning, argumentative, anti-establishment age, which flourished in Great Britain, had its impact even in the old-fashioned north, even amongst the more traditionalist groups of Northern Ireland Catholics. In a period when accepted attitudes were no longer regarded as acceptable simply because they had lasted for generations, the NICRA caught the mood of the period as well as the more particular complaints of the Catholic minority. For a minority to retain its status unmoved and unchanged required not only the determination of the majority to oblige it to accept that status, but the acquiescence of the minority in that status that it was expected to accept. In Northern Ireland in the 1960s not only was the majority split over its policy towards, and concept of, the minority as 'Liberal Unionism' emerged under the premiership of Terence O'Neill; the minority, or a substantial proportion of it, was determined that its previous acquiesence in its status must be challenged, and if possible, changed.

The NICRA succeeded beyond any predictions, even of its most optimistic supporters, in moving minority status from the sterile years since partition; the mobilisation of mass support did not take the form of orthodox political organisation, for the minority was, as always, electorally in a minority. The NICRA was a vociferous, clever, well orchestrated pressure group which, like any such group, gained its success through its effective propaganda, especially in Great Britain, where the Unionist case was almost swamped by NICRA media effort; and also by its tactic of applying pressure where its opponents were weakest, and where they must of necessity concede to superior power. London might not want to get too deeply involved in the affairs of Northern Ireland; but the price of non-involvement was seen to be the cajoling of Unionism into concessions to the minority. This process placed intolerable strains on the Unionist party and government. And it was the astonishing spectacle of Stormont, the institution which the minority held in a mixture of fear and contempt, crumbling before British pressure, and the solidarity of the formidable Unionist party also crumbling as it split into pro and anti reformers, that finally destroyed the old Nationalist Party, and enabled the new Catholic leaders to found a successful, modern political party, the Social Democratic and Labour Party, in 1970.

This party seemed to conform to the character of nationalist parties in the United Kingdom generally in the late 1960s and 1970s, in that it was social democratic, somewhat left of centre (in Irish terms at least), and with a sophisticated and well-honed electoral machine; and above all, frequent and, on the whole, sympathetic media coverage. Its leader, John Hume, was a plausible and even charismatic figure, able to perform equally convincingly on British, American and world television, and in his own Bogside constituency. He quickly emerged as the Catholic leader who could interpret, not only Roman Catholic, but Ulster politics to a bewildered world outside. But he still represented a minority that was, in the nature of things, a very oddly placed minority. Unionist opposition to reform had undoubtedly soured the Catholic political experience between 1968 and 1970; yet the main objectives of the original NICRA had been achieved by 1970.[7] The problem now lay in the obstacles and the opportunities that the politics of reform had generated for Catholic politics in 1968–70. The obstacles, Unionist fear and opposition – at times violent – to the NICRA, culminating in the serious disturbances of August 1969, had helped provoke a recrudescence of the old idea that the Catholics must look to themselves for self-defence: and that meant reorganising and revitalising the Irish Republican Army structure. The presence of the British Army, at first welcomed by the minority, in some areas recalled the old, but not forgotten battles of long ago, when the same army helped fasten the ligature of partition on the minority it was now sent to protect.[8] This ambivalence was soon felt by the army, which was confronted with a deteriorating relationship with the Roman Catholics whose areas it policed, patrolled, or occupied – depending on the point of view. When 'nationalism', as distinct from Catholic social democratic politics, began to re-emerge in 1970 then the SDLP had to look to its credentials as a party that was not to be outflanked by a small, but increasingly volatile, minority within the minority: Irish Republicanism.

The politics of reform had also generated opportunities; or rather, had exposed weaknesses undreamt of by Catholics in the Unionist state. Here was Unionism, divided, paralysed, resenting Westminster yet calling upon it for help in the crisis of August 1969. Even if the original programme of reforms had been envisaged as a final settlement of Catholic grievances, the spectacle of a disordered and discredited Unionist government stirred Catholic opinion, and opened up new objectives. These objectives – to insert a wedge into the Unionist party, and exert pressure upon it so that Catholics could think the unthinkable – a share in the actual government of the state – were not formally conceived nor proposed. But they were the product of the fragility of the Unionist government, which under Brian Faulkner – no friend to nationalists – found itself obliged to offer some changes in the administration, but not the structure, of government in the shape of two Catholic salaried chairmanships of certain key committees, those dealing with social services, industrial development and environmental matters. This was first tentatively accepted, and then rejected, as the SDLP encountered opposition from some of its own supporters, many of whom were now convinced that Stormont had been dealt a fatal blow by the crisis of 1969–70, from which it could not easily recover.[9] Moreover, Roman Catholic political unity was not as solid as it appeared. For while the SDLP could count on the Catholic vote, it was aware of the increasing appeal of military action, especially after the Unionist government's introduction of internment as a means of combating the IRA in August 1971. Catholic unity was best created in opposition, not in participation in some minor way in a still Unionist state, and with accusations of a sell-out lurking in the background. Thus between 1971 and 1972 Catholic politics lapsed once more into the refusal to have anything to do with Northern Ireland government, and the restatement of historical grievances against its very existence.

In 1972 the fall of Stormont placed nationalist politics into a new mould, while not entirely freeing them from an old one. Militant Republicanism and general nationalist disaffection had made it intolerable for the British government to prolong much longer the existence of a Unionist regime whose security activities were bringing obloquy on Westminster as well as Belfast. Militant republicanism would continue its campaign unabated, and its lack of support throughout the 1970s in most sections of the Catholic population hardly deterred it from its objective of taking Northern Ireland out of the United Kingdom altogether. But now that the British government had embarked on the search for a form of administration in Northern Ireland that would receive widespread and general allegiance from both nationalists and Unionists, the SDLP found itself with new ambitions, but also new dangers. Between the power-sharing executive of 1974, which lasted only a few months, and the Hillsborough Agreement of November 1985, constitutional nationalist politicians pursued goals which appeared on the face of it contradictory. They sought to win a place in the political system, or in any political system that might be devised to run the province. Yet at the same time they demanded what came to be called the 'Irish dimension' – some role, however shadowy or ill-defined, for the Republic in the internal affairs of the North.

This dualism in political goals has earned the SDLP much criticism, and not only from Unionists in the north. It might be attributed to a simple desire to turn the tables on the Unionists, and rub salt into their wounds; but such an explanation does not account for the fact that the SDLP has pursued this Irish dimension in circumstances – such as the power-sharing agreement of Sunningdale – that seem to work against its primary aim, to establish a foothold in Northern Ireland government. It also owes a great deal to the SDLP's vital necessity to survive the challenge of the militant wing of northern nationalism, Sinn Fein, which in June 1983 took 40 per cent of the total anti-Unionist vote.[10] But it owes much to the paradox of nationalist politics in the north after the partition of Ireland.

The identity problem

The nationalist population was faced with two major contradictions. It could pursue the path of constitutional opposition, and thus accept permanent minority status. It could reject this status and attempt to overthrow the state and gain reunification by force. But this would invite the kind of murderous Unionist reprisals that occurred in 1920, and then again in 1973, the latter dismissed by a Protestant paramilitary spokesman as an 'emotional reaction'.[11] The militant option, moreover, usually met with indifference or outright hostility in the south of Ireland. But the constitutional option inevitably led back to the resented role of permanent minority. Yet Dublin always held open the theoretical right of the Northern Ireland Catholic to think of himself as a member of the rightful majority in the island.

It was a bewildering role that must inevitably provoke occasional, and at times serious, questions about the national identity of Northern Catholics. Northern Ireland is a distinct region with a special character and history that marks it off, not only from Great Britain, but from the rest of Ireland as well. Such a region might be expected to produce local sentiment, piety, even patriotism. And the 1970s witnessed the manifestation of a phenomenon that might be called 'Ulster nationalism', or at least a special brand of northern patriotism.[12] But this was a sentiment held by Protestants alone; and its development only exacerbated the minority predicament, for the minority could feel no response to this sense of 'Ulsterness', and might resent its implications. The civil rights period taught the minority that it need not expect any new disposition on the part of many Unionists to welcome them as full citizens of the north; and their position as a minority must always cast doubts upon any chance or hope they might have of establishing themselves in some kind of permanent political power. The only way that constitutional nationalism could overcome its minority position was by looking to Dublin for some kind of guarantee that it would never again be relegated to a permanent political second place.

But it was not only the calculations of Irish political arithmetic that mattered. For the Catholic population of the north was from the 1970s suffering from a kind of identity crisis. What was its identity anyway? John Hume sought to give it some definition when he declared in 1972 his 'right in my own country to say I am an Irishman and to work for the unification of this country.[13] Some nationalists sought identity in the traditional nationalist symbols of Irish street names and the Irish language, however remote these might seem to the everyday experience of the urban Catholic working classes. But the Catholic identity was best expressed in the words of the Ulster poet Seamus Heaney, quoted by one leading SDLP councillor, some ten years after the fall of the power-sharing executive of 1974:

> Where does the SDLP, with Seamus Heaney,
> draw the line
> At being robbed of what is mine,
> My *patria*, my deep design
> To be at home
> In my own place and dwell within
> Its proper name ...?[14]

An Irish dimension, then, to the Catholic nationalist was not merely a political pawn, nor a blow at Protestants (though it would of course offer that satisfying experience), nor a guarantee of Catholic rights; it was a necessary part of the Catholic attempt to reassert a confidence and an identity denied them by their sudden severance from the nationalist population of the whole of Ireland in 1921, a predicament best summed up in Heaney's brief, but vivid, description of an encounter with the police in his young manhood:

> ... the air
> All moonlight and a scent of hay, policemen
> Swung their crimson flashlamps, crowding round
> The car like black cattle, snuffing and
> pointing
> The muzzle of a sten-gun in my eye:
> 'What's your name, driver?'
> 'Seamus ...'
> *'Seamus?'*[15]

But while nationalists draw attention to the fact that Unionists were the 'real' minority in the whole island of Ireland, and the more racially-minded among them dismissed the Unionists as mere 'colons' to be cast back where they belonged,[16] this did not shake the facts of demography and political geography. For while Unionists comprised a minority in the island, Dublin's indifference about the ending of partition, its impracticality as a political prospect, and the experience of over fifty years of self-government, left the Unionists unlike the nationalists with certain assurances, however much these may have been shaken since 1972. Robert McCartney, a liberal-minded Official Unionist, could still describe the north as 'our house',[17] a phrase whose significance he hardly noticed – but whose lack of notice was itself significant and spoke more about Unionist assumptions than many volumes of the more strident Paisleyite Unionist rhetoric.

This question – of whose 'house' the north really was – posed itself not only to the SDLP. The attempt by a section of the minority to assert identity and majority feelings opened prospects for the militant republicans to claim continuity between their campaign and that of the Irish separatists who had demanded an Ireland Gaelic and Free in the 1916 Rising, and then fought for it again in the 1919–21 independence struggle. This continuity was rejected by most southern Irish nationalists, and by Republican veterans, uneasy at the equation between the heroic deeds of Michael Collins and Patrick Pearse, and the bombing of innocent men, women and children by the IRA. But it was given a new impetus by the hunger strike of 1981 which ended with the death of ten prisoners between May and August and provided scenes reminiscent of earlier Irish political martyrdom: indeed, IRA propagandists looked back to earlier examples, and one leading Republican explained that Bobby Sands, the first martyr of 1981, saw his case as 'a microcosm of the way the Brits are treating Ireland historically and presently'.[18] IRA prisoners were seen as special, the victims rather than the cause of the troubles: dormant Republicanism was reawakened. This posed particularly difficult problems for the SDLP, faced with a by-election in Fermanagh-South Tyrone which the hunger striking Sands contested as a candidate for the IRA.

The SDLP's decision not to contest the seat was defended by Hume with a mixture of procedural points (the SDLP's constitution does not allow the executive to override the local constituency on such issues), and expedient politics: 'If you are going to take them on, take them in a place of your own choosing'.[19] But the real issue was whether the SDLP could afford to open a kind of second front in Northern Ireland politics, and be seen to be fighting in some sense the British battle against the IRA. Of course it could be argued that the real battle was between violence and constitutionalism; but in the heightened atmosphere of 1981 these were rather thin and abstract terms, unable to compete with the idea of a suffering people, historically bound hand and foot by the British in 1921.

Endemic dilemmas

The fashionable term to describe the political mentality of the nationalist people in the wake of the 1981 hunger strike was 'alienation'; but whatever the difficulties involved in this overworked expression[20], it was one that most nationalists felt described their predicament. This posed problems for the SDLP, though not of course for Sinn Fein and the IRA, which sought military victory and the final solution of the Protestant question. If the SDLP was to demand that the Unionist 'veto' on moves towards a united Ireland be abandoned by the 'guarantor'[21], the British government, then it risked the accusation that it was not, after all, substantially different from the militant Republican movement; but to modify its Irish unity aspiration would cost it support in Catholic areas, now moved with the concept of 'alienation'. However, to avoid identification with its Sinn Fein opponents, it agreed that moves towards unity must be by consent. But the problem was that consent might include the right for Unionists to refuse to move towards unity; this part of the consenting process must therefore pose great difficulties for constitutional nationalists.[22]

The dilemmas are better understood if the real nature of the nationalist minority's ambitions, as well as its predicament, are appreciated. Its status as a minority obliges it either to accept that position – which its experience has taught it is an unenviable one – or seek to establish a new self-respect based on a majority outlook. But in these circumstances the question of unity cannot readily be abandoned, and moves towards the Unionist 'consent' are fraught with difficulty. Its political ambitions pose equally daunting problems. For while the language of political commentators in describing hopes of a settlement in Northern Ireland are couched in terms such as 'reconciliation' – terms which the SDLP themselves would use – the fact remains that the Ulster crisis is a struggle for power, not reconciliation. The search for power might not be an absolute one and reconciliation might follow; but the necessity for the minority to seek power, its assertion of its right to power, its ability to use power to dismantle the continuing in-built discriminatory character of the Northern State (frequently described as 'irreformable') must necessarily shape its tactics and also, as a democratic party, its public political language. Such tactics have earned criticism, and one former SDLP executive member has declared that the SDLP's absentionist stance after 1982 'indirectly encouraged support for the IRA and Sinn Fein since the Nationalist electorate were no longer being given an alternative which stressed the value of participation'.[23] 'It is impossible to turn the clock back to 1920'.[24]

But this criticism misunderstood the real and central need of the post-hunger strike SDLP: the need to reassert not only its leadership of the minority, but to reassert its own confidence. The main place where this confidence could be found was Dublin and the New Ireland Forum, where constitutional nationalism, north and south, examined its traditions, discussed those of its opponents, and above all turned the political spotlight back on the centrality of the constitutional political method.[25] Here the SDLP could enjoy its 'real' majority status, formally inscribed in the Forum Report, which declared that the parties in the Forum represented 'a large majority of the people of Ireland'[26] and which hoped to convince Unionists that the majority saw their tradition as an essential part of a joint endeavour. The majority status of the SDLP was reinforced in the Forum's recommendation of a unitary Irish state which would 'restore the historic integrity of Ireland and end the divisions in the country', ending also 'the alienation and deep sense of injustice felt by nationalists'.[27] This rediscovery of confidence (described, hopefully without irony, by one political scientist as 'surprising'[28]) was enhanced by the Anglo-Irish Agreement of 1985, and indeed enabled that Agreement to be made in the first place. Moreover, the Agreement, opposed by Unionists and Sinn Fein alike, placed Sinn Fein at the obvious disadvantage of apparently siding with the Unionists: in a BBC Newsnight poll in January 1986 10 per cent of Sinn Fein voters said they strongly supported the Agreement, and a further 22 per cent tended to support it.[29] At last Roman Catholic constitutional politicians had recovered the initiative; and rediscovered a sense of the rightness of their cause, so badly wounded by the hunger-strike crisis.

But the Anglo-Irish Agreement, or any political arrangement that might emerge from it, still leaves the nationalists in the north in a predicament shaped by their history in the Ireland that emerged after the troubles of 1916–23. The nationalists were always a minority in the political, social and economic life of the north even before 1920; after partition their potential development, social, political, economic, was arrested, halted; and to these disadvantages was added the psychological handicap of their permanent second class – or possibly even non-citizenship: to the Unionist government the standard citizen of Ulster was a Protestant and Unionist, and the prevailing tone of social and cultural life (as expressed, for example, in BBC Northern Ireland) was one with a distinctly Protestant tone, or emphasis. It was easy to forget there was a minority. It was certainly convenient to do so.

The minority has thus lived in an environment very different, not only from that of the Unionist majority, but from the majority in the rest of Ireland, which was able to find its confidence and identity in its separate statehood, especially under the dramatic and vigorous leadership of Eamon de Valera. But the northern nationalist had no such leader, no such experience. The growing indifference in the south to a united Ireland reinforced the northern Catholics' isolation; but even if there were a united Ireland, the Roman Catholic from the north would find himself in a very different relationship to his new Ireland: his citizenship would have to be established, his presence would not be wholeheartedly welcomed, his political style might disturb the even tenor of Leinster House ways. And he would still have to live in the north (assuming that the Unionists would not have driven him from his homeland in their fury and anger at a united Ireland, the option the Protestants dread above all). But if disbelief is willingly suspended, and a peaceful united Ireland imagined, then the future of the Northern Ireland nationalist would be shaped by his past: he would, in a real sense, remain a minority of his majority in all Ireland, as in Northern Ireland. Even his nationalism, at its most extreme expression in the political wing of the IRA, Sinn Fein, differs from that of his southern counterpart; as one commentator has remarked, anyone who journeys from the south to the north only realises he is in Northern Ireland when he sees the Irish tricolour flag, which is virtually absent in the independent Republic of Ireland.[30]

The history of minority nationalism in Northern Ireland is of more general interest. Minorities in Western Europe have, in recent times, sought privileges and rights denied to them by the majority in the state in which they happen to live; but they have not sought separate nationhood.[31] European integration has also lessened the opportunity for separate statehood, or transfer to another state, even if that option were desired. No western European state encourages irredentist feelings. But

Ireland is still, politically and culturally, on the fringe of Europe, membership of the EEC notwithstanding; and she offers an example of a minority nationalism that can look to a bordering state for help and encouragement for majority, irredentist feelings, even if this support barely goes beyond lip-service, and even if those southern politicians whose constitution lays claim to the north are careful not to set a precise timetable to the British withdrawal that some of them argue is the only solution.[32] The Roman Catholic of Northern Ireland still stands poised between the alternatives of pursuing the irredentist goal, by peaceful or violent means, or a combination of the two; and seeking a role in some power-sharing devolved government (without of course necessarily abandoning his long-term hopes of realising his 'natural' majority status). His most acute problem therefore lies not in the choice, but in the danger that these choices may not be compatible. And while the violent faction presses on with its full claim, both Sinn Fein and the SDLP may find themselves, not only embarrassed, but paralysed by their paradoxical history: that of a minority nationalism with majority feelings.

Notes

1. D.G. Boyce, *Nationalism in Ireland* (London, 1982), p.275.
2. D.G. Boyce, op. cit, pp.275–8.
3. John Bowman, *De Valera and the Ulster Question, 1917–1972* (Oxford, 1983), p.312.
4. I. McAllister 'Political Parties: traditional and modern', in I. Derby (ed.) *Northern Ireland: the Background to the Conflict* (Belfast, 1983).
5. G.S. Walker, *Harry Midgley and the Failure of Labour in Northern Ireland* (Manchester, 1985), p.219.
6. John Hickey, *Religion and the Northern Ireland Problem* (Belfast, 1983), pp.102–3, 121.
7. Padraig O'Malley, *The Uncivil Wars: Ireland Today* (Belfast, 1983), p.207.
8. Ibid., pp.207–9.
9. Ibid., p.310.
10. Harvey Cox, 'Who Wants a United Ireland', *Government and Opposition* (1985), vol.20, p.44.
11. O'Malley, op. cit., p.13; see also pp.316–17. The UDA murdered about 400 Catholics between 1971 and 1976.
12. D.G. Boyce, 'Ulster: Some Consequences of Devolution', *Planet*, no.13, Aug.–Sept. 1972, pp.8–9.
13. B. White, *John Hume: Statesman of the Troubles* (Belfast, 1984).
14. Brian Feeney, *Fortnight* (Belfast), October 1984, pp.4, 8.
15. Seamus Heaney, *Selected Poems, 1965–1975* (London, 1981 ed.), p.130: 'The Ministry of Fear'.
16. O'Malley, op. cit., p.298. It is significant that IRA violence is most aggressive in areas with large Catholic majorities (in excess of

90 per cent), contiguous with wider territorial areas also with large Catholic majorities (Michael Poole, 'The Demography of Violence', in Derby (ed.), op. cit., pp.165–8).

17. Ibid., p.168.
18. See the material reviewed by D.G. Boyce, 'A Callous Story and a Dirty Deed', in Alan O'Day and Jonah Alexander (eds.), *Ireland's Terrorist Dilemma* (Dordrecht, 1986), pp.25–6.
19. O'Malley, op. cit., pp.123–4.
20. Michael Farrell, *Fortnight* (October, 1984), p.5.
21. See the SDLP manifesto for the Westminster election of 1979: 'The question is not *whether* Britain should disengage from Ireland, but *when* and *in what circumstances*' (Richard Rose, 'Is the United Kingdom a State', *Strathclyde Studies in Public Policy*, no.114 (Glasgow,1983), p.26.
22. O'Malley, op. cit., pp.111–12.
23. Brendan McAllister, *Fortnight* (21 Jan., 3 Feb. 1985), p.12. It must be stressed that the SDLP did not see its tactics in this light. See S. Elliott and Richard A. Wilford, 'The 1982 Northern Ireland Assembly Election', *Strathclyde Studies in Public Policy*, no.119 (Glasgow, 1983), pp.31–2.
24. McAllister, op. cit., p.12.
25. This was emphasised by the SDLP in its 1983 campaign; see Elliott and Wilford, op. cit., p.31.
26. *New Ireland Forum: Report* (Dublin, 1984), p.19.
27. Ibid., pp.28–9, 31.
28. Michael Poole, 'Demography of Violence', in J. Derby (ed.), op. cit., p.160.
29. Jim Cusack, *Fortnight* (October, 1986), p.11.
30. Harvey Cox, op. cit., p.44.
31. An exception are the Basques. But Spain, like Ireland, is formally in the EEC, but culturally very much on the fringe of Western Europe.
32. O'Malley, op. cit., p.94–7.

Chapter four

Northern Ireland: The Unionists

Simon Murphy

Unionism in the 1980s

Political Unionism in Northern Ireland is not a monolith. It was not after
its emergence as a parliamentary force during the Home Rule debates of
the 1880s, and it certainly is not in contemporary Northern Ireland.
There exist two competing strands within Unionism which constantly
vie with each other for political support amongst the majority
community of Northern Ireland.

The Ulster Unionist Party, more commonly known as the Official
Unionist Party (OUP), was established in 1921. Its roots are to be found
in the Ulster Unionist Council of 1905. The OUP is the traditional face
of Northern Irish Unionism. Up until the late 1960s, the OUP was the
only Unionist political party of any electoral note, exercising as it did
electoral domination over the Northern Irish political system.

In most of the parliaments from 1921 to 1972, the Unionists held
around forty of the fifty two seats in the Northern Ireland House of
Commons, and usually held at least ten of the twelve Westminster
seats. It was unquestionably a party of government, and many
Unionist MPs never had to fight an election.[1]

Up until the 1960s, the OUP was a predominantly united party,
devoid of any significant splits and experiencing only minor internal
pressures. It received the support of the great majority of Northern
Ireland's Unionists, becoming, in fact, synonymous with the Northern
Irish state itself.[2]

Within the OUP of the 1980s, there exist two competing factions.
The party's official policy line, as advocated by the leader, James
Molyneaux and by the former MP for South Down, Enoch Powell, is for
the total integration of Northern Ireland within the UK state. In effect
this would lead to a situation where Northern Ireland would be treated
by central government in the same manner as any English county.
Coexisting with the official party integrationism, is a pronounced de-

volutionary current. This is represented by deputy party leader, Harold McCusker. Advocates of such a policy wish to see a devolutionary parliament returned to Northern Ireland, as was the case prior to the introduction of direct rule from Westminster in March 1972.

The OUP is perceived very much to be a conservative, middle-class party, though for the forty-five or so years of its electoral supremacy, it drew virtually all the working-class Unionist votes. It also normally wears the label of more moderate pragmatic Unionism, though it is by no means as moderate as the Alliance Party of Northern Ireland. The Alliance Party is a party of the Union, but which does attract cross-communal support. The OUP is often viewed by its political rivals, along with the predominantly Catholic and Nationalist Social Democratic and Labour Party (SDLP), as the party of the 'fur coat brigade', i.e. as bourgeois and somewhat 'soft'. Nevertheless, the OUP remains the single largest party in Northern Ireland. Being the traditional face of Northern Irish Unionism, it has continued to retain a substantial core of loyal supporters, despite the rapid emergence to electoral prominence of the Democratic Unionist Party (DUP). In the 1970 Westminster general election the OUP polled 54.1 per cent of the votes cast. In the 1983 Westminster general election, the OUP polled 34.0 per cent compared to 20.0 per cent for the DUP.

The vote lost by the OUP between 1970 and 1983 has found its new electoral home with the DUP, which is bent on challenging the OUP for the mantle of leader of Northern Irish Unionism. The DUP is a relatively new and inexperienced political party. It was established on 29th September 1971, as a response to the perceived appeasement and 'un-Unionist' policies of the OUP. Its leader is the charismatic and imposing figure of Dr Rev. Ian Paisley, probably the political figure with the highest profile to have emerged in Northern Ireland since the 1960s. The DUP is sometimes referred to as the Loyalist, or Protestant, party of Northern Ireland. Loyalism identifies those people and organisations which are particularly fundamentalist religiously or in their views on the constitutional status of Northern Ireland. In terms of the norms and masses, a Loyalist is more likely to reject any compromise with the Nationalist community, e.g. power-sharing, to reject an institutional role for the Irish Republic in the affairs of Northern Ireland, and to demonstrate a pronounced line of independence, in both thinking and action, where the dictates and policies of the Westminster parliament are involved. He/she is more likely to belong to a fundamentalist Protestant religious sect. This is not to say that the OUP does not demonstrate many of these tendencies, just that the DUP has built its electoral success around them.

Ian Paisley himself emerged in the early 1960s as a vociferous, if slightly eccentric Bible-bashing fundamentalist Presbyterian preacher.

He was largely disregarded by the body politic of the day, being seen mainly as something of a freak whose electoral appeal would be regulated and curtailed by his overt religiosity and bigotry. But Paisley has out-distanced many a more moderate Unionist politician and now stands as the single most popular Unionist politician in Northern Ireland. At the 1979 European elections he polled 170,000 votes, or 30 per cent of the first preference votes cast. This put him 80 per cent ahead of the total amount of votes polled by the two OUP candidates.[3] Indeed, in the aftermath of the June 1984 European elections, when Paisley polled more first preference votes than any other politician in Europe (over 230,251), some of his supporters began referring to him as the most popular man in Europe!

The DUP's official party policy revolves around two predominant concerns. The first is its oft-stated preference for devolution for Northern Ireland. The party has repeatedly called for the renunciation of direct rule, accompanied by the return of devolution to Northern Ireland, along the lines of the 1921–72 Stormont parliament. This devolutionary stance is expressive of a not insubstantial independence streak within the party. The DUP has always advocated Northern Ireland being administered from a locally sited legislative assembly. The DUP has demonstrated a willingness to participate in assembly-type politics. The DUP did not boycott the Prior Assembly (the 1982 Northern Irish Assembly, established under the guidance of the Secretary of State, James Prior) as the OUP did after the Darkely Chapel murders in November 1983. This favourable disposition towards assembly-type politics can also be construed as an indication of a DUP desire to become an experienced political party in as short a space of time as possible.

The second concern of the DUP is with the security aspects of the present inter-communal conflict and instability in Northern Ireland. The DUP asserts that a workable and durable solution to the problems of Northern Ireland will only be possible after the paramilitary threat has been disposed of. Therefore the DUP's preoccupation with the restoration of law and order is frequently at the expense of the search for cross-communally supported political structures. This is not to say that the OUP is not concerned with the security problem. But rather that the OUP has demonstrated itself to be more willing to engage in politics while the violence continued, especially during the 1971–4 period. This willingness in itself was a contributory factor to the split within Unionism.

It is possible to draw a comparison between the respective political elites of both communities in Northern Ireland. The OUP and the SDLP have demonstrated themselves to be much more prepared to consider radical solutions to old imponderables than either the DUP or the

Provisional Sinn Fein (PSF). Both the DUP and the PSF organise around, and function to, certain inherited atavistic truths. The realisation of which, they assert, can be the only possible signal to progress in other, perhaps unrelated, fields. In addition, the OUP/SDLP and the DUP/PSF draw their respective electoral support and governing ideologies from differing constituencies. Basically, this is reflected in the more working-class base to the electoral support of the DUP/PSF bloc. Thus the DUP's appeal is largely as a working-class party. One of its co-founders asserted that it would be 'right wing in the sense of being strong on the Constitution, but to the left on social policies'[4]. By this it was meant that the DUP would resist very firmly any deviations from the constitutional status of Northern Ireland within the UK and outside the Irish Republic, but that it would work for the improvement of the social and economic conditions of the working class in a way that the OUP had never been capable of. The DUP also receives the support of the majority of the more fundamentalist Protestant religious factions.

As such, the DUP is very much the manifestation of political Protestantism. In 1951, Paisley himself created a Protestant sect, the Free Presbyterian Church, and has been its sole moderator ever since. This is a small, vociferous, extreme Presbyterian sect within the ranks of the Protestant faith: 'Where the mainstream protestant denominations dither, Free Presbyterianism fills the vacuum and converts it into political action. In consequence, political Protestantism has become a force'.[5] Due to the essentially religious *Weltanshauung* of the Free Presbyterians, 'Every Catholic action is part of a conspiracy to achieve unification, and where the reality does not bear out preconceptions, reality is simply rearranged so as to confirm a larger scheme of deception'.[6] The suspicious nature of political Protestanism will be examined in greater depth below. Its disproportionate influence, however, is indicative of the wider role played by the fundamentalist Protestant sects in the political activity of Northern Ireland since the late 1960s.

The DUP's *raison d'être* is its fear that middle class, 'fur coat' Unionism will sell out the shibboleths and aspirations of traditional Protestant Unionism. Such sentiment was clearly illustrated by Paisley's reaction to Capt. O'Neill's intention to 'build bridges between the two traditions' in Northern Ireland in the 1960s. Paisley retorted that 'a traitor and a bridge are very much alike for they both go over to the other side'. The DUP is a static, religiously inspired and fundamentalist force in Northern Irish politics. It is inherently suspicious of any changes in the status quo. The reasons for such obstructionism will be examined at length below. It very much reflects some of the psychological components of Unionism. The spectre of a sell-out by moderate pragmatic Unionism, the British Foreign Office, the British people, or any combination of the three, constantly haunts the DUP and political Protestantism. As O'Malley notes, 'It is the politics of paranoia'.[7]

The significance of the intra-Unionist tensions may be lost on many passive observers. But these strains have constantly exercised a pronounced regulatory influence upon the course of Unionist political development and behaviour, especially since the mid-1960s. In particular, the liberal, revisionist tendencies of Official Unionism have lost it electoral support to 'Ultra' Unionist political organisations such as the DUP. Northern Ireland amply demonstrates that in divided societies, 'the strength of Ultra sentiment, of course, reduces the leaders' latitude for consociational initiatives to an absolute minimum'.[8]

The roots of the intra-Unionist divide are to be found in the pre-Partition days, when 'The basic problem of the poorer Protestant was that to secure his independence from the Irish Republic he had to support politically those he neither liked nor trusted'.[9] The Ulster Unionist Party portrayed itself as the only means by which Northern Ireland's Protestants could ensure the continuation of the British link and exclusion from the social, economic and religious shackles of the Irish Free State. So long as this remained the case, fundamentalist Protestants and working-class Unionists were prepared to place their trust in the established Unionist elite. An outwardly appearing Unionist electoral monolith was created, impervious to socio-economic issues that might have affected cross-cutting loyalties, united by the constitutional status of Northern Ireland. But this apparent unity was of a highly conditional, contractual nature. If the established Unionist elite demonstrated any propensity to waver in its defence of inherited, traditional Unionist beliefs, then the contract could be reviewed. It is precisely such a review which began to emerge through the 1960s liberalism of Capt. O'Neill. The breakdown of this contract altogether had a very profound effect in 1974, when a general strike appeared to defy the policies of the established Unionist elite.

The DUP will resist any changes in the balance of power within Northern Ireland, if that change is perceived as having detrimental effect upon the religious and/or political status of Northern Ireland within the UK 'Unsound' Unionists such as O'Neill in the late 1960s and Brian Faulkner in 1974 were defeated and expurgated. The following observation in 1972 concerning the fates of two constrasting Unionist politicians, William Craig and Capt. O'Neill, further illustrates the issue:

> The manners of the two men correspond to their positions. O'Neill has an English accent and smiles a good deal. Craig has an Ulster accent and hardly smiles at all in public. O'Neill was at one time very popular in the South – he was Man of the Year in a poll run by one of the Dublin mass circulation papers at the end of 1968 and was

pleased by this. Craig is unlikely ever to be Dublin's Man of the Year, and would suspect a trap if he were. Craig is still a force in Ulster politics, O'Neill is no longer one.[10]

Indeed, even Craig's excellent Unionist credentials were unable to prevent his marginalisation in Northern Irish politics in the mid-1970s, at the hands of yet more fundamentalist Unionist politicians.[11] As Professor Rose has pointed out, 'To seek friends amongst one's enemies is to risk making enemies of one's friends'.[12]

Intra-Unionist division is a constant regulator of the orientation of political Unionism. Compromise affecting inherited values, relative power structures, and patterns of intercommunal interaction, can be severely stifled by an omnipresent need to cater for Ultra sentiment in societies divided along rigid ethnic, religious or linguistic cleavages. In May 1974, the concessions of the pro-Sunningdale Unionists were destroyed by the emergence of coherent, Ultra Unionist opposition. During the hunger strikes of the first half of 1981, no Unionist deviation from the path of no compromise was permissible, or electorally and personally advisable. Similarly, in February 1986, a clear indication of guarded concession by the leaders of the two Unionist parties, Ian Paisley and James Molyneaux[13] (two men who established their political reputations on obduracy and defence of traditional Unionist values), was immediately reversed on their return to Northern Ireland due to Ultra pressure. Consequently, in the light of the observations that have been made so far, it is possible to assert that, 'There really are two Protestant minds. Relations between the two main Protestant bodies have been at times far from cordial. A coolness persists to this day, and there is of course still a subtle social difference'.[14] The implications of the existence of the two contrasting Unionist states of reality mean that, 'The psychology of political Protestantism which is intent on keeping Northern Ireland out of a united Ireland at all costs, is quite different to the psychology of Unionism, which is intent on keeping Northern Ireland within the United Kingdom at all costs'.[15] This, as we will see later, has implications for the relationship between Westminster and Unionism.

The religious fundamentalism of political Protestantism, as represented by the DUP, is translated into a near spiritually inspired rejection of any initiatives which could be perceived as making the anathema of Irish reunification more probable. This obduracy is considerably at odds with the pragmatic streak within Unionism (as illustrated by factions within the OUP), which nevertheless remains adamant in its rejection of Irish unity. In terms of political practicalities, this pragmatism within the OUP has led at times to a greater preparedness on the part of OUP elites and non-elites to consider new structures of accommodation within Northern Ireland: for example, consociationalism, in the form of power-sharing, in the early 1970s. However, it is only fair to point out that since 1974, the OUP has demonstrated a more obdurate nature where the consideration of new structures for the government of Northern Ireland is concerned than it did during the preceding decade.

But the relevance of the intra-Unionist split is that it contributes to an understanding of the nature of the intractability of division and conflict within Northern Ireland. 'It is because Protestant distrusts Protestant, not just because Protestant distrusts Catholic, that the Ulster conflict is so intense'.[16]

Unionist motivation and political consciousness

The noted Northern Irish historian, A.T.Q. Stewart, in an emotional exposition of the Loyalist feeling of betrayal after the Anglo-Irish Agreement, noted that Hollywood always knew how to captivate an audience. Be it in 'Zulu', or in the 'Alamo', 'We are always on the side of the besieged, not the besiegers. Unless, that is they happen to be Ulster Protestants'.[17] And he concludes with the following lament for the predicament of Ireland's Unionist, Protestant community.

> As the sentries peer out from the ruins of the abandoned mission station, they see rising from the plain the spectral armies ranged against them – politicians, the press, serried ranks of clergy, the EEC and behind them again row upon row of Irish-Americans, their saddle bags stuffed with dollars,...[18]

This is a perfect cameo case illustrating that, psychologically, the Unionist community exists in a perpetual state of 'siege' (suggesting a close comparison with the Afrikaner laager mentality).

This mentality, with its concomitant fear of betrayal, subjugation and even pogrom, in part accounts for the peculiarly suspicious, apprehensive, intransigent, aggressive, and at times, bigoted nature of Unionism. The fear of being sold out, unwanted and under threat, plagues the Unionist psyche, producing also a resolve to draw on the community's own resources. As Andy Tyrie, commander of the Ulster Defence Association (a loyalist paramilitary organisation), put it:

> We are betrayed, maligned and our families live in constant fear and misery. We are a nuisance to our so-called allies and have no friends anywhere. Once more in the history of our people, we have our backs to the wall, facing extinction by one way or another. This is the moment to beware, for Ulstermen in this position fight mercilessly, till they or their enemies are dead.[19]

The inherited historical analysis of the Unionist community ensures that these emotions and fears all remain omnipresent features of contemporary Unionism. This is especially so within that branch of Unionism which is more fundamentalist and radical in its religious and political orientation.

The prognostications and actions of British governments since Gladstone and Lloyd George have done little to allay the fears of these Unionists. Take for example this quote from Mrs Thatcher: 'Northern Ireland is ... a fundamental part of the United Kingdom. If the majority of the people of Northern Ireland wish not to be, obviously we would honour their wish, whether it was to be independent or to join up elsewhere.'[20] For Unionists this contains a glaring contradiction. How is it possible for Northern Ireland to be a fundamental part of the UK, if the British Prime Minister is openly prepared to let it leave in certain circumstances? This equivocation concerning the long-term status of Northern Ireland as a component of the UK is a spur to Unionist intransigence and, as will be seen shortly, to Unionist independence. One eminent observer has noted: 'Nationalist claims that unionists are made intransigent by the "steel wall" of a British guarantee are the reverse of the truth; it is because the guarantee is not made of steel that Unionists need to show so much intransigence.'[21]

In relation to British reasons for keeping Ireland, Unionists believe that this is due as much to political expediency as to any emotional commitment to Ireland as an integral part of Britain:

... but their arguments [British party leaders] for staying on are more often based on the pragmatic argument that withdrawal could produce a bloodbath, than on the patriotic ground that Northern Ireland is inhabited by Britons and is part of the national territory. This makes the Unionists' position permanently insecure.[22]

As a consequence, Unionism demonstrates a pronounced propensity to be suspicious of all, and to abide only by its own version of the truth. This has a strong unifying influence upon political Unionism, especially during times of inter-communal tension, and can help to explain the apparently incongruous cross-class loyalties of Northern Irish Unionism. Consequently, 'Whatever basis there may exist for division between different classes of protestants, the first question that is asked is: "Who is using the division?"'.[23] Such a response points to another feature of the Unionist psyche. If an event, or a pronouncement, is perceived as incongruous to the rationale of the inherited folklore of the community, e.g. a Nationalist politician renouncing reunification, then it is disregarded as false or as a plot. Such a 'Trojan Horse' syndrome regards any apparent concession from enemies, or even from allies, who may be potentially treacherous, as mere sinister trickery. Friendly positioning from traditional enemies is rearranged to fit into the wider Unionist mentality of siege and betrayal.

Examples of such rearrangements are common. The Anglo-Irish summitry from 1980 onwards could be viewed as improving the economic and political links between two traditionally interdependent members of the European Community. To the Unionists, the summitry had a more sinister primary aim, viz. the extraction of Northern Ireland from the UK via a process of clandestine Anglo-Irish negotiation. 'Hence the hysterical reactions of Unionists; "special relationships" suggest clandestine activities, goings-on behind closed doors, secret deals; "reconciliation" is a euphemism for "unification" and "new institutional arrangements" are code words for an all-Ireland state'.[24] Similarly, the concept of consociationalism, or power-sharing, whilst it may have had success elsewhere around the world, was totally incongruous with a Unionist ethos which had always viewed its survival as dependent upon excluding the minority Catholic community from social, economic and political power. Power-sharing was a ploy, paving the way for the introduction of the Irish dimension and eventual unification.

For the Unionist, 'Every Catholic action is part of a conspiracy to achieve unification, and where the reality does not bear out preconceptions, reality is simply rearranged so as to conform to a larger scheme of deception'.[25] This paranoia is not experienced uniformly throughout the Unionist community. It is strongest amongst the more religiously inspired Unionists, as personified by Ian Paisley and the DUP (indeed, the above observation was written of the DUP). Paisley epitomises Unionist fears and perceptions of reality. He may not directly represent the views of all Unionists, but his psychological appeal, with its warnings of the consequences of compromise and concession, is pervasive. He has been attacked for exploiting the fears of religious and working-class Unionists for his own personal and political ends. Nevertheless, his atavism, deeply suspicious nature, intransigence and aggressive posturing, are all traits common to the Unionist community of Northern Ireland to a greater or lesser degree. Thus fundamentalist, radical Unionism sets the pace and acts as the spiritual and historical conscience of those Unionists inclined to greater pragmatism. Their fear, of losing electoral support to the more radical wing, is a genuine and pressing one. The fates of Capt. O'Neill and Brian Faulkner in the 1960s and 1970s testify to that. Intra-communal suspicions only add to the hold of siege and Trojan Horse mentality.

Any willingness to contemplate change can be readily undermined by appeals to past images and events, mobilising these archetypes in the Unionist political consciousness. Consequently, the rejection of the Sunningdale Agreements in 1974 (culminating in the Ulster Workers'

Strike) and the Anglo-Irish Agreement of 1985, should be totally comprehensible to the outside observer. The apparent pragmatism and moderation of both (especially the latter), and their truck with the Irish Republic, all too readily evoked the Trojan Horse syndrome and called forth, as an automatic reflex, the sloganeering of the more fundamentalist Unionists: 'No Surrender', 'Ourselves Alone', 'No Popery Here', 'Quis Separabit' (the defiant motto of the UDA), Je Maintiendrai (the motto of William of Orange), and 'Ulster Says No'. All these Unionists catch-phrases speak volumes for the influence of the siege mentality upon contemporary Unionism. '.... For the heart of the Unionist case beats to a seemingly immutable tune: not an inch, not now, not ever'[26]. A testament to its power is its capacity to always re-introduce unity, at a time of possible change and challenge, where there is party political division (OUP and DUP).

Conditional British identity and Ulster nationalism

The suspicion and fear inherent in Unionism have created a paradox where its national identity is concerned. Nowhere else in the United Kingdom is allegiance to the Crown and the Protestant faith, traditionally the symbols of British national identity, so fervently adhered to than in Northern Ireland. Outwardly, Unionists constantly demonstrate their Britishness by employing easily recognisable symbols with regular frequency. But caveats need to be made.

First, insistent Union Jack waving, and pledges of loyalty to Crown and faith, are ways for the Unionists to reassure themselves of their identity, in the absence, as they feel it, of a genuine emotional commitment to them on the part of the British on the mainland. Second, the fact that the Unionist population is loyal to the symbols of a British national identity does not necessarily mean that these same Unionists are invariably loyal to the British state. In Unionist eyes British governments have consistently demonstrated their indifference towards the Unionist predicament, their dangerous ignorance of the realities of Ireland, and that their undertaking to the British identity of the Unionist community is only partial and conditional – which justifies a similar loyalty to the British state by Unionists.

The practical manifestations of this conditional loyalism are to be found in a history of Unionist rejections of the legislative pronouncements of the Westminster Parliament, e.g. 1912, 1974 and 1986. In conjunction with this, coursing the veins of all good Unionists, to a greater or lesser extent, is a very independentist streak. Born out of the siege mentality, and the psychological self-reliance and inherently suspicious nature that this has engendered, Unionism is a markedly isolationist, 'loyal unto ourselves, God and the Crown' creed. If the shibboleths of Unionism are being threatened by a treacherous British government, then resistance, even if this involves direct, violent confrontation with the agents of the British state, is seen as morally justified. And, if required, there has always been a significant strand within Unionism, as represented contemporarily by the DUP, certain sections of the OUP, and Loyalist paramilitary organisations such as the UDA and the UVF, which would support an independent Northern Ireland in preference to the acceptance of abhorrent Westminster legislation, i.e. any which was seen as legislating Ulster into a united Ireland.

In the aftermath of the introduction of direct rule from London, 24th March 1972, new evidence of this strongly independent, self-reliant Unionism surfaced. A pamphlet, entitled 'Ulster – A Nation', argued that the Ulster Loyalists were 'an old and historic community' for whom union with Britain had never been 'an end in itself', but 'was always a means of preserving Ulster's British tradition and the identity of her loyalist people'. Further, British politicians, by 'dismantling Ulster's capacity for resistance to friend [sic] or foe' had 'unwittingly forged a nation that cannot entrust to them its security or national destiny'.[27] A leading Unionist politician, William Craig, stated on behalf of a United Loyalist Council, circa 1973/4:

> As British citizens we have a right to all the provisions and protection of any other part of the realm. It is because we have no guarantee of these that the Ulster Loyalist demands his own Parliament with powers to maintain the Union. If Westminster does not want the Union, then Northern Ireland has a moral right to opt for terms which will maintain its heritage.[28]

A similar separatist streak characterises the Ulster Clubs, established in late 1985, whose aims according to their spokesman, Alan Wright, are four: '... the right to self-determination for the Ulster people, to maintain the Union as long as it's in our best interest, to combat the encroachment of Irish nationalism, and to unify the talents, abilities and resources at our disposal'[29].

All this is evidence of a '... matter of fact nationalism, perhaps a nationalism of despair, a nationalism arising out of immediate events and circumstances, not out of long term social process'[30]. The end product of such a sense of identity and nation is that 'loyalty' is described as being 'not a unilateral relationship'. It is perceived to be no disloyalty to the Queen to refuse loyalty to 'ministers or governments that fail in their duty to give loyal subjects the blessing of the Queen's Peace'. British politicians have 'inspired no confidence in their honesty of purpose or their resolve to do other than to betray the trust they undertook to discharge'. They 'have robbed Ulster of her own means of protection and then ... have failed in the moral duty to supply it them-selves in honour of their explicit undertaking'.[31] A sense of remaining British in spite of, rather than because of, the British guarantee is detectable. 'We want to stay British, whether you bloody English like it or not'.[32] Or as Miller has noted, 'Ulster chooses to remain British', rather than 'Ulstermen are like Britons'.[33]

The bilateral nature of Unionist British national identity, based on a contractual attitude to the state, is associated with the phenomenon of negative nationalism. Such identity is as much a symbol of Unionist resistance to Irish reunification as it is of any sense of belonging to a UK 'collective conscience'. In this respect, Unionist adherence to a British national identity is an act of defiance, rather than a positive assertion of British nationalist sentiment. 'The Ulster state came into being solely because of the opposition of Northern Protestants to Irish unification: negative nationalism had its way'.[34] Unionism, and especially its more fundamentalist brand, is loyal unto itself first. This is the real significance of the label of Loyalism. According to the Northern Ireland Attitude Survey of 1978, 85 per cent of respondents deemed that a 'loyalist is loyal to Ulster before the British Government'.[35]

The highly symbolic nature of the Unionists' Britishness and their conditional loyalism and negative nationalism, present a paradox. Is it that the Unionist community is not British at all? Or is it that it is the most British part of the UK? Certainly Union Jack waving, noisy loyalty to Crown and fundamentalist Protestant faith, all tend to set Ireland apart from the rest of the UK. Nowhere else on the mainland of Britain are these traditional symbols of Britishness so visibly and audibly proclaimed. In this respect Hartzian Fragment social theory may be enlightening; i.e. a community which leaves the motherland and estab-lishes itself in some distant land, will not necessarily be subject to the social development occuring in the home territory. A type of time-warping could be said to occur. The Unionists can be seen as falling into this category of Hartzian Fragment, because of their fervent adherence to the symbols, especially the now near-redundant fundamentalist Protestant faith, of traditional even archaic, Britishness.

It is consequently possible to assert that the regional peculiarism of symbolic and emotional Britishness in Northern Ireland, coupled with the siege mentality, contains within it the seeds of a new national identity. 'The end of the 50 year ambiguity about the autonomy of Ulster [i.e. direct rule] has given rise to the growth of a separate sense of Ulster nationality and the increased popularity of the idea of independent Ulster'.[36] Additionally, 'Two different communities in Great Britain and Ulster at different stages of development by virtue of different historical experience, possess different scales of reference by which to measure, weigh and judge'.[37]

An application of a six-point guide to nationhood, in the case of Unionism *vis-à-vis* mainland Britishness, further enhances an understanding of the community's quite separate identity. First, the requirement of a common government, either as a past memory or future aspiration, provides an initial dislocation. All Unionists are aware of the fifty years of virtual self-government in Ireland and there are many who advocate a return to such arrangements. The present reality of the existence of common government in Northern Ireland since 1972, i.e. direct rule, has at times been psychologically and physically distressing for Unionists. Common government with the British mainland is increasingly regarded by Unionists as being the potential vehicle for the incorporation of Northern Ireland in the Irish Republic.

The second requirement, of relatively close contact between all parts of a nation, is tempered by geographical fact. Northern Ireland is after all separated from Great Britain by the Irish Sea, which contributes to a distancing of the mainland body politic from Irish affairs. Third, in respect of a territory which they regard as 'home', Unionists regard the islands of Britain and Ireland as a geographical unit. Whilst such a point of view does not lack credibility in mainland Britain, the average mainland Briton's mind's-eye view of Ulster is as a part of the island of Ireland. Fourth, there is a significant cultural distinctiveness, a combination of language, religion, literature, customs and history. Fifth, where the requirement of common interests and goals is concerned, many mainland Britons would be happy to see troublesome Ulster incorporated into the Republic. Unionism's preoccupation with the maintenance of the Union hardly concerns the mainland British mind, apart from in Westminster and Whitehall.

Finally, there is a consciousness of being a 'nation' in their own minds, i.e. 'different'. This may be explained in the following way:

> There is ... among Ulster Protestants, a reasonably general, clandestine affection for the Irish label and a willingness to acknowledge, under certain circumstances, that the label is appropriate to them ... Conversely, when the Irish are under some form of attack, it is difficult for the Protestant Ulsterman to entirely disassociate himself from the force of the attack because of his curiously partial attachments'.[38]

The Unionist sense of Britishness thus exists in an uneasy relationship with what is perceived as being British on the mainland. In times of intercommunal tension, or perceived British prevarication concerning the status of Northern Ireland, the siege mentality, negative British nationalism, Ulster nationalism, and conditional loyalism, all come to the forefront and join together. They are omnipresent features of the Unionist make-up and contribute to the independent streak within

Unionism, which is prepared to defy the British state if necessary and is increasingly developing as an emergent nationalism in its own right. All this underlines the enormous complexity of the Ireland situation.

Notes

1. W.D. Flackes, *Northern Ireland – A Political Directory, 1968–1983*, Ariel, London, 1983.
2. M. Diskin, 'The Development of Party competition Among Unionists in Ulster 1966–1982', *Studies in Public Policy* no.129, University of Strathclyde, 1984.
3. W.D. Flackes, op. cit., p.174.
4. D. Boal in W.D. Flackes, op. cit., p.76.
5. P. Arthur, 'Church and State in Northern Ireland. Which Church? Which State?', Paper presented to the Conference of the Political Science Association of Great Britain, Southampton, 1984.
6. P. O'Malley, *The Uncivil Wars – Ireland Today*, The Blackstaff Press, Belfast, 1983, p.189.
7. ibid., p.189.
8. A. Lijphart, 'The Northern Ireland Problem', *British Journal of Political Science*, vol.5, 1975.
9. R. Harris in J. Whyte, 'Interpretations of the Northern Ireland Problem', *Economic and Social Review*, vol.9, July 1978, p.277.
10. C.C. O'Brien, *States of Ireland*, Hutchinson, London, 1972, p.165.
11. W. Craig, controversial Unionist politician, one of the instigators and planners of the UWC Strike. He fell from popular grace in the wake of the Constitutional Convention, when his proposal of voluntary coalition in Northern Ireland for a limited period was rejected by the main body of the Northern Unionist elite at the convention.
12. R. Rose, *Northern Ireland: a Time and a Choice*, London, 1976, p.16.
13. Ref. Press Conference given by Ian Paisley and James Molyneaux, February 1986, after meeting with Prime Minister Thatcher in Downing Street.
14. A.T.Q. Stewart, 'The Mind of Protestant Ulster' in D. Watt, ed., *The Constitution of Northern Ireland: Problems and Perspectives*, Heinemann, London, 1981, p.36. Also see chapter 1, section on Class and Class Relations.
15. P. O'Malley, op. cit., p.200.
16. J.H. Whyte, op. cit., p.278.
17. A.T.Q. Stewart, article in the *Irish Times*, 14th January 1986, p.8.
18. ibid.
19. A. Tyrie in A. Guelke, 'Northern Ireland: The Territorial Dimension and International Legitimacy', paper presented to the 8th Annual Conference of the U.K. Politics Workgroup, Oxford, August 1983, p.282.
20. Newsweek, 16th May 1983, in A. Guelke, op. cit., p.282.
21. J.H. Whyte, 'Why is the Northern Ireland Problem so Intractable?', *Parliamentary Affairs*, vol.34, no.4, 1981, p.249.

22. ibid., p.422.
23. F. Wright, 'Protestant Ideology and Politics in Ulster', *European Journal of Sociology*, vol.xiv, 1973, p.25.
24. P. O'Malley, op. cit., pp. 40–4.
25. ibid., p. 189.
26. ibid., p. 167.
27. D.W. Miller, *The Queen's Rebels*, Gill and Macmillan, Dublin, 1978, pp.153–4.
28. ibid., pp. 153–4.
29. *Fortnight*, Issue 233, February 1986, p.4.
30. D.W. Miller, op. cit., p.154.
31. ibid., p.155.
32. H. Jackson, 'The Two Irelands', *Minority Rights Group*, London, 1979, p.3, irate old lady's comment.
33. D.W. Miller, op. cit., p.157.
34. P. O'Malley, op. cit., p.149.
35. E. Moxon-Browne, *Nation Class and Creed*, Aldershot, Gower Press, 1983, p.86.
36. F. Wright, op. cit., p.237.
37. D.W. Miller, op. cit., pp.154–5.
38. K. Heskin, *Northern Ireland: A Psychological Analysis*, Gill and Macmillan, Dublin, 1980, pp.49–50.

Chapter five

Brittany

Vaughan Rogers

Overcoming the fascist contamination

Since 1945 the fortunes of the Breton movement ('Emsav' in Breton circles) have undergone a profound transformation. The combined effect of the upsurge in French national sentiment at the Liberation and the notoriety of those Breton activists who collaborated with fascism in one way or another, led to a post-war political climate hostile to the cause of Breton specificity. So damaging was the legacy of collaboration that, as late as 1974, a popular magazine was moved to describe the nationalist organisation responsible for blowing up the TV mast at Roc'h Tredudon, in protest at the insufficient air time accorded to the Breton language and culture, as 'une séquelle du nazisme'.[1]

Yet by the latter part of the 1970s a Breton nationalist party, the Union Democratique Bretonne (UDB) had succeeded in gaining recognition by the Communists and Socialists as the third component of the Union of the Left alliance in Brittany and as a result had made considerable progress in local government representation.[2] With achievements such as this, as well as the unifying and regenerating influence brought to bear by the UDB on other elements of the Emsav it could be justifiably claimed in 1982 that, 'The UDB is part of the political landscape. Its influence in Brittany is increasing, since it has become the focal point for the whole of the movement. This phenomenon, due just as much to its own militant qualities as to the collapse of the various forms by which traditional nationalism has tried to keep itself afloat, appears to provide the basis for bringing about what was always the ambition of the Emsav: its unification. The history of the UDB is thus one of success, quite unique within the Emsav, after twenty years of existence'.[3] The fortunes of the Breton movement in the 1980s, however, have failed to match up to this positive appraisal and implied prognostication. But before examining the recent problems, it is important to say a word about the legacy of collaboration and notably how it was overcome, leading to the emergence of the UDB.

The 1930s saw the development of fascism in the Breton movement, in the form of the Parti National Breton, composed of Emsav's separatist elements. By 1937 the PNB had clearly become a party embodying the essential features of national socialism, including the corporate state, rejection of the class struggle, the cult of force, discipline and elitism, and racism as shown in the following rejection, as France again prepared for war with Germany, of the Union Sacrée practised by the Breton movement in the Great War: 'Paysans! Pendant que tu seras au front, un nègre ou un bicot prendra ta place à ton foyer'.[4] The overtures of the PNB after 1940 towards the Nazis cannot be accounted for simply in terms of opportunism, but also reflect a major ideological convergence.

Still other 'moderate' nationalists, such as Yann Fouéré, who never favoured direct collaboration with the Nazis, did work closely with the Vichy government in the hope that the provincialist rhetoric of Pétain, heavily influenced by the doctrine of Charles Maurras, would lead in the direction of regional autonomy for Brittany. Fouéré was largely responsible for obtaining from the Vichy government the creation of the Comité Consultatif de Bretagne in 1942, a consultative body entitled to express its views regarding the Breton language and culture, and the creation of one weekly radio programme in Breton lasting one hour, as well as certain optional examinations in the Breton language.[5] At his trial, his defence lawyer argued that Fouéré was a moderate, opposed to the anti-French separatism of the PNB, and that his loyalty to France was beyond question. What this omitted was the role under Vichy of his newspaper, *La Bretagne*. Thus when the *Journal Officiel* began to name high-ranking freemasons in France generally with a view to taking measures against them, the paper published the names of Breton freemasons, and on occasion it even divulged information in order to remedy the inefficiencies of Vichy repression.[6]

The discredit which the Breton movement had brought upon itself meant it was not until 1957 that an overtly political organisation to promote the cause of Breton autonomy, the Mouvement pour l'Organisation de la Bretagne (MOB), was created. This move was itself enormously facilitated by the activities of CELIB (Comité d'Etude et de Liaison des Intérêts Bretons), which in the 1950s was the spearhead of the regional economic expansion movement in France generally, promoting the inclusion of a regional dimension in government economic planning. The presence at its head of former Prime Minister René Pleven and a host of eminently respectable Breton politicians, and the resolutely apolitical image which it strove to maintain, conferred on CELIB a degree of credibility which no Breton organisation could have hoped to attain in 1945. CELIB succeeded in bringing to public attention the specific needs of the Breton population, particularly the problem of emigration, without being accused of separatism or fascism.[7] This success was based on a number of factors. The 'eternal morass' of Fourth Republic politics, with its unstable governments and shifting parliamentary alliances, made it possible for the Breton deputies of whatever party to exert considerable political influence at the centre by voting together as a group on issues directly concerning the region. The CELIB's parliamentary commission, by exerting pressure in this way, succeeded in establishing for a while an authentic dialogue between the regional representatives and central government and led to the promise of a regional development plan for Brittany, the famous *loi-programme*.

It was the apolitical functional regionalism practised by CELIB which created the conditions for Breton political activism to re-emerge. The MOB skilfully exploited the opportunities created by the activities of CELIB, presenting itself as a political extension of the economic regionalism represented by CELIB. A kind of symbiotic relationship developed between the two organisations and the CELIB itself defined the complementary roles as follows:

> Whereas the CELIB strictly limits its activities to the economic, social and cultural problems of Brittany, the MOB adopts positions on questions of an institutional order. It recommends a reform which would allow Brittany, through regional decentralisation of its structures, to control a part of its own interests in a federal France.[8]

The prestige and respectability of CELIB made it possible for the MOB to advance as moderate, responsible requests, demands for the institution of federalism in France (a crime for which for a long time one could be prosecuted!).

The symbiotic relationship came to an end in 1962 in the aftermath of the Gaullist victory at the general election. The bi-polarisation of political life in France broke up the Breton parliamentary alliance and Breton deputies dutifully respected the exigencies of party discipline. The promise of the *loi-programme* was broken. The lie had been given to the illusion that the two organisations were merely different dimensions of the same decentralist tendency. The logic of CELIB's strategy, whatever its leaders may have thought, was to promote the integration of the Breton economy into the expanding French and international economy.[9] The convergence between this and the modernising ideology of Gaullism, plus the new left–right polarity, led to the political integration of hitherto uncommitted CELIB leaders such as Joseph Martray, who joined the Gaullists, and Michel Phlipponneau, who joined the French Socialists. The objectives of the nationalists in the MOB, on the other hand, were at bottom disintegrative. The apparently moderate federalist stance was none the less tantamount to promoting the dismantling of the French state in its unitary form.

Abandoned by its former ally, the MOB found itself in a crisis. Some of the younger elements had for some time been disenchanted with what they perceived as the ideological bankruptcy of the MOB, highlighted by the reaction amongst its leaders to the Algerian crisis. The MOB student section at Rennes University saw the activities of the FLN in Algeria as a struggle for national liberation, to which Breton nationalists must lend their support. The MOB leadership could not comply with this demand and the conservative tendency expressed itself in MOB's newspaper, *l'Avenir de la Bretagne*, in 1958: 'We cannot give up our national and cultural solidarity with the white men of Christian heritage who are threatened with losing everything if Moslem fanaticism triumphs'.[10] This current, then, had an order of racial priorities which led it to become the objective ally of virulent French nationalism which denied the right to self-determination on the basis of ethnic distinctiveness to the citizenry of the Republic.

The concept of social class provided a further source of conflict in the early 1960s. The MOB, against a background of intensifying class-based conflict in Brittany, organised particularly by the CFDT and the CGT, consistently refused to incorporate the concept of class into its analysis and programme, declaring that its objectives were to bring together the Breton people, whatever their opinions and political persuasion, in the assertion of their rights and liberties. The students at Rennes reacted in a hostile fashion to this refusal.[11]

The MOB, increasingly isolated and torn by internal dissension, began to sink back into obscurity. The Young Turks who had been questioning the MOB's failure to define its position on the left–right spectrum, departed to form the Union Démocratique Bretonne in 1964.

The move to the left : the ascendancy of the UDB

The advent of the UDB opened a·new era in the history of the Breton movement. On the basis of an ideological renewal and a strategic re-orientation, the UDB spearheaded the emergence of the nationalist movement into the political arena with unprecedented success. Building on the idea that the position of Brittany was essentially colonial, the UDB made it a cornerstone of its prescriptive analysis.[12] The colonial model made it possible for the UDB to bring together all the elements constituting the 'Breton problem' under one heading, thereby imbuing nationalist ideology with an apparent coherence which it had previously lacked. The cultural, socio-economic and political oppression suffered by Bretons was attributable to the combined effects of the capitalist system and the imperialism of the French state. The colonial theme had the added advantage of highlighting the notion of the people, rather than that of the nation. This was particularly important because it paved the way for the UDB to establish Breton nationalism as a political phenomenon of the Left. Instead of insisting upon the Breton nation as an eternal entity independent of economic and social variables, the traditional concept of nationhood so dear to previous manifestations of Breton nationalism, the UDB placed the historical experience of the Breton people in the context of colonial domination, thus facilitating a convergence between the idea of national liberation and the concept of social class. The UDB conceded that the processes of assimilation and acculturation had eroded the specificity of Brittany effectively and asserted therefore that it was inappropriate to postulate the existence of a Breton nation. Instead the UDB emphasises the 'national vocation' of Brittany to be realised through a process of liberation from centralist domination and capitalism, thus casting those elements of the Breton population facilitating the operation of the system of colonial domination and the elements of the Breton movement which rejected the concept of class struggle, as the class enemy.[13]

The ideological renewal generated by the UDB rests, however, on shaky foundations. The specific character of the Breton problem, which it is crucially important to establish in order to justify the existence of the UDB at all, is substantiated by attempting to answer the argument that many other regions suffer from very similar problems and that Breton specificity cannot be established through an enumeration of the economic, social and cultural problems of the region. The UDB's answer to this argument goes as follows:

> Certainly the Bretons have several problems in common with other regions. Let us mention the best known of them – under-industrialisation in Western Basse Normandie and in Brittany, the farming problem in Alsace, in the west and particularly in Brittany, because of its peripheral position in relation to the developed regions of France and the EEC, rural exodus in inland Guyenne and in Brittany, demographic disequilibrium due to emigration on a massive scale in Corsica, in the Auvergne and in Brittany, alcoholism in Normandy, Alsace and Brittany, military installations of great strategic importance, in the Limousin and in Brittany, the language question in the Basque country and in Brittany. We observe that only in Brittany are all these difficulties to be found at once. It is these conditions taken together which constitute the specificity of the Breton problem. It cannot therefore be reduced to the mere French regional question'.[14]

Quite apart from the factual errors of omission in this enumeration – the Massif Central and the South West for example, were no doubt very happy to learn that their agricultural crisis had disappeared and the Corsicans must have been overjoyed to learn that their linguistic problem had evaporated – apart from errors like this, the UDB's justification pays scant attention to the exigences of logic. The criteria of colonialism selected are, for example, totally arbitrary.[15] At no stage is it made clear exactly why the particular problems selected for inclusion in the enumeration constitute the basis for a situation of colonial domination. Also, the terms in which the Breton problem is defined as specific and not reducible to the French regional question effectively deny to other ethnically distinct groups the status which the UDB claims for the Bretons. By dint of contradiction and tautology, the UDB took the base metals of Breton nationalism, transformed them into the gold of national liberation ideology and forced them into a socialist mould. The significance of this 'alchemy', as Louis Quéré has observed, went far beyond the boundaries of Brittany, and the colonial analogy developed by the UDB was incorporated by many other ethnic minority movements on French territory.[16] The UDB therefore provided further proof that ideological coherence is not a prerequisite for political success.

The strategic re-orientation inspired by the UDB was aimed in two directions, first the nationalist movement itself and second the French left. For the UDB, one of the greatest sources of the weakness of the nationalist movement was its chronic divisiveness. To combat this, the UDB adopted a muscular policy of unification, by applying the principle of democratic centralism and party discipline within its own ranks and attempting to outstrip its rival in the Breton movement. It has always been most vociferous in its condemnation of what it regards as the irresponsible, unrealistic and counter-productive activities of the Front de Libération de la Bretagne. It would have no truck with other organisations in the movement which it considered doctrinally unsound, such as the Party Strollad Ar Vro, a re-incarnation of the MOB which emerged and quickly disappeared again in the 1970s.[17] The UDB's insistence on discipline encountered considerable resistance from some nationalist quarters which accused it of Stalinism. Nevertheless, this had the effect of reinforcing its image as a no-nonsense respectable organisation of the left which was a crucial factor in establishing its credibility with the French Communists and Socialists, the second major aspect of the UDB's strategic renewal.

Basing its strategy on the conviction that the colonial situation of Brittany could be eliminated only through socialism, the UDB cultivated an association with the French left. This option became increasingly credible as the political circumstances in France began to evolve, first of all with the growth of a rejuvenated Socialist Party and second with the establishment of the Union of the Left on the basis of a Joint Programme of Government, including a commitment to genuine regional decentralisation. This new set of circumstances gave the nationalist movement a new sense of purpose since, for the first time, they had the opportunity to participate in the development of an alternative to the government of the day, an alternative which promised more in terms of self-determination than had ever previously been envisaged. For the French left, association with the UDB brought assistance from enthusiastic, hard-working militants and the possibility of attracting support in an area where, with a few very notable exceptions, the population had remained largely impermeable to the appeal of socialism. The alliance began with the UDB supporting left-wing candidates at elections in Brittany and later developed into participation in elections on a Union of the Left ticket. This led in 1977, when the Socialists made significant gains in the local elections in Brittany, to the election of thirty-nine UDB local councillors and a share in the administration of cities like Rennes, Brest and Nantes.[18] As a result, Ronan Leprohon, a UDB founder-member, was elected on to the Regional Council. He soon launched a scathing attack on it, as a place where prominent politicians indulged themselves by continuing arguments begun in Parliament in Paris.[19] The UDB considered the Council wholly inadequate, with insufficient powers or resources, indirectly elected, and suffering from the notorious '*cumul des mandats*' of its members, which encouraged absenteeism and irresponsibility.[20] The UDB counted on the French left to rectify such deficiencies.

While the alliance with the left soon paid practical dividends, certain longer-term dangers began to manifest themselves; in respect of both political action and ideology. The considerable success achieved by the UDB in persuading the French left to incorporate in its analysis and programme a more radical perspective on the Breton problem may have represented a significant advance for the cause of regionalism, but it constituted a growing threat to the nationalist movement. The danger for the UDB was strikingly illustrated in the regional manifesto published by the Finistère federation of the Socialist Party in January 1978, which adopted a line of analysis amounting, not so much to an accommodation of certain nationalist demands, as to a deep encroachment into the ideological territory hitherto occupied by the Breton movement. The stifling of the Breton culture, for example, was closely linked by the Finistère Socialists to, 'The process of capitalist exploitation which, by forcing generations of our compatriots to emigrate, has condemned our region to economic stagnation'.[21] To this, and other, clear evocations of the colonial theme developed by the UDB, the manifesto added a forceful affirmation of the right and need to 'live and work in our own homeland', another slogan frequently employed by the UDB. The only means of achieving this, according to the manifesto, was through the establishment of socialism: 'This old and yet brand new idea', which 'by liberating the Bretons from the dual exploitation from which they suffer, as Bretons and as workers, represents for them a dual opportunity'.[22] Here, the Socialists were 'borrowing' another theme popularised by the UDB, based on the famous dictum of Yann Sohier, founder of the cultural movement Ar Falz, according to which 'The Breton is doubly proletarian, as a proletarian and as a Breton'.

The UDB began to realise in the late 1970s that the alliance with the French left had led, not only to a substantial erosion of its ideological specificity, but that it had also severely restricted its freedom of action as an independent political party. In placing all its eggs in one basket, the electoral victory of the left, it had tied its own fortunes too closely to those of its partners and its room for political manoeuvre outside of this strategic framework was now severely limited. In March 1978, Ronan Leprohon, anticipating the defeat of the by then disunited French left in the parliamentary election of April, declared 'We have been struggling in Brittany for fourteen years with the victory of the Union of the Left as our starting hypothesis. We must now admit that, objectively, four-teen years of UDB activity are currently being sanctioned by failure'.[23] The party began to perceive that its *raison d'être*, the expression of autonomist aspirations in Brittany, was in danger of disappearing.

In response to this danger, the 1978 Party Conference endorsed a motion recommending a radical break with the strategy hitherto pursued and called upon the party to explain to the Breton population that 'Deconcentration, regionalisation and decentralisation are traps and that only socialist autonomy will allow the Breton people to assume its full role in the international struggle against capitalist oppression'.[24] The disarray of the French left was presented as an opportunity to 'preserve our ability to redefine a strategy capable of building a socialist society which takes account of the needs of Breton workers' and for the UDB to 'affirm more powerfully the need for the existence of the party as an indispensable instrument in the decolonisation of the Breton people'. This implied the development of 'a programme which cannot be taken over by the French Left and the Socialists in particular'. However, the motion stressed that 'the affirmation of our specificity must not lead our party to cut itself off from the tactical gains previously attained, such as our presence in a few municipal councils'.[25] Yet the resolutions adopted by the Brest conference overtly referred to the 'national question', or 'the right of the Breton people to separation' and envisaged an 'autonomous status for Brittany which will guarantee legislative, executive, administrative and judicial sovereignty for the Breton people'.[26] After having spent fourteen years overcoming the damning image of the Breton movement in which separatism and treachery were confounded, the UDB was now clearly implying a new commitment to the creation of a Breton state. In anticipation of the inevitable criticism that it was thereby demonstrating the dubious nature of its socialist credentials, the party resolved to include in its constituent charter a new clause which was a clear rebuff to the French left. 'The UDB condemns chauvinism, the negation of nationality, and bourgeois nationalism, in opposition to which it advances revolutionary nationalism'.[27] As Nicolas has observed, if the UDB was seeking to develop a programme which the French left could not take over, then it had made a considerable start.[28]

The party's new line was re-affirmed at its St Nazaire Conference in 1980 and the 'cold shoulder' attitude towards the French left given concrete expression in the decision which was taken to begin negotiations with representatives of the other ethnic minorities of metropolitan France and the Overseas Departments and Territories with a view to presenting a candidate representing them all at the 1981 presidential election.[29] This plan, however, came to nothing when negotiations broke down, demonstrating the immense difficulty experienced by the UDB when it sought to exert a telling influence outside the alliance.

The UDB and the Socialist government

Precisely at the point where the UDB began to distance itself from the left, the objective for which the party had striven from its inception until the late 1970s was attained: the accession of a socialist government in France. The party hailed this as a great victory for the left as a whole, in which, of course, it included itself. Claiming some of the credit for the Socialists' success for itself, the party engaged in a policy of 'critical support' for the new government. However, as the 'socialist experiment' unfolded, relations between the UDB and the new majority became increasingly sour and it is to the dynamics of these relations that attention must now be turned.

In his major study of the Breton movement, Michel Nicolas identified the dilemma facing the Emsav in the following way.

> Participating in the French political process implies the necessity to contract electoral, if not programmatic, alliances with powerful partners .... Conducting a strategy of this kind presents the Emsav with the risk of failure through having its nature perverted by integration into a logic which has as its effect the reinforcement of (French) national unity'.[30]

The need to avoid succumbing to the centripetal and assimilatory forces to which the UDB laid itself open in contracting an alliance with the French left must not, however, lead the party into the introspective isolation of the 'nationalistic impasse, which constitutes the principal danger generally haunting movements of this nature'.[31] The way forward for the Emsav, Nicolas maintained, must lie in 'subverting' not only the economic and administrative processes of French society, but also 'the ideological principle which lies at their heart, [French] nationalist ideology: hence the need for an internationalist perspective which goes beyond the level of discourse'.[32] Nevertheless, the success of the Emsav depends upon the consolidation of the elements which characterise the Breton minority (awareness of cultural distinctiveness, social conflicts with specific characteristics), which the Emsav must identify and with which it must closely associate itself.[33] The application of this conceptual framework to the experience of the UDB in the 1980s goes a long way to explaining the recent difficulties of the party and to providing a basis for a prognosis.

The problem of devising an effective role for itself under the Socialist government rapidly became acute for the UDB as the party sought to re-establish its credentials as a component of the left whilst at the same time affirming its independence of analysis and action. This enterprise took the form of a systematic monitoring of the proposals for reform emanating from the government, especially, of course, those relating to the decentralisation programme. The disappointment felt by many militants when the government's blueprint was published, highlights the problematic position of the party. The party quickly observed 'the discrepancy between the electoral promises and the first proposals of the Government'.[34] Severe reservations were expressed concerning the technocratic character of the proposed reforms, regretting the subordination of economic and political questions to issues of administrative efficiency. In respect of the reform of the functions of the prefectoral corps for example, the UDB commented that 'First of all they talked about abolition, then a change of title, but now all we have is a modification of their power'.[35] The department of Loire-Atlantique, containing the historic capital of Brittany, Nantes, was not to be included in the Breton region and would remain in the region of the Pays de la Loire. Corsica was to be accorded special status with extra powers devolved to its regional bodies, but Brittany would retain its status as a region just like any other. Once more, the party emphasised that there was a fundamental distinction between the concept of decentralisation which, as the decentralisation programme itself underlined when it was eventually adopted in February 1982, 'far from weakening national unity will, on the contrary, reinforce it',[36] and autonomy conceived of by the UDB as a process of decolonisation, carrying with it the dismantling of the French unitary state as far as Brittany was concerned.[37] A further preoccupation of the UDB, in its response to the blueprint, concerned the accession of the region to full local authority status, which, as the reform stipulated, would only become effective on the election of the Regional Assembly by direct universal suffrage. The lack of haste of the minister responsible to take the steps necessary for holding such elections was the object of sharp criticism.[38] Despite all these areas in which the reform received the UDB's strong condemnation, thus putting a considerable distance between itself and the Government, the need to avoid isolating itself led the party to affirm that, 'In summary, the application of the Socialist programme would be a great step forward' and must be supported by the militants:[39] 'It is up to us to put our shoulders to the wheel of a change which must not be restricted simply to the institutional domain'.[40] Regarding regional elections, the UDB affirmed that 'The Parti Socialiste cannot go back on such an important promise'.[41] The UDB was continually faced with the Hobson's choice of remaining in critical support of the government but with negligible influence, or dissociating itself and returning to complete isolation. At the Party Conference in 1982, 'solidarity but not alignment' was the catchphrase of the leadership in an attempt to square the circle.[42] The tension caused by this stance, however, resulted in the departure of long-time 'tête pensante' of UDB strategy, Ronan Leprohon, who joined the Socialist Party in a flurry of recrimination. For Leprohon, the position of the UDB had become untenable:

> It should either have participated directly in the policy of de-centralisation, which the line adopted at St Nazaire made impossible, or it should have clearly opted for the Opposition camp, which was intolerable because the Breton people had voted in favour of the Left'.[43]

The impotence of the party in these circumstances had already caused a crisis to erupt in the Brest federation of the UDB (Leprohon's own), recognised for a long time by the party as its 'guiding light'. Its rejection of the official line was countered by the leadership by its dissolution and the requirement to rejoin the party on an individual basis with a clear commitment to the independent line adopted at St Nazaire.[44]

And yet, in the Rapport Politique drawn up for the 1982 Conference, the UDB appeared quite lucidly to accept the validity of Leprohon's analysis when it decided against a course of systematic criticism of the government, a course which, as we have observed, it had already begun to follow.

> This attitude would be very likely to isolate us. As the little terriers of the Left, we could only snap at a few heels and, eventually, collecting a few kicks in return, take refuge in a semi-opposition as uncomfortable as it would be undesired.[45]

The lucidity of the party's perception was not matched by strategic inventiveness and the situation envisaged by the leadership in its striking little metaphor was precisely what was to come to pass.

The aftermath of the 1982 Conference saw a hardening in the attitude of the UDB towards the Socialists, exemplified by the account in *Le Peuple Breton* of Leprohon's departure, which was denounced as 'treachery', the re-affirmation of the autonomous strategy and severe criticism of the 'austerity' measures which the Socialists had already begun to introduce with regard to the economy.[46] Despite the fact that the exigencies of affirming its own independence as a party were pushing the UDB further and further away from the government, the electoral alliance with the Socialists was still pursued. Not surprisingly the preparation of the 1983 municipal elections saw the eruption of considerable animosity between Breton Socialists and UDB militants over the issue of the placing of the UDB candidates on Union of the Left lists. The considerable fall in the government's popularity, coupled with the UDB's critical stance, caused the Socialists to be much less enthusiastic than hitherto about allowing the UDB to figure prominently. The consequence of this was, as the UDB saw it, that UDB candidates were insufficiently represented on the electoral lists; or figured too far down to have much hope of being elected.[47] In fact, the situation was far from uniform across Brittany, with the alliance holding up extremely well in some municipalities, whereas in others the animosity which had developed led the UDB to abandon the strategy of alliance and present its own lists, protesting at the 'hegemony' shown by the Socialists; so that relations degenerated still further.

In those areas where the UDB sought to fight alone, its results were derisory, amounting to an average share of the vote of 3 per cent.[48] Without the strategy of alliance, the UDB failed to make a significant electoral breakthrough, strikingly illustrating the observation contained in the 1982 Conference report of the Bureau Politique, which admitted: 'For the UDB itself, the conquest of autonomy is difficult'.[49] In those areas where the alliance remained solid, considerable progress was made and the party more than doubled its number of local councillors. It was one of the UDB's most successful candidates, Iffig Remond, who was elected mayor of the small municipality of St Hernin in Finistère, as head of a United Left list, who put the 'success' of the party into perspective in the following manner: 'This is not the way to take power. We must work to take over at grass roots level. That is how the Left managed to implant itself in the rural community'.[50] But progress in this direction was very disappointing, as the party's own 1982 Conference report perceptively conceded: 'Our party finds it difficult to publicise the overall analysis which would make it possible for every worker to make the link gradually and simply between his day-to-day experience and the objectives which we propose'.[51]

The consequences of the analytical and strategic contortions indulged in by the UDB and its demonstrable inability either significantly to influence government policy from its position of 'critical support' or to emerge as a credible independent force had already begun to make themselves felt in several important ways. By 1983, for example, the membership level of over 2,000 card-carrying militants enjoyed by the UDB before the advent of the Socialist government had dwindled to approximately 800.[52] Since 1981 the party's right to pride of place in the nationalist movement had begun to be challenged by the emergence of several rival organisations, such as the Parti Républicain Breton, Emgann (le Combat) and POBL (Parti pour l'Organisation d'une Bretagne Libre).[53] Already by 1983, the Breton movement was beginning to move back to the position of fragmentation and disarray from which the UDB had, it seemed, extricated it in the 1970s. The problems extended to the party's newspaper, *Le Peuple Breton*, whose financial situation was reaching crisis point. In early 1984 the party launched an appeal for money to 'save *Le Peuple Breton*'.[54] The significance of the crisis was particularly serious in that the UDB placed enormous emphasis on countering the disinformation it imputed to the predominantly Parisian but also regional press (the paper's front cover has the slogan, '*Aujourd'hui, être libre c'est être informé*'). But subscriptions were not being maintained and the annual Fête du Peuple Breton, organised on the model of the Communists' Fête de l'Humanité, had made a financial loss[55], both suggesting the UDB's declining credibility as a political force.

In 1984 the issue of the party's future relations with the French Left came to crisis point. For the first time in the UDB's history, rival motions were presented to the annual Conference. The motion presented to delegates by the self-styled 'regionalist' leadership recommended the maintenance of the policy of critical support for the government. Against this, the Léon and Brest federations of the party, described by their opponents as the 'nationalists', called for a much more independent line and stressed the inadequacies of Socialist policy. 'Contrary to certain declarations,' the 'dissident' document affirmed, 'it is our duty to keep an account of the Left's derelictions of duty in Brittany'.[56] To put greater pressure on the government to meet the UDB's demands, the insufficiencies of its policies in Brittany should be publicly highlighted. The strategy of the UDB must be to act 'without the slightest servility', and use elections as a bargaining counter, refusing to stand down in favour of the candidate of the left at the second ballot unless negotiations took place on a range of issues, such as economic policy and its effects in Brittany, measures in favour of the Breton language and culture, and, the regional elections which had once again been postponed.[57] The dissident faction went on to reiterate a long-standing principle of the party which, in practice at least, had ceased to figure prominently in the UDB's position.

The struggle for socialism is indissociable from the struggle for autonomy. In failing to recognise this, we give priority to the efforts of French parties in Brittany, which is a further stage in the process of assimilation and a further retrograde step for the Breton question.[58]

The leadership's response was to appeal for the principles of 'democratic centralism' to be respected. Henri Gourmelon, for the Bureau Politique emphasised that the party had already debated the issue, adding that 'Democracy means accepting that one is in the minority'[59]. (Fortunately for him, the opponents of the survival of Breton distinctiveness have not adopted this ill-considered remark as their battle cry!). The call for unity and respect for democratic centralism was ignored by the dissidents, who attributed the sharp decline in membership to the close ties with the French left. The 'regionalists' rejected this analysis and, while conceding that it was possible to discern 'an accentuation in the Jacobin tendencies of the Socialists and Communists' since their accession to power, insisted that this did not preclude the continuation of joint action.[60] The proposal to break more radically with the French left was defeated and the Léon federation walked out, issuing a communiqué announcing that 'they had left the Conference, but not the UDB'.[61] The party leadership, in somewhat Stalinist fashion, made no mention of the dispute in the Conference report in *Le Peuple Breton*. In an attempt however, to contain the dissent which had been expressed, the UDB proceeded to adopt a policy which was entirely consistent with the analysis of the dissidents. It was decided to abandon the practice of unconditional support for the left at the second ballot, which had been adopted in different circumstances, with the right in power and the left in opposition but capable of taking power and willing to undertake specific commitments. 'Today we see that the promises have, for the most part, not been kept ... and that obtaining further promises is to a large extent illusory'.[62] In order to demonstrate its new combative stance, the party refused to participate in the forthcoming European elections. It justified this decision in the following terms: 'We shall not be present at the European elections, by the express wish of the Government of the left which we contributed to bringing to power'.[63] The electoral system for the European Parliament adopted by the Socialist government was thoroughly castigated by the party leadership for its undemocratic character in treating France as a single constituency with no specific regional representation, despite the vote by the European Parliament in favour of proportional representation on a regional basis for all countries in the Community. The loss of UDB support at the European election was presented by the party as a 'warning' to the left.

In effect, therefore, despite the determination of the party leadership to maintain the option of electoral alliance with the left and to defeat the push for a clean break, the UDB was staggering in an ungainly fashion towards the opposition camp. This was further underlined when, in October 1984, in pursuing its more combative stance, the UDB organised a demonstration at St Nazaire, the choice of venue being dictated by the very high incidence of unemployment in this area (19 per cent) and the continuing determination to affirm the Breton identity of the Loire Atlantique department. The spokesman for the UDB in Loire Atlantique after the demonstration put considerable distance between the party and the government when, in an interview for *Ouest-France*, he replied to the question 'Do you place yourself in the category of those let down by socialism?' by replying

> If there are those who feel let down by socialism, then they can only be the Socialists themselves. We, in fact, only called for support for Mitterrand at the second ballot, although we found encouragement for the regions in the proposals of the Socialist candidate. However, we realised very quickly that the government of the Left would not go very far in this direction. We are not disappointed, we simply have the bitter satisfaction of having been proved right too early.[64]

The party, presenting itself as the mouthpiece of economic grievances in Brittany, put forward a five-point plan for reducing unemployment in the region: (1) Two development contracts must be established between the state and the region to invest in shipbuilding and electronics. (2) An essential boost to the capacity of the region for investment would be achieved through an increase in the resources available to the Regional Council and the creation of a regional investment bank. In support of this demand, the UDB observed that, in the case of banks such as the Credit Mutuel de Bretagne, out of 2.35 thousand million francs raised in a single year, only 620 millions had actually been invested in the region. (3) An authentic Breton agricultural policy must include the passing of a law to regulate the accumulation of land and to facilitate the entry into agriculture of young farmers. (4) A more solid fisheries policy would improve circuits of distribution. (5) State investment in the tertiary sector in Brittany was essential to absorb the labour resources being 'released' by industry, along with state-financed incentives to produce further industrial decentralisation in favour of the region. These proposals were accompanied by a virulent critique of the 'social democracy' practised by the government and the 'chit-chat of the politico-technocrats and our impotent local politicians'.[65]

The UDB, in organising the demonstration, was pursuing the strategy referred to by Nicolas of attempting to develop close links with the immediate economic difficulties experienced at grass-roots level. The inability to achieve credibility in this respect was shown by the turn-out for the demonstration against regional unemployment, 300 protesters.[66] This failure was echoed in relations with the government, when ministers failed to receive a UDB delegation to discuss the development plan early in 1985. As a result, the UDB implemented its threat not to give way to the Socialists at the second ballot of the 1985 departmental elections and relations reached a new low. These developments took place against a background of continuing internal disarray. In January 1985 the leaders of the dissident Léon federation of the party were finally expelled. The decision was only taken after a delay of six months, which attested to the reluctance of the leadership to proceed to this ultimate sanction against prominent figures in the Breton movement, such as Réné l'Hostis, President of Diwan, the organisation which had been so dynamic in its promotion of nursery schools in the Breton language.[67] It was clear, however, that the UDB was resorting to the proto-Stalinist reflex which for so long had characterised its internal workings when the authority of the leadership was questioned.

With its credibility attacked from without and within, the UDB began to embark, in the aftermath of the 1985 departmental elections, upon a new strategy as an alternative to the now moribund alliance with the French left. In an editorial in its April edition, *Le Peuple Breton* began to promote the theme of uniting all elements and organisations which had 'comparable aspirations' for the future of the Breton people in preparation for the regional elections now set for 1986. These potential partners would include 'progressive, ecologist, cultural and trade union forces'. The preoccupation with the need to re-establish contact with grass-roots opinion and discontent was thus given concrete expression in the attempt to create a new political consensus in Brittany between the alienated, the disenchanted and the disenfranchised. 'The policy of the Socialist Government has discouraged and demobilised trade union, cultural and political activists.' However, by alienating small organisations, the Socialists had created the conditions under which such organisations could come together and present a united front. 'The classic forces of the Left have left vacant a space in the political arena. It is up to us to occupy it before the legislative and regional elections of 1986.'[68] The party proceeded, on the basis of its new strategy, to make overtures, not only towards the ecologists and small left-wing groups in Brittany, but also towards other elements in the Breton movement. In a key phrase, Henri Gourmelon, emphasising the need for unity, revealed the desperation of the UDB in its fight for survival, when he declared the party was ready to seek alliances at local level, 'even if certain elements of our analysis have to be questioned'.[69] The great strength of the UDB since its inception, and especially since the adoption of democratic centralism in 1970, had always been its attempt at rigorous analysis and vigorous discipline. This, as we have seen, has not always endeared the party to its members and supporters, but it was a crucial factor in the emergence of the UDB as infinitely more successful in terms of ideological and political impact than any previous emanation from the Breton movement. That it should consider such a compromise in its basic position is a measure of the low ebb to which its fortunes had sunk.

In 1985 an analysis in *West European Politics*, argued that, in the main, 'the dialectic of unity through diversity' underpinning Socialist policy towards the regions and cultural minorities had created 'a real possibility for the reincorporation of the more moderate elements [of the ethnic minority movements] – representing the majority – into the mainstream of political life. The author's main contention was that 'the Socialist strategy of drawing the alienated back into the fold has been largely successful'.[70] In the case of the Breton movement, however, it would appear that the forward progression implicit in the term 'dialectic' has been markedly absent in the 1980s, as disillusionment, despair and desperation have grown and the movement has receded (far from the mainstream) towards fragmentation, disarray and impotence. A record low in the fortunes of the movement was reached at the regional elections, called at the very last possible moment by the government to coincide with the parliamentary elections of March 1986. The performance of the 'Convergence Bretonne' lists in which the UDB participated was inferior even to the most pessimistic predictions, with a share of the vote of 1.51 per cent.[71] The UDB, with its characteristic lucidity, analysed the disaster as follows: 'These elections reveal the fundamental difficulty for a "different Left" to exist in competition with the Socialist Party, which at present benefits from its image as the only effective barrier against the Right'[72]. This analysis remains valid. Thus the Breton movement had returned to square one, in a situation apparently as weak as that before the UDB was launched to become the most successful organisation in the history of the Emsav.

Notes

1. Télé 7 Jours no. 722, 24 fevrier 1974. Quoted in Alain Déniel, *Le Mouvement Breton de 1919 a 1945*, Paris, 1976, p.15.
2. Hervé Guillorel, 'Problème Breton et Mouvement Breton', *Pouvoirs*, no.19, 1981, p.95.
3. Michel Nicolas, *Histoire du Mouvement Breton*, Paris, 1982, pp.297–8.
4. Alain Déniel, op. cit., p.204.
5. Yvonnig Gicquel, *Le Comité Consultatif de Bretagne*, Rennes, 1961.
6. Alain Déniel, op. cit., p.249.
7. J.E.S. Hayward, 'From Functional Regionalism to Functional Representation in France: The Battle of Brittany', *Political Studies*, March 1969.
8. Renaud Dulong, *La Question Bretonne*, Paris, 1975, p.136.

9. Jill Lovecy, 'Protest in Brittany from the Fourth to the Fifth Republics: From a Regionalist to a Regional Social Movement', in P.G. Cerny (ed.), *Social Movements and Protests in France*, London, 1982.
10. Michel Nicolas, op. cit., p.191.
11. Ibid.
12. Union Démocratique Bretonne, *Bretagne = Colonie. Avec l'UDB pour que ça cesse*, Brochure, 1974.
13. G.V. Rogers, 'Ethnicity, Inequality and Integration: Ethnic Activism in Post-War Brittany', in Peter Morris (ed.), *Equality and Inequalities in France*, Nottingham, 1984.
14. Union Démocratique Bretonne, op. cit., p.7.
15. Alain Le Guyader, *Contributions à la critique de l'idéologie nationale*, Paris, 1978, p.187.
16. Louis Quéré, *Jeux Interdits à la Frontière*, Paris, 1978, p.300.
17. G.V. Rogers, op. cit., p.138.
18. Ibid.
19. *Le Peuple Breton*, No.178, Septembre 1978.
20. Ibid. 'Cumul des Mandats' refers to the possibility of holding any number of elected offices at local, departmental, regional, national and European levels (now reduced to just two 'mandates').
21. *Le Breton Socialiste*, 28 janvier 1978, p.2.
22. Ibid.
23. In Michel Nicolas, op. cit., p.345.
24. In Michel Nicolas, op. cit., p.346.
25. Ibid., pp.346-7.
26. Ibid.
27. Ibid.
28. Ibid.
29. Ibid.
30. Michel Nicolas, op. cit., p.354.
31. Ibid., p.355.
32. Ibid., p.355.
33. Ibid., p.356.
34. *Le Peuple Breton*, No.211, juillet 1981, p.2.
35. *Ouest-France*, 3.7.1981.
36. In Michel Nicolas, op. cit., p.11.
37. *Le Peuple Breton*, No.211, juillet 1981, p.2.
38. This theme is present in almost all the publications of the UDB from July 1981 onwards.
39. *Le Peuple Breton*, No.211, juillet 1981, p.2.
40. *Ouest-France*, 3.10.1981.
41. Ibid.
42. *Ouest-France*, 13.4.1982.
43. *Ouest-France*, 10.5.1982.
44. *Ouest-France*, 7.1.1981.
45. *Le Peuple Breton*, janvier 1982, p.28.
46. *Le Peuple Breton*, juillet 1982.
47. *Ouest-France*, 21.12.1982.

48. *Le Monde*, 18.5.1983.
49. *Le Peuple Breton*, janvier 1982, p.26.
50. *Le Monde*, 18.5.1983.
51. *Le Peuple Breton*, janvier 1982, p.27.
52. Le Monde Dossiers et Documents, *Les élections municipales de mars 1983, L'avertissement à la gauche*, p.35.
53. Ibid.
54. *Le Peuple Breton*, fevrier 1984.
55. Ibid.
56. *Libération*, 1.3.1984.
57. Ibid.
58. Ibid.
59. *Ouest-France*, 19.4.1984.
60. *Ouest-France*, 24.4.1984.
61. *Ouest-France*, 24.4.1984.
62. *Le Peuple Breton*, juin 1984.
63. Ibid.
64. *Ouest-France*, 4.12.1984.
65. *Ouest-France*, 22.10.1984.
66. *Ouest-France*, 22.10.1984.
67. *Ouest-France*, 24.1.1985.
68. *Le Peuple Breton*, avril 1985.
69. *Ouest-France*, 10.6.1985.
70. John Loughlin, 'A New Deal for France's Regions and Linguistic Minorities', *West European Politics*, no.3, vol. 8, July 1985, pp. 108–11.
71. *Le Peuple Breton*, avril 1986, p.7.
72. Ibid, p.19.

Chapter six

Corsica

Peter Savigear

The 1982 Special Statute

'So Corsu, ne so fieru' reads a motor-car sticker widely seen on the Mediterranean island of Corsica since the 1970s. 'I am Corsican, and proud of it' is a slogan which nevertheless suggests a touch of uncertainty, a need to proclaim an identity of which others might not be aware and the assertion of something which is actually rather unclear.

However, some aspects of Corsican identity are not only clear but strongly asserted. The deliberate use and encouragement to develop the language has been one result of this pride. Demand for more broadcasting time, publications, education using the language, have all been loud and probably can never be satisfied by any mere increase in the quantity of print or time. There has been a proliferation in studies of the culture, Corsican architecture, agriculture, husbandry, ploughing and baking. Traditions and customs have been rescued and examined in a depth and with an enthusiasm not seen since the earliest years of a remarkable local publication, the *Bulletin de la Société des Sciences historiques et naturelles de la Corse* which first appeared in 1881. Moreover a large diaspora has been self-consciously promoting attachment to their island. Corsican associations of all kinds thrive in the cities of mainland France, the 'continent' as they call it. The strength of this affection on the part of Corsicans living, working or studying away from the region, has turned a practical necessity into an exile.[1] At a cultural and social level, the identity of Corsicans is self-evident. This is not the case at a political level where the Corsican national identity remains obscure.

The once indivisible French Republic permitted a special constitutional status for the Corsican region in 1982, apparently in large measure a response to nationalist demands for an identity. This moment of achievement has been followed by the most intense questioning of the nature of Corsican nationalism since the 1930s. The direction of the nationalist impulse was no longer clear. What such a movement might mean is uncertain. Familiar questions required more precise answers; how strong is support for Corsican nationalism, what precisely did the nationalists now wish to achieve?

A degree of obscurity about the nationalist movement had existed before 1982. The demands of separatists and nationalists merged with those of regionalists seeking some element of self-government, and with those expressing the frustrations of economic decline and social changes. The creation of a devolved executive and an elected regional assembly gave a new importance to the distinctions between nationalists and regionalists, autonomists and separatists. The Special Statute for Corsica provided for the election, by proportional representation, of 61 deputies for the two departments, Haute-Corse and Corse-du-Sud. A regional executive was elected from and by these deputies and its powers defined by the legislation introduced by the Socialist government in Paris. Thus a regional government of Corsica was to be constitutionally responsible for matters such as the regional budget and local borrowing and taxation, economic planning and development including tourism, the environment, housing, education and culture, internal communications and a number of related matters. There is a new, regional, tier of administration. Committees of the regional assembly were created to debate and scrutinise these competences which had been made over by the central government in Paris. This was a radical change, the first of its kind since the Revolution of 1789, and brought to an end one era of regional discontent and nationalist agitation. All Corsican nationalists and regionalists were brought face to face with new realities.

The first of these new factors was the fact of the concession of a major part of the constitutional demands of the regionalists and autonomists in the reforms of 1982. A measure of autonomy had been granted and all groups could participate in the regional elections with some hope of success under the proportional system. The first elections were held in August 1982. This forced upon the supporters and advocates of constitutional change the decision whether these new institutions were indeed what they had sought and whether they were adequate. The largest and most important of the regionalist groups, the Union of Corsican People, UPC, enthusiastically geared its members for the election; 'on n'est plus des militants, on est élus' was their position.[2]

However, the wording of the constitutional innovations of 1982 invited further consideration. The Statute recognised the peculiar nature of Corsica. Article 2 referred to the 'specificités de cette région' and required the new executive to concern itself with the respect for and protection of this identity. This was particularly invited in the provision for regional responsibility in cultural matters and for employment and professional planning and career structures in the economy. Corsicans now had to find answers to the questions, what was their cultural identity and what exactly did the employment of Corsicans mean? Who in fact were Corsican? Such issues touched on a fundamental change that was brought about by the 1982 reforms. Where there had been regionalists and autonomists before 1982, there were increasingly only nationalists. By early 1987, the talk was of the 'nationalist family', but new tensions were already appearing in this muddled, many-faceted movement which through recent decades had been active in demanding political change.

The ingredients for a nationalist movement had a long history in Corsica. Slow beginnings in the nineteenth century led through the consciousness of economic and social pressures, often presented as a colonial oppression, to the release of new energies in the organisations of the 1950s and 1960s. With these came some violence and finally concessions and new institutions. Yet the form of these institutions raised doubts whether this has been the latent aim of two centuries and more of national aspirations. Could an election for a regional assembly with some devolved powers be accepted as the culmination of a vibrant nationalism which looked back to a history of struggle against the Genoese, to a moment of national independence in the eighteenth century with a great cultural and military leader, Pascal Paoli? His name and his legend, the emblem and the belief in a historical identity, were upheld by the nationalists of the twentieth century. The Corsicans have their language. The identity of the people is seen in their music, customs, in their distinctive view of death (always an interesting measure of social bonds) and the traditional forms of property.[3] After the Second World War there came an increased awareness of poverty on an island which had long been the most deprived part of metropolitan France. This took the form of rural and mountain depopulation, and of the lack of organised local opportunity for work and for further education and training on the island. Above all there were the French, the 'continentals'. They lured Corsica's best children away to be educated, to fight and administer for France. The French had come to Corsica, had treated it with disdain, had used it, built villas on its coastline and dumped 18,000 *pieds noir* (white French from North Africa) there after the independence of Algeria in 1962. In short, autonomists and nationalists argued that the French had treated Corsica as if it were a colony and not an integral part of France. In so doing, the French administration had encouraged and seduced some Corsicans into participating in this humiliation of a people by working with the imposed institutions. A series of events between 1962 and 1975 galvanised these feelings and inherited assumptions into an active political movement, giving expression to the latent nationalism, especially among the young who were most affected by limited educational and vocational opportunities. But the new institutions changed all these attitudes because they recognised Corsica as a quite special part of France; at least a change of attitude was invited. Many might now see the Special Statute as the culmination of protest, activism and a programme of uneven but definite concessions through the 1970s. In future the irritations of the Corsican people might be expressed through the elections and the regional government. The political position had therefore changed in a significant manner. Corsicans now had representation.

Another reason for the change of context that followed the institutional innovation of 1982 was the need to face a further precise question: how strong was support for nationalism on the island? Until 1982 this question was fudged. Thousands might attend rallies, as they had done in the frenzied summer of 1975 at the height of autonomist fervour, the year of Aléria.[4] Hundreds processed through the streets at times of crisis, demonstrating a high level of unity in the face of the administration. But none of this was more than *ad hoc* reaction, high-points of regional feeling, and there was no true measure of support. The elections which had been fought by autonomists before 1982, had never brought them any significant support. But they could be dismissed as corrupt, controlled by established interests which had long dominated the politics and institutions on the island. These interests were identified as the much loathed clans, with origins dating back to the late middle ages, unprincipled and essentially concerned with office rather than money, with power and influence rather than change. Under the new system of proportional representation, with much credit for bringing the constitutional change going to the autonomists, the question of support for the nationalists, and thus the extent of rejection of established interests, became precise and important. However, in this respect the nationalist impulse has had to come to terms with another new factor – their electoral support has not been impressive.

Nationalist problems after 1982

There have been six separate elections since 1982 and the Special Statute – three regional elections for the assembly, in 1982, 1984 and 1986, cantonal elections in 1985, and legislative elections in 1986 and 1988. In addition there have been further legislative and regional elections in the departments of Haute-Corse, in August 1986 and in March 1987, as a result of malpractice in March 1986. Across these several consultations the nationalists and autonomists have seen their support decline in a consistent manner. The high-point was 1982, not surprisingly. They obtained 12.6 per cent of the vote in those regional elections, a total of 17,268 votes. The drop has been steady since that election, with only 10,804 votes (7 per cent) obtained in the legislative elections in 1986, although they did rather better in the consequent regional elections, with 13,997 votes, 8.9 per cent. Overall there has been a 40 per cent drop in the nationalist vote.[5]

A number of particular explanations can be offered for this fresh dilemma facing Corsican nationalism. Perhaps the most obvious, but underestimated in importance, has been the issue of leadership. For many years the autonomist/nationalist movement has been led by two brothers, Edmond and Max Simeoni. Both doctors, vivacious, intelligent and very publicly committed to the regional cause, had been the spearhead of the first stirrings of contemporary activism in the 1960s. Max Simeoni contested elections in those years, but without much success. They dominated the newly formed political group, the ARC, Corsican Regionalist Action, and its successor the present UPC. But gradually Dr Edmond Simeoni assumed the prominent role, particularly in the move towards direct action. In February 1973 he was arrested for his activism. He became ever more forceful as the leader of the autonomist movement, a process that reached a climax in 1975 with the occupation of a wine 'cave' at Aléria, resulting in a clash with the gendarmerie, leaving two dead. Edmond Simeoni's arrest, trial and imprisonment were keenly followed by autonomists and others on the island in 1975 and 1976, the year of trial and conviction. Max Simeoni celebrated the anniversary of Aléria by a dramatic and individual act, the destruction of another wine depot belonging to a *pied noir*. He then disappeared into the Corsican maquis. Although this act reconcentrated attention on the original issue of fraud in the Corsican wine trade, it did not place Max Simeoni securely at the head of the movement. His brother remained the respected leader and his return from prison was widely welcomed. He remained the leader of Corsican autonomism through the years of agitation and finally of consultation which preceded the reforms of 1982, working closely with his brother, Max. Edmond Simeoni was elected among the deputies of the first regional assembly. He worked hard to build up an electorate, the new institutions and framework for the region. However in 1984 he became seriously ill and more or less withdrew from political activity. He was replaced only then by his brother Max, as the leader of the UPC. But Max Simeoni has not achieved the same charisma. The peak of 1982 has long gone and no dynamic new leader has appeared. Moreover Pierre Poggioli, leader of the Cuncolta Naziunalista, formerly the now-banned MCA, has not provided a popular replacement for Edmond Simeoni. The shaky alliance between the autonomists (UPC) and nationalists (once the MCA) has come under severe strain.

The element of electoral indigestion after five elections in as many years, and seven in Haute-Corse where more than half the electorate vote, has produced a growing abstention rate. This has been more striking in Haute-Corse. In the legislative elections in August 1986 only 60,997 votes were cast whereas there had been 85,411 in the March election.[6] A general increase in abstentionism had been assumed to favour the autonomist/nationalist candidates, but this has not occurred. A respected Corsican commentator observed that the nationalist electorate had shown itself no more active than the rest of the voters. The autonomist/nationalist share of the vote remained the same, *c*.8.4 per cent, in Haute-Corse, and nothing has prevented the steady decline in their share since 1982. All of this suggests that the new institutions have not significantly affected the voting patterns and habits of the Corsicans. Moreover, Corsica has not been able to rid itself of the slur of electoral malpractice, although this is by no means unknown elsewhere in France, hence the repeat elections in Haute-Corse. In August 1986, two voters in the commune of Altisanti carried off the urns, in protest at electoral fraud.[7] Furthermore it would seem that the balance of political forces in the assembly and among the deputies for the region sitting in the National Assembly in Paris, continued to reflect the traditional clan interests and strengths. The regional balance of power still favours the coalition parties of the right in the late 1980s, headed by the local RPR (Gaullists). They are presided over by Jean-Paul de Rocca-Serra in the regional assembly, as the deputies were in the previous assembly, i.e. by a man recognised as the 'chef de clan' of the political right and of the south of the island for some three decades. The Giacobbi family and supporters continued to lead the Socialist/left grouping in the region, in effect the opposition.[8] Thus it appeared that constitutional reform had not resulted in a transformation of the electoral balance.

There has also been a degree of disappointment with the reformed institutions and the nationalists and autonomists have not easily been able to respond to that disappointment. The transfer of competences was not immediately accompanied by a transfer of funds to accomplish policies. The region is too poor to mount major loans; there are not the resources to cover substantial interest and capital repayment. In addition there has been confusion and overlap in the allocation of responsibilities. The regional and other, often older organisations, have ill-defined areas of competence. The regional development agency, Société de développement régionale, established in 1981, still retained competence in economic and industrial planning, yet this was also an area of competence of the regional executive. Tourism, an important source of wealth and a subject requiring careful structural planning with consequences for the environment, was a regional matter, but the older regional agency for tourism and leisure remained in existence after 1982. There have also been direct clashes between the region and central government in which the regional opinion has been ignored or its decision overruled. Communications and transport between the island and France have been controlled by Paris. The power cable linking Corsica and Italy was rejected by the regional executive, but pushed forward by Paris. Such issues have given a disappointing start to the devolved government, and this disappointment may be reflected in the declining interest in the reformed institutions and in regional elections. The nationalists who had been so prominent in encouraging the government in Paris to move towards autonomy and especially enthusiastic about Socialist party proposals for these reforms since a draft constitution for Corsica in 1976 was backed by them, must adjust to this spreading disillusion.

Some support for the regional movements has also been withered by the concessions to Corsican demands made during the last decade. There is no doubt that internal communications have been improved by the spending of large sums on roads. Although not adequate and still bedevilled by administrative and costing problems, the sea and air links with France have also improved, and there are extensive plans for detailed improvements into the next decade. The university has been re-established at Corte (after closure in 1770) and students are in residence, taking courses, despite a number of disruptions following political and other agitation. A variety of economic development programmes have been started, particularly in irrigation and crop diversification. Support, however meagre, has been given to small rural industries and crafts, although there are disagreements about the economic value and social significance of such support. In these ways many Corsicans and island residents are encouraged to believe that real changes have occurred and that there is a serious commitment to future change on the part of government in Paris. It has therefore become an important matter for nationalists to explain a clear view on future development and the significance of reform. This has not been presented in a united and decisive manner.

A further divisive issue for the nationalists and autonomists has been the persistence of violence. In searching for an explanation of the recent decline in support for the nationalists of the UPC/Cuncolta Naziunalista, the joint party list, the impact of some eighty bomb attacks during the night of 21st March 1987, before the elections in Haute-Corse the following day, cannot be discounted. There had been an increase in bomb and other violent attacks in the department associated with the nationalists, and these aroused fears of worse to come (although these did include the Bastia tax office). The continuing deterioration in the control of violence worked against the electoral prospects of the nationalists. This high level and the varied forms of terrorism has had two effects. The first has been to place the nationalists in an ambiguous position. On the one hand they have formally condemned the bombings, the increase in gangsterism, the occasional assassinations and racial attacks (both of these have remained rare). On the other hand there has never been any doubt that there has long been an element among the nationalists which favoured violence. This has been acknowledged. It had led to the prohibition of armed organisations like the FLNC, the Front for the National Liberation of Corsica, and of sympathetic political groups like the ARC and the MCA. The UPC has tried to distance itself from the violence, rejecting the argument that only violence can force change and urging economic and other reform as a means of ending a violence arising from social discontent. But there has been some overlap in membership between the various groups, and the present nationalist movement has not firmly clarified its view. This dilemma has been made more acute for the nationalists because of the merging of politically motivated violence and crime with no political motive. There has been a substantial increase in the latter, with major gangs and rackets (notably the world of the 'Brise de mer' with ramifications in the gangsterism of the mainland). There has therefore been no question of violence declining after the 1982 reforms, and this has further called into question the value of regional constitutional change.

The result of these doubts has been to rally support around the established political parties and their leaders in condemning the violence as an affront to the dignity of Corsicans. The leaders and the clans have spoken loudly and in unison and thereby drew support for their interests. This too has disadvantaged the nationalists. They cannot accuse the regional executive of failing to respond to continued violence, although it had no authority over policing. The clans and established parties were able to denounce violence and terror without incurring the displeasure of the Corsicans because they could not end it. Policing of the region was one of the major competences which had not been transferred from central government to the region. Dealing with crime, with the destruction of villas and with murder and gang commerce was therefore still in the hands of gendarmerie and the police commissioners on the island, and the Commissaires de la République, formerly the Prefects. No blame or direct responsibility can be attached to the regional executive in the fight against violence.

Such pressures have eroded nationalist support and changed nationalist and autonomist objectives; the essence of the movements may not have changed, but the issue of translation of a people's identity into practical institutions has been affected. The Corsicans are seemingly more autonomist than nationalist. The recognition of their identity as a people among French peoples, the respect for the language (long delayed) and the quite remarkable position that they have been given in contemporary France, have all helped to allow the majority to live happily with the traditions of loyalty to France. This loyalty is also a proud element in the island's history, represented by sacrifices in war, service to the state and the resolute opposition to fascism (Corsica was the first liberated department of France, achieving this in 1943). Widespread support can be roused where the people's identity is apparently threatened. This has been seen in the government's attempt to replace the senior controller of the Corsican broadcasting station on the FR 3 network, Sampiero Sanguinetti. An estimated 2,000 marched in protest in February 1987. On an issue such as this, the Corsican public can be motivated and the expression of opinion seen to be effective, despite the accusation that M. Sanguinetti's handling of broadcasting 'systematically favoured the anti-French separatists'.[9] But an emotional response to the preservation of the language, the employment of Corsicans, to educational opportunity and the historical identity (articles devoted to episodes of Corsican history are abundant in the island's press), are not the same as a coherent and consistent political programme.

The autonomist/nationalist cause has a growing difficulty in presenting a programme. While the idea of a separatist political solution has some appeal, it cannot be an immediate electoral 'winner'. The political aim of constitutional change within the French state has now been attained, and this experience has not been unequivocally encouraging for those who demand further constitutional change or even separatism. Correctly or not, the impact of the 1982 reform has been to discourage constitutional change among those who once wished it. The content of autonomist and nationalist programmes was not significantly different from those of other parties. The issues raised in the recent elections were the familiar ones, unemployment, economic development, transport, violence. All the parties had programmes for dealing with these distressing difficulties and they divided broadly along the traditional left/right barrier. It was therefore less easy for the nationalist family to stake out their electoral territory and keep this distinct from that of the other parties. Even quite specific problems rarely had a distinct nationalist solution. The protection of the small Corsican producer in the agricultural sector, including the wine growers, has been taken up as coherently and forcefully by the Communist Party as by the nationalists, especially since the increase in European Community subsidies for the uprooting of vines has altered the basis of many livelihoods on the island.

Plus ça change

The evolution of politics in Corsica since 1982 has had the effect of increasing uncertainty and has worked generally in favour of the established interests. The uncertainty came from the fate of nationalism. Both features, nationalism in crisis and the strength of the established political practices and forms, were the results of the small size of the region's political community. Relatively isolated from the rest of France, the electorate remained at just over 200,000 for the two departments. Democracy has existed in Corsica on a small scale. The political leaders are still the four deputies and the new sixty-one regional deputies (two of the deputies elected for the National Assembly in March 1986 also held a mandate in the regional assembly at Ajaccio), and the cantonal and communal officers. The whole remains a compact elite, and democracy in the hands of the few. All are known to each other. The air of cosy familiarity has long made this an extremely difficult world to enter. Apparently anachronistic groupings like the Bonapartists in Ajaccio can exist in this tight and controlled political atmosphere. Their names and clan alignment are known and unambiguous. Once elected to the new regional assembly, the autonomists found that they were either drawn into the world of Corsican politics, needing to negotiate and communicate with the established interests, or had to divide themselves from this reality and be cut off from the thrust of the island's politics. Formal attitudes had little to do with the bargaining that took place in Ajaccio, where control has remained in the hands of leaders who originally rejected the proposed constitutional reforms of 1982.[10] The need to compromise led to a split within the UPC in 1984 and the isolation of the bulk of their members.[11] The future fortunes of the nationalists are not easy to see; the limits of their participation are uncertain, and they hold none of the key vice-presidencies of the assembly, of which there are nine. The dilemma that they face is similar to that of the Green Party in the Land and Federal assemblies in the German Federal Republic. Extensive participation implies a compromise and co-operation with elements of which they disapprove. The existing party groups have conducted Corsican politics through a high level of consensus, and office, and 'spoils' have been acceptably allocated. This division among the clans has been the target of autonomists since their first political stirrings over twenty years ago. On 19th March 1987, three days before the elections in Haute-Corse, Max Simeoni denounced the mediocrity and influence of the clans in much the same language that he had used in the municipal elections in Bastia in March 1967. However the history of the regional assembly has so far made one feature of Corsican politics completely clear: the clans have not disappeared despite proportional representation and new institutions.

The appearance of new names, of politicians in a new mould, has not broken the traditional system. There was some optimism. A new personality might have achieved such a transformation. There were hopes that José Rossi, elected to the Conseil Général in Corse-du-Sud in the cantonal elections in March 1985, might bring a fresh approach, but he has shown himself too astute a politician to think of confronting the practice of decades or the established position of a man like Jean-Paul de Rocca-Serra or the Giacobbi influence.[12] Similarly the growth in support for the extreme right Front National in Corsica has been as much about the position and credibility of the two leading party figures as about policies or a loosely defined racism. MM. Pascal Arrighi and Jean-Baptiste Biaggi have been experienced in Corsican politics and the politics of Corsicans for many years, indeed since their role in an era before Algerian independence in 1962, when there were as many Corsicans in the cities of Northern Algeria as there were on the island. Their position is unequivocal. The 1987 elections confirmed the vote for the Front National, giving them four seats in all, and enabled Jean-Paul de Rocca-Serra to secure an overall majority in the regional assembly with a broad rightist coalition. But since then the electoral success of the Front National has declined. Pascal Arrighi has disassociated himself from the party and the group scarcely exists in the assembly. The clans have adjusted and continued to influence Corsican politics, perhaps not only because they are part of the Corsican identity, but also because of the size and nature of the island's political base. Even the policy of extending proportional representation to all elected bodies, favoured by the nationalists and autonomists, might not affect the politicisation of such institutions by the clan interests. Where the number of politically active citizens is so small, and the electorate so easily influenced, the application of proportional representation to the chambers of commerce, tourist agencies and those for rural and agricultural development, would be unlikely to shake the position of established interests. In these circumstances the path for nationalists and autonomists is by no means clear.

Corsican nationalism and regionalist activity has been loyal to the idea that political change must come before economic or social develop- ment. They confront the clans who have made politics remarkably stable on the island, through the 'esprit des clans'. Contrary to popular myth (especially assumptions outside the island) their violence has not been random or uncontrolled, but deliberate and calculated in a time-honoured manner. The arbitrary is totally alien to the world of client politics. Thus regionalism and nationalism have not been able to escape the role of the clans as a guiding principle of politics, paradoxical though this form has been. The paradox lies in the combination of inertia and the infinite flexibility and adaptation of the clan phenomenon.[13] The lure of this 'institution' and the need to confront it, has kept Corsican nationalism remote from other influences, notably from Marxism. Their argument about colonisation has been essentially political, directed towards the system of client interests, and not based on class or on the control of the economy. They have been quite distinct from Sardinian groups in this respect and sustain few contacts of that kind. The need for political change was the principle on which Corsican nationalism grew after 1945. The many concessions from which Corsica benefitted, were regarded as peripheral. In the eyes of the nationalists, economic and social reforms, more grants following the many surveys of the island's economy and the development charters of the 1960s and 1970s, educational reforms and greater respect for the language, were dismissed as secondary. It was irrelevant that this 'frontier' region, this portion of the French periphery did not develop because of its remoteness from the 'core', the view so beloved of economic and human geographers. Even the constitutional reform was incapable of touching the crucial factor, that is the restricted nature of the political elite and the primary concern with office, influence and political power, concerns encouraged by the association with the French state.

However, the disappointment following the reforms of 1982, may have brought not only puzzlement but a more fundamental change in the emphasis of Corsican nationalism and autonomism. One stimulus has been the pernicious effect of violence which cannot be rapidly terminated, and has not been a product of clan-orientated interests. Gang strife, intimidation for the purpose of commercial and personal rivalry as well as for the purpose of raising a political levy, has concentrated attention on the need for structural reform in the economy. The rejection of economic development and social reforms is less appropriate than it seemed to the autonomists of the 1960s and 1970s. Such reforms may be welcome as the vehicle for ending violence and accelerating political change at the expense of the clans. Such reforms might include more extensive employment of Corsicans and the effective democratisation of institutions. This process had begun within the trade union organisations on the island. The major national unions, like the CGT, have been losing ground to the STC, the Syndicate of Corsican Workers, especially among the employees of growth sectors of the economy, in jobs related to tourism and among supermarket staff. Therefore there is a pressing need for the autonomists and nationalists to revise their principles and assumptions in order to retain the confidence of their supporters and to survive the critical developments of the turn of the decade.

The nationalists' achievement has been to survive, to keep the message alive through the active and varied autonomist/nationalist press, and to retain the loyalty of supporters. Much has remained familiar in the nationalist movement, the demands for the recognition of the Corsican people, denunciation of clans and the need to face the strength of non-radical, conservative centre-right politics. In 1988, three of the island's four deputies leant on that traditional electoral support, and in May 1988 the majority of the votes cast in Corsica in the presidential elections was for M. Chirac (54 per cent). The nationalists and autonomists have acknowledged the need to co-operate despite their differences and there is a growing sense of political compromise. The FLNC 'truce' of 1988 was a further example of this sense and of the need for a political formula which might enable the island to cope not only with many forms of violence, but also rapid economic and environmental change. A fresh debate is opening in Corsica between government, nationalists and the people.

Notes

1. Pascal Marchetti 'Compatriote non éminent', *Kyrn*, December 1975, pp.35–6.
2. Edmond Simeoni in conversation with the author, 1982.
3. No traveller in Corsica can miss the elaborate, walled cemeteries outside the villages. They show the great respect for family and its association with land. Many studies have been undertaken of this phenomenon. See M. Caisson 'Les morts et les limites', in *Pieve a Paesi*, CNRS 1978, pp.159ff.
4. In August 1975 Dr Edmond Simeoni occupied a wine depot at Aléria owned by a *pied noir* in an attempt to draw attention to fraud and corruption in the Corsican wine-trade, essentially to 'chapitilisation' (excessive sugaring of wine). He hoped to force the administration to prosecute offenders, thereby defending the small-scale indigenous producers and punishing the big exploiters. The occupation ended in tragedy as security forces tried to bring it to an end. See E. Simeoni *Le piège d'Aléria*, Paris, Lattes, 1975, and Jean-Paul Delors and Stephane Muracciole, *Corse, la poudrière*, Paris, Moreau, 1978. In English the impact is assessed in P. Savigear 'Corsica 1975: Politics and Violence' *World Today*, November 1975, pp.462–8.
5. The percentages obtained by the autonomist/nationalist groups have been as follows:

    regional elections 1982......12.62 per cent
    regional elections 1984......11.22 per cent
    cantonal elections 1985....... 7.44 per cent
    regional elections 1986....... 8.97 per cent
    legislative elections 1986... 7.02 per cent
    legislative elections 1988... 7.09 per cent (in 3 of the
    4 seats contested)

    In 1982 the UPC obtained seven seats in the regional assembly. In 1984 and 1986 the joint list of the UPC and MCA obtained six seats. There have been no regionalist/nationalist deputies elected for the National Assembly in Paris.

6. Abstentions have always been high in Corsican elections. In the legislative elections of June 1986, the rate was above the national average, as high as 41.5 per cent in Bastia on the first round of elections. The figures for the two regional elections in the Haute-Corse were 86,110 votes cast in 1986 and 64,696 in March 1987. The nationalist vote was 8.38 per cent and 8.45 per cent respectively. *Kyrn*, April 1987, pp.16–18.

7. *Nice-Matin* 26th August 1986.

8. The political balance in March 1987 was as follows:

   Union RPR, UDF, CNIP and various right = 27 seats
   Front National = 4 seats
   Movement des Radicaux de Gauche = 10 seats
   Union socialiste et radicale = 6 seats
   Communist Party = 8 seats
   UPC/Concolta Naziunalista = 6 seats
   Total 61 seats

9. M. Giacobbi quoted in *Le Monde*, 1st/2nd March 1987.

10. Jean-Paul de Rocca-Serra voted against in the National Assembly, Chamber of Deputies, and M. Giacobbi voted against in the Senate.

11. Two UPC deputies intended to co-operate with the majority in an attempt to influence policy and decisions, MM. Lucien Felli and J.F. Ferrandi.

12. 'L'éléction de Jose Rossi est un coup de tonnerre dans la classe politique insulaire. Pour la première fois on a le sentiment que quelque chose a craqué dans le système claniste'. Antoine Olivieri '1985: la remontée des départements' *Kryn* April 1985, p.18. The hopes thus expressed were perhaps too hasty.

13. Few works have explored this theme better than José Gil, *La Corse entre la liberté et la terreur*, Paris, Editions de la Difference, 1984. Thus his comment 'Le systeme clanique moderne s'est non seulement adapté mais aussi partiellement confondu .... avec l'appareil de l'Etat. Mais, parce qu'il est 'bi-front' comme on l'a dit souvent, presentant un visage corse aux populations insulaires et un visage francais à l'Etat, d'une part; parce que, d'autre part, il s'est rabattu sur le système ségmentaire populaire, il a longtemps freiné l'irruption des tendances nationalistes du peuple', p.22.

Chapter seven

The Basques

Jean Grugel

The greatest threat to the post-Franco order in Spain comes from the Basque country (Euskadi) and the struggle of the Basque people to realise their right to self-determination.[1] In the same way, the single biggest test facing the Socialist government in Madrid in the late 1980s is not the heated debate over the military bases or the performance of the Spanish economy but whether it can negotiate a peaceful solution to the conflict in Euskadi. It is not just that ETA (Euskadi and Freedom) is the largest terrorist/armed struggle movement in Europe after the IRA. Rather, nationalist sentiment is rooted deep in Basque and Spanish history, and dominates politics and government in Euskadi with broader, Spanish issues playing a subordinate role. Basque nationalism is peripheral in Spain in only a geographical sense, and whatever else may be said about ETA, there is no doubt that it took the nationalist debate out of Euskadi to Madrid and the corridors of power.

Regionalist movements can be found in Cataluna, Galicia and the Canary Islands; but nowhere are separatist tendencies as strong as in Euskadi. The *raison d'être* of Basque nationalism has always been separatist, and its expression has been almost always party political. In order to understand why this is so, we need to know something of the nature of the development of Euskadi in the Spanish context, and the extent of the repression under Franco's authoritarian state.

The development of nationalism

Basque nationalism can be interpreted as part of the revival of minority nationalism in multinational states, a phenomenon with reverberations throughout Europe. But nationalism is neither new nor recently reborn in Euskadi and must also therefore be interpreted within the specificity of Spanish development. The Spanish state was unable to complete the process of centralisation which accompanied state-building in Western Europe until the establishment of the Francoist dictatorship, and then only temporarily, through force, and imperfectly. Consequently, the process of identification between the state and nation in Spain was never completed. Juan Linz writes:

> For important minorities, Spain has been and will probably continue being a state ... but it is not their nation and therefore it is not a nation-state. The minorities which identify with the Catalan nation and more especially with the Basque nation ... illustrate the incapacity of Spain and her elites in building a unitary nation, however successful they may have been in building a state.[2]

In the case of Euskadi, integration into Spain occurred later than the other provinces. Until around 1840, it was almost completely independent, and it was not until 1876 that the Basques lost the last elements of their independence, the *fueros* or foral rights. The Basque sense of grievance against Spain dates from the loss of relative municipal, military and fiscal autonomy which the *fueros* involved. The loss of the *fueros* has since become what has been termed 'the justifying myth of the Basque cause'.[3]

The incorporation of Euskadi into Spain under the hegemony of the province of Castile and the loss of the *fueros* led to the first manifestations of Basque nationalism. The Basque Nationalist Party (PNV) was formed in 1893 under the leadership of Sabino Arana. The precepts elaborated by Arana were to dominate the PNV until the civil war and remain to some degree influential today. Sabino Arana's interpretation of nationalism was fundamentally different from the centralising, capitalist, liberal nationalism of nineteenth-century Europe. It was also different from the cultural assertiveness of Cataluna. Instead, Arana looked back to the past. The slogan associated with the PNV in this period was 'God and the Old Laws', referring to the PNV's defence both of catholicism against the onslaught of incipient secular values and of Basque autonomy through the *fueros*.

The first expressions of Basque nationalism coincided with the development of an industrial base in the region, especially in the provinces of Viscaya and Guipuzcoa. Urbanisation and migration, including from other regions of Spain, were the inevitable consequences of this. According to Arana, this meant that the danger of disappearance through assimilation was added to the problems of cultural and political oppression by the Spanish state. The maintenance of ethnic purity became the paramount issue for him. He was far more concerned about the 'degeneration' of the Basque 'race' from the influx of Spaniards into the cities than he was about the resulting erosion of euskera (the Basque language). Hostility towards Madrid was thus transformed into a distrust of the Spanish. The nationalists coined the word 'maketo', which was used in a derogatory sense to describe the Spanish 'foreigners'. Arana went as far as rejecting industrialisation and city life in general, which he saw as fatal for Euskadi in that they inevitably increased economic interdependence between Euskadi and Spain. Hostility between the town – representing the Spanish and secular values – and the country-side, which was catholic and euskera speaking, is a strong leitmotif of Aranian nationalism.

By the end of the nineteenth century, the development of heavy industry, especially around Bilbao, together with the expansion of mining had radically altered the social structure in Euskadi. Industrialisation took place unevenly, occurring chiefly in Viscaya and Guipuzcoa, whilst Alava and Navarre remained primarily agrarian provinces. It was in the industrialised zones where nationalist sentiment took root, and given the comparative prosperity of these areas, it is difficult to argue that Basque nationalism emerged as a direct consequence of economic deprivation.

In its initial stages, Basque capitalism was dominated by a fairly small, cohesive bourgeoisie who successfully sought economic conces-sions from the Spanish state, including protection for heavy industry. This sector of the Basque bourgeoisie, generally termed 'oligarchic', was thus absorbed into the dominant capitalist class in Spain and rejected nationalism.[4] However, as the cycle of industrialisation deep-ened, a local capitalist class developed, which, together with the Basque petit bourgeoisie, formed the basis of the nationalist vote. Alfonso Perez-Agote has argued convincingly that the local or national bour-geoisie in Euskadi was not linked to other centres of capital accumula-tion outside the Basque provinces, and tended to establish paternalistic relations with its employees.[5] These factors encouraged identification with the PNV, and also enabled the party to retain some traditionalist elements in its ideology. In Guipuzcoa where local capitalism was far stronger and industrialisation occurred on a smaller dispersed scale than in Viscaya, radical Basque nationalism has its heartland.

Nationalism out of the ashes : from the civil war to the end of the dictatorship

After 1920 the PNV displaced the oligarchic sector of the bourgeoisie to become the hegemonic force in Basque politics. Urbanisation and in-dustrialisation continually increased the importance in Basque society of tradesmen, professionals, administrators, bureaucrats, etc., who provided most of the PNV's leadership. In the 1933 elections, the PNV became the largest single party for the first time. It articulated the hostility in Euskadi towards the secularism of the Republic, reflecting that, in addition to representing sectors of the bourgeoisie, the support was based on the catholic vote. None the less, the PNV was republican; but its catholic commitment meant almost inevitably that it was anti-socialist and anti-communist. Relations between the Basque nationalists and the Socialists, who were also strong in Euskadi and who followed almost entirely the centralist line of the Madrid party, were extremely poor. It was not a complete accident that Euskadi only received a statute of autonomy from the Republic months before the outbreak of the civil war, while the Catalans were granted autonomy in 1932; though in fact, a total of three different statutes of autonomy had been proposed for Euskadi between 1930 and 1936, which failed to become law due to opposition from Alava and Navarre (Navarre rejecting the very concept of home rule).

Bilbao was captured by the Spanish Nationalists in June 1937, with the inevitable consequence that the statute of autonomy was immediately abrogated, and the PNV suppressed along with the other republican parties. In the period following the civil war until the 1960s, Baltza distinguishes four distinct phases in the PNV's history:

1. 1939–45, during which the nationalist government was in exile in Paris and London, and its future precarious due to the possibility of an Axis victory;
2. 1945–7, when Allied hostility towards Franco indirectly increased the prestige of the Basque Republicans in Western Europe and the United States;
3. 1948–52, which was characterised by the onset of the Cold War and the beginning of the rehabilitation of Franco in the eyes of the west, which caused a consequent downturn in the fortunes of the Republican camp as a whole;
4. 1953–60, years during which the PNV's presence inside Spain was reduced and it was unable to respond to the challenge of offering opposition internally.[6]

Two important points emerge out of Baltza's periodisation. First, the PNV was the only legitimate representative of Basque nationalism until the 1960s, and second, the fate of nationalism was bound up with the possibilities of a return to democracy in Spain. This is important in understanding political alignments in the last years of the dictatorship.

Within Euskadi itself, the Franco years were a time of coercion and repression of any sign of Basque language, culture or identity. It has recently been argued that the degree of repression was unique in Spain, and the nature of the Francoist state was qualitatively different in Euskadi. According to Stanley Payne, Francoism commanded consistently less support from Basque political elites than from those of other regions of Spain, and that recruitment to the security forces was lower than elsewhere, with the result that the paramilitary police force, the *guardia civil*, took on for the Basques the character of an army of occupation.[7] And significantly, although in general the final years of the dictatorship were marked by a softening of the repression and an informal opening up of the political system, in Euskadi the repression actually increased, torture of detainees remained commonplace and states of exception were continually in force.

The harshness of the dictatorship, combined with the weakness of the PNV as a vehicle of opposition, brought about a dramatic change in the nature of Basque nationalism : for the first time it took on board radical and Marxist elements. The first signs of dissatisfaction with the leadership offered by the PNV came in 1952 with the creation of the group and journal EKIN, and culminated in 1958 with the formation of ETA. Initially, the young people of EKIN were concerned primarily with rediscovering Basque culture, language and literature after a generation of suppression, and the movement's orientation owed much to Aranian nationalism, in that it was characterised by a strong anti-Spanish mentality. EKIN was also concerned with the need to take action, to preserve all that was Basque in defiance of the Francoist state. ETA grew directly out of EKIN's concern with activism, and was to become the most dynamic expression of Basque nationalism in the 1960s and early 1970s.

The revival of nationalism in the 1960s constituted a challenge not only to the Francoist regime but also to important sectors of the Basque bourgeoisie. The big industrial bourgeoisie, together with the large financial and banking groups, located primarily in Bilbao, identified strongly with the economic and cultural policies of Francoism. The new nationalism of ETA was directed equally against the pro-Spanish groups within Euskadi as it was against Madrid. This, more than anything else, accounts for the confusion within the Spanish opposition as to the true nature of ETA's goals: ETA was always primarily concerned with liberating Euskadi from Spain, rather than liberating Spain from Francoism.

Although ETA maintained a fairly anti-communist line until around 1964, by the late 1960s it had been incorporated into a loose anti-Francoist coalition, consisting of the political parties of the left, in particular the Communist Party, the trade union movement, students and the Catalan nationalists. ETA was responsible for the single most audacious blow to the authoritarian state in December 1973, when Prime Minister Luis Carrero Blanco was assassinated in Madrid. This event, more than any other single act, became the symbol of resistance to the dictatorship.

The transition to democracy in Euskadi

The democratic transition in Spain took place as a result of a remarkable compromise between the Crown, the left and some of the more modernising sectors from within the Francoist camp, who, grouped together in the Union of the Democratic Centre (UCD), distanced themselves from the armed forces and assumed positions which could be termed centre-right. The years following the death of Franco have been distinguished by negotiation and compromise, reflecting what is nothing less than a massive ideological transformation of Spanish society. Instead of the polarisation of Republican politics before 1936, almost all political parties now find themselves contesting the centre ground. A similar transformation of parties, platforms and social values has not taken place in Euskadi. A poll taken in October 1986 indicated a consistently higher level of identification with the left and the extreme left within Euskadi than Spain as a whole: 62 per cent of the Basques identified with the left, compared to 45 per cent in Spain as a whole.[8] Indeed, Mario Onaindia of Euskadiko Ezquerra, goes as far as questioning the notion of a transition in Euskadi:

> It is not as if the same transition takes place in Euskadi later or even more slowly ... It is, rather, a different transition. And more, there exists some doubt as to whether a transition as such takes place at all there.[9]

The period of transition in Euskadi has been marked by tension and conflict, between the nationalists, especially ETA, and Madrid, and between the Basques themselves. Since around 1968, when ETA undertook armed struggle, Basque politics have developed at their own rhythm, independent of developments in the rest of Spain. ETA's activities, the guerrilla struggle and the consequent repression, radicalised politics in the region, especially in the urban centres of Viscaya and Guipuzcoa. According to Onaindia, during the last years of the authoritarian state, ETA

> played a role in Euskadi similar to the role played by the Communist Party in the rest of Spain: the struggle was led by a small group because the dictatorship prevented the emergence of mass struggle until almost the end. ETA was able to keep alive the sacred flame of the fight for freedom.[10]

Levels of political mobilisation and class consciousness were higher in Euskadi than in the rest of Spain, and small ultra-left parties mushroomed in the region after 1968. Some of these were later incorporated into Herri Batasuna in 1979.

It is indicative of the gulf between Euskadi and the rest of Spain that, of all the political parties, only the Basque nationalists boycotted the referendum for the new democratic constitution, on the grounds that it did not recognise the right to self-determination of the Basque people. As a result, the constitution was rejected in Euskadi by over 65 per cent of the electorate, if we add the 'no' vote to the abstentions.[11] This pattern is different from political developments in Cataluna, where the transition to democracy has proved to be a turning point in centre-periphery relations.

Nevertheless, an acceptance of the need to disperse power territorially in Spain is understood as an essential element in the democratisation process. Only the die-hards within the right-wing Popular Alliance have opposed any degree of decentralisation. The main area of disagreement relates to the pace and/or degree of autonomy granted to the regions, particularly the historic nationalities of Euskadi, Cataluna and Galicia. While the autonomy debate in Madrid covers the spectrum from centralism to the statute of Guernica in its present form, in Euskadi, the debate begins with the statute of Guernica in its present form and moves towards independence. In effect, therefore, the two debates are separate ones, with the present state of affairs constituting the only meeting point between the parties in Madrid and those in Euskadi. It is in this sense that the statute is sometimes referred to as a compromise or pact between the signatories. In the case of the PNV and Euskadiko Ezquerra, the statute has been accepted with some reluctance as a point of departure, but it has been rejected in its totality by the radical nationalist formation, Herri Batasuna, who described it as 'embracing the Moncloa'.[12]

The provisions of the statute of Guernica include the creation of an autonomous parliament in Vitoria, to which was ceded the right to self-government in administrative, fiscal and educational affairs, with the autonomous community paying a fixed sum to Madrid in recognition of the services provided by it. It also created a Basque police force alongside though not instead of the national police, a television channel in Euskera and recognised Euskera as an official language in Euskadi as well as Spanish. Basque citizenship under the statute was granted to all those who reside within the bounds of the autonomous community; that is, the concept of the Basque people as constituting a distinct ethnic group was ignored. The statute applies to only three of the Basque provinces: Viscaya, Guipuzcoa and Alava, with Navarre retaining the right to integration should the Navarrese so desire. It was approved by only 53.2 per cent of the electorate.

The statute was negotiated in an atmosphere in Madrid which if not totally favourable to the expression of regionalism, was certainly prepared to make concessions and was hopeful that autonomy could be made to work, particularly in the sense that it would bring about the collapse of ETA. Its success has been limited, however; it has failed to deal a death-blow to ETA, and perhaps more significantly, all the nationalist parties, with the partial exception of Euskadiko Ezquerra, continue using the separatist political discourse of the past. Disillusionment in Madrid with the effectiveness of decentralisation, combined with a fear of antagonising the ultra-right in the aftermath of the coup attempt of February 1981, led to the slowing-down of the autonomy process. The *Ley para la armonizacion del proceso autonomico* or LOAPA, as it is known, was passed without prior consultation with nationalist representatives of any of the regions. In view of this, the likelihood of further substantive devolution is slight, certainly in sensitive areas such as the judicial system or policing, or even of the anti-terrorist legislation, about which Amnesty International has expressed concern.[13]

The Basque party system

The Basque party system which has emerged out of the dictatorship is complex and fragmented. It is no longer possible to talk of one hegemonic party representing the nationalist cause, as was the case in 1936. Instead there are four parties which contest the nationalist vote. At the same time, the Socialist Workers' Party – the Socialist Party of Euskadi (PSOE–PSE) commands significant support within the system and is currently the largest single party within the autonomous parliament due to the division of the PNV. Other Spanish parties are also present. The system is thus very different from Spain as a whole, where two or perhaps three parties are dominant.

The party system in Euskadi conforms to Giovanni Sartori's description of a 'pluralised polarised system'[14]. Pluralism refers to the number of parties present within the system, and describes a system where more than two parties are 'relevant' or 'influential', through for example, a capacity for coalition-building. The extent to which a party system is polarised depends upon the ideological difference which separates those parties which lie at the extreme poles of the system. In the case of Euskadi, the system is polarised in two distinct but converging senses: along a left–right continuum, and along a separatist–centralist one.

The nationalist parties within the system are: the Basque Nationalist Party (PNV), Euskadiko Ezquerra (EE), Herri Batasuna (HB), and the recently formed Eusko Alkartasuna (EA).

The PNV remains a multi-class party in terms of its electoral constituency, is populist and employs separatist rhetoric, especially during electoral campaigns, but is none the less perceived as representing a moderate (i.e. not separatist) nationalism of a centre–right persuasion. Without dismissing the anti-liberal and anti-Spanish legacy completely, something the PNV has never done, the party's long march towards pragmatism and consensus with Madrid can be traced back to the 1930s and the *modus vivendi* it accepted with the Republic.

The dual strategy of separatist rhetoric in conjunction with practical compromise can be seen emerging for the first time in this period.

The PNV controlled the autonomous parliament in Vitoria from when it began to function until the elections of November 1986. Good relations were established with the UCD governments, and perhaps more suprisingly in the light of the hostility between the nationalists and the Socialists in the 1930s, the PNV's relations with the PSOE government were also reasonably good. The PNV is currently in deep crisis due to the secession of an important sector of the party grouped around the charismatic figure of Carlos Garaikoetxea, who formed the Eusko Alkartasuna (EA). The ideology of EA is similar to that of the PNV: the split was the result of personal antagonism and conflicts on the one hand, and dissatisfaction with the lack of democracy inside the PNV. In the short time that EA has existed, it has presented itself as a modernising party, untainted by contact with the Madrid-based parties, and more genuinely nationalistic than the PNV.

Euskadiko Ezquerra (EE) is considerably to the left of the PNV, but, like the PNV, has preferred with some reluctance to accept the reality of the constitution and the statute of Guernica. Despite their considerable ideological differences, both EE and the PNV offer territorial-based opposition within the rules of the democratic game. Like Herri Batasuna, EE claims to be Marxist in its inspiration, but it is much closer to PSOE-PSE, given that the primary issue in Basque politics relates not to goals but to means – pacific and parliamentary or violent. Euskadiko Ezquerra won only 8 per cent of the vote in Euskadi in 1984, which it increased to 10.88 per cent in 1986. Its influence, however, lies less in its popular appeal, and more in the support it receives from the intellectual elite of Euskadi, which has earned it the reputation as somewhat of a think-tank of nationalism. EE has been notably unsuccessful, though, in winning the ultra-nationalist vote from Herri Batasuna.

Herri Batasuna, ETA and the alternative KAS

ETA is a product of the repression of the Francoist era, and was radicalised by the student movements of the 1960s in Europe. In the first instance, its ideology was determined by the legacy of Aranian nationalism, but by the late 1960s, the theories of imperialism, development and underdevelopment and the corresponding strategies of national liberation which were current at the time, and which found a receptive audience in the peripheral regions of Spain where repression was a daily reality, meant that ETA came to analyse the Basque situation in terms of an imperialist centre (Madrid) and a colonised periphery (Euskadi).

Euskadi was seen as producing wealth for capitalist enterprises which have their headquarters in Madrid and which export their profits to Madrid. As a result, ETA moved away from many of the traditional elements of Basque nationalism, especially its anti-Marxism and its confessionalism. Instead, ETA talked of the need to synthesise national liberation with class struggle in language which acknowledged influences from the Third World, particularly the struggles in Cuba, Vietnam and Algeria:

> History has shown us that national independence depends upon the committment of the oppressed to bring about their own liberation. This committment is revealed in action, through violence ... the oppressed must use force in order to win recognition for what is in fact their right.[15]

Since 1968, ETA have adopted a form of urban guerrilla warfare as a strategy of liberation from Spain. In the period 1968 to June 1984, ETA claimed responsibility for the deaths of 428 people, and approximately 124 ETA members had been killed. By the end of 1986, ETA had claimed responsibility for nearly 40 more deaths.

ETA sees the autonomy process as palliative and superficial, and aims to bring about its collapse by revealing its contradictions and forcing the Madrid government to show its 'true' repressive face, which should in turn radicalise the Basque people and orient them towards the option of independence. It was relatively successful in these respects before the transition; since 1977, however, it has been less so. The ending of the Francoist states of exception together with the statute of autonomy have made the goal of winning enough support for the option of an armed struggle for independence an ever more remote possibility.

With the adoption of a national liberation perspective, other new elements were incorporated into nationalist ideology. ETA favoured a strictly secular society, for example, in spite of the catholicism of the original members and the support it has received on occasion from sectors of the Basque catholic church. ETA also modified the original nationalist positions *vis-à-vis* immigrants living in Euskadi, in its public declarations at least. For the first time, the immigrant is not seen as the eternal enemy and the Basques are not conceptualised as a completely homogeneous race. Instead, class becomes a primary determinant of nationality, with language remaining a secondary determinant. These ideological changes were part of the transformation of nationalism which made it possible for ETA to appeal to the student movement in the early 1970s and to the industrial working class. At the same time, however, the incorporation of 'workerist' elements has introduced a measure of permanent tension into the movement. ETA's history of fragmentation is attributable in part to the struggle between the

Socialists and the extreme nationalists. In 1974, the movement split in two: ETA *politico-militar* (ETA p-m) and ETA *militar* (ETA-m). ETA p-m renounced armed struggle after the abortive coup attempt in February 1981 in an effort to shore up Spain's democracy and remove one major potential point of rupture. ETA-m, meanwhile, disputed any analysis which argued that the operation of the state in Euskadi had in any way changed since the ending of the authoritarian state. Indeed, the hard-line faction of ETA proposed negotiations take place between their organisation and the Spanish armed forces, who are the real power in Spain. At the same time, the *linea blanda*, or the 'wets' in ETA are known to favour open dialogue with the Spanish government, and have engaged in discussions with the other nationalist parties.

ETA's relationship with Herri Batasuna (HB) has been compared to that of the IRA with Sinn Fein. Formed in 1979, HB is a coalition grouping together many of the small ultra-left or ultra-nationalist parties which emerged clandestinely in the early 1970s. It competes in elections to the autonomous parliament and to the Cortes in Madrid, but has so far refused to occupy any seats it wins in either. Like ETA, HB rejects the statute of Guernica and proposes instead the *Alternative KAS* (*Koordinadora Abertazale Socialista*), which serves simultaneously as a political programme. The main points of KAS are :

1. a complete amnesty for all political prisoners;
2. the expulsion from Euskadi of all Spanish police and security forces;
3. an improvement in the standard of living for all the 'popular' classes of Euskadi, especially the working class;
4. the reunification of Navarre with the other provinces of Euskadi;
5. recognition of the links which exist between north Euskadi (part of France) and south Euskadi (part of Spain);
6. recognition of the right of Euskadi to form an independent state;
7. the control by the Basque government of the armed forces which are stationed in Euskadi.

HB can command a steady 15 per cent of the total vote in Euskadi, a far from inconsiderable percentage in a pluralist party system. It is particularly strong in Guipuzcoa, where in November 1986 it won almost 19 per cent of the vote. None the less, few studies of exactly who votes for HB have been undertaken. It is generally thought that its appeal is greatest to young – under 25 – voters, and especially to young men, living in urban areas, without university education. In 1986, HB, for example, may have benefited proportionally more than other parties from the incorporation of 75,000 first-time voters to the electoral register. It is also possible that HB can attract those sectors of the electorate who identify in the rest of Spain with the United Left coalition of Communists, anti-nuclear organisations, feminist groups etc. This is interesting, because it implies that HB has electoral potential as a broad left mobilising party in Euskadi, not only as a nationalist party associated with ETA; but as yet sufficient empirical evidence is lacking to substantiate the argument.

What is most remarkable about ETA and HB is not their existence as such, but the degree of support they have succeeded in building in Euskadi, and even more important, their legitimation in the region. This is what differentiates ETA from Terra Lliure, the small national liberation group in Cataluna, with whom ETA has on occasion collaborated. There is considerable support within Euskadi in favour of the government negotiating directly with ETA. In a recent opinion poll, 77 per cent of the Basques rejected any analysis which reduced ETA to a law and order problem in the region, and favoured a 'reinsertion' of ETA into the political system. Only 32 per cent were in favour of the expulsion and extradition from France of members of ETA who have sought refuge there.[16]

This is indicative of the prevailing sense of nationhood within Euskadi, rather than direct support for terrorism. The statute of Guernica has not delegitimised ETA inside Euskadi. In turn, this pressurises the PNV and EA to adopt postures which are far more extreme, at least at the level of rhetoric, than are their natural inclination, in order to avoid marginalisation and the label of 'selling out' to Madrid.

The evolution of Basque identity

How has the Basque sense of nationhood changed over time, especially in response to the continuous process of industrialisation and the waves of immigration which Euskadi has experienced over the last 100 years? What are the factors which have determined the sense of Basque nationhood in south Euskadi (Spain) and not in north Euskadi (France)? How does Basque identity differ from regional identity in the rest of Spain, for example in Cataluna, which can also be considered a separate nation? These are the central questions which this section will attempt to address.

The Basques who inhabit south Euskadi share some racial, cultural and linguistic links with the French Basques, but their history has been very different. First, south Euskadi was incorporated late and imperfectly into Spain, unlike north Euskadi into France. Second, the French Basques lack the profound sense of injustice and oppression which exists in south Euskadi. This sense of oppression is multiple and has taken different forms: racial, economic, cultural and actual physical oppression are entwined. Quite simply, the French Basques have not suffered forty years of authoritarianism. Part of the current crisis between Euskadi and Madrid relates directly to a loss of sympathy in the rest of Spain for the Basque sense of national oppression.

The first expressions of Basque nationalism reflect the perception of the Basques as a people in danger of extinction through forcible integration into the Spanish state. The original Aranian formulation was anti-industrial, catholic and elitist. It was a traditional ideology in that it was rural and looked back to a supposed golden past. However, nationalist sentiment, even at this early stage, was not linked to the use of euskera. In view of the traditional elements of nationalism, it is perhaps surprising that nationalism did not take on any fascist or corporatist characteristics in the 1920s and 1930s. Instead, when nationalism became a political force under the Republic, the PNV had identified itself as a catholic but democratic party, representing the Basque petit bourgeoisie and local capitalists.

The growth of ETA in the late 1960s, and the emergence of two distinct left-wing parties, Euskadiko Ezquerra and Herri Batasuna, in the post-Franco period added a new dimension to nationalist ideology – a Marxist perspective of class oppression under peripheral capitalism. Thus the nationalism articulated by Herri Batasuna and ETA comes closest to the nationalism of revolutionary movements in the Third World. It differs from non-revolutionary Third World nationalism in that it is class-based, rather than populist.

One of the factors which distinguishes nationalism in Euskadi is a correlation between nationalist sentiment and the political and economic projects of specific social groups and classes. Consequently, specific groups or classes are identified as making up the Basque nation to the exclusion of others. Basque identity is not a result of merely living or being born in Euskadi or speaking euskera. In this respect, Basque nationalism is very different from nationalism in Cataluna, where it is conceptualised on the basis of birth, territory and language, irrespective of class. Francesc Hernandez noted:

> There exists a generalised idea within Cataluna that nationality has a multi-class dimension, independent of political confrontations between conflicting class interests. All Catalans have accepted in the course of their socialisation as nationalists a degree of solidarity towards their fellow Catalans, regardless of their social position and their ideology.[17]

Nationalism is thus far more sectarian in Euskadi than it is in Cataluna. This is perhaps ironic, given that data collected by Juan Linz indicates a much higher affective identification in Euskadi than in Cataluna, irrespective of class:

Only 15 per cent of the inhabitants of Cataluna describe themselves as solely Catalan, while in the Basque country 40 per cent define themselves as Basque : this difference cannot be attributed to replies from immigrants from other regions, since 20 per cent of those born in Cataluna define themselves as Catalan, compared with 50 per cent of those born in Euskadi and Navarre who define themselves as Basque.[18]

The paradox of Basque nationalism is that regional identity is far stronger in Euskadi than in any other part of Spain, yet it is also a more divisive force there than in any other part of Spain because it is complicated by class and territorial cleavages and because of the absence of factors of convergence. Linz's conclusion is that a sense of dual nationality, which operates in Cataluna for example, is absent in Euskadi.[19] In so far as the statute of autonomy was designed to foment a dual nationality in Euskadi and a sense of being Spanish as well as Basque, it is difficult to escape the conclusion that it has failed.

Conclusion: the future of Euskadi

Elections for the renewal of the autonomous parliament were brought forward to November 1986 because of the split in the PNV and its consequent loss of a majority. The results, however, did nothing to end the tensions within the Basque party system and within Basque society.

The nationalist parties, if we take the total of their votes together, increased their representation, confirming a pattern established since 1979. In the case of Herri Batasuna, its share of the total vote was enough to make it the third-largest party in Euskadi, after the PNV and PSOE-PSE. The Socialists' share of the vote was lower than in either the general elections of 1986 or the autonomous elections of 1984, but they none the less won more seats than any other single party. Long weeks of intense negotiations brought about a formal alliance between the PNV and PSOE who now jointly control the Basque legislature.

Increasingly, however, the search for a solution to the problems in Euskadi centres upon the need to defeat ETA and put an end to the atmosphere of violence and confrontation which impedes negotiation and compromise. The Madrid government has tried to isolate ETA and Herri Batasuna politically and tactically by promoting an anti-terrorist pact which has been signed by all the nationally-organised parties and by most of the Basque parties, the exceptions being Herri Batasuna and Eusko Alkartasuna, both of which continue to insist that the problem is not one of law and order and that therefore a solution must come through a renegotiation of the relations between Euskadi and Spain; in effect, a renegotiation of the statute of autonomy. Furthermore, a willingness on the part of Madrid to extend Basque autonomy in at least some areas, argues Garaikoetxea of Eusko Alkartasuna, would increase the latent divisions both within ETA and between ETA and Herri Batasuna, which should in turn weaken the 'extremist' nationalists within ETA because of their growing isolation. This strategy is in keeping with Garaikoetxea's long-term goal of incorporating the radical nationalists within Herri Batasuna within the democratic framework without changing the nationalist elements of their discourse, but it is not a course of action which enjoys consensus inside Spain.

One area where autonomy could be deepened without needing to renegotiate the statute of Guernica is policing. The Basque police force, the Ertzaintza, has only 3,100 members and, primarily because of a fear that the Ertzaintza could be infiltrated, it has little access to confidential information kept in Madrid on the identities and movements of ETA members. As a consequence, its effectiveness and its credibility are much reduced. It is perhaps ironic that the Ministry of the Interior is prepared to keep a foreign government (that of France) better informed about ETA than the Basque police force. The proposal by the moderate nationalists of increasing the size of the Ertzaintza meets with little enthusiasm in Madrid.

The Madrid government's strategy is premised on the belief that the current level of devolution is sufficient and focuses its attention on the struggle to defeat ETA. It has adopted a two-pronged strategy. First, it prioritises the weakening of ETA by the police and the Spanish state. To this end Gonzalez has signed a series of agreements with France which have led to the expulsion of Basques living in France who are known to have connections with ETA and the extradition of others. The arrests in France have weakened ETA logistically and psychologically.

The second part of the strategy is negotiation with sectors of ETA with the aim of bringing about the reinsertion of ETA members into civil society and convincing them of the validity of democratic channels of dissent. Negotiation and reinsertion proved successful with sectors of ETA p-m, while others simply joined ETA-m. The Madrid government has in fact entered negotiations periodically with ETA, but it is only recently that it has begun to do so openly. The possibilities of a negotiated solution to Euskadi's problems, however, depend not only on a willingness to enter dialogue, but also a willingness to compromise, and it is unclear in which areas Madrid is prepared to cede terrain. And, last but not least, successful negotiations depend upon the hard-liners in ETA losing control of the movement and it has yet to be demonstrated that this has happened. Peace and justice would still seem to be some way ahead for Euskadi.

Table 7.1 The Basque parliament, 1980–6

Parties	Mar 1980		Feb 1984		Nov 1986	
	%	seats	%	seats	%	seats
Basque Nat. Party (PNV)	38.0	25	41.7	32	23.64	17
Socialist Workers' Party (PSOE)	14.1	9	23.3	19	22.04	18
Popular Coalition (UDC/SDC)	4.8	8	9.4	7	8.39	4
Euskadiko Ezquerra (EE)	9.8	6	8.0	6	10.80	9
Eusko Alkartasuna (EA)					15.8	14
Herri Batasuna (HB)	16.5	11	14.6	11	17.47	13

Sources. Cambio 16, 6/10/1986; *El Pais*, 1/12/1986.

Notes

Acknowledgement: the author would like to thank the Leverhulme Trust, which made the research possible, and Rob Robinson for discussing many of the ideas contained here.

1. It should be noted that this article will only deal with the ideology and struggles of the Basque people who live in south Euskadi, inside Spain.
2. Juan Linz, 'Early State-Building and Late Peripheral Nationalism against the State : the case of Spain' in S.N. Eisenstadt and S. Rokkan (eds), *Building States and Nations*, London, 1973.
3. Gurutz Jauregui Bereciartu, *Ideologia y Estrategia Politica de ETA*, Madrid, 1985.
4. The incorporation of the oligarchic bourgeoisie of Basque extraction continued throughout the Francoist period, with the result that by 1970, 30 per cent of Spain's monopolistic enterprises counted with the investment of capital accumulated originally in Euskadi. Moreover, the internationalisation of Basque capital invested in banking and financial houses during the late 1950s and the influx of foreign capital into Spain strengthened the centralist tendencies of this sector of the bourgeoisie.
5. Alfonso Perez-Agote, *La reproduction del nacionalismo: el caso vasco*, Madrid, 1984.
6. Baltza, *Nacionalismo vasco y clases sociales*, San Sebastian, 1976.
7. Stanley Payne, *Basque Nationalism*, Reno, 1975.
8. *Cambio 16*, 27/10/1986.
9. Mario Onaindia, 'Transicion Democratica en Euskadi', *Leviatan*, Autumn 1985, no.21.

10. ibid.
11. 55.3 per cent of the electorate abstained; 30.86 per cent voted 'yes'; and 10.51 per cent voted 'no'. In Spain as a whole, the constitution was approved by 89.7 per cent of the electorate.
12. Manifesto of Herri Batasuna, 1/6/1983. The Moncloa is the seat of government in Madrid.
13. Amnesty International, *Spain: A Question of Torture*, London, 1985.
14. G. Sartori, *Partidos y sistemas de partidos*, Madrid, 1980.
15. Gurutz Jaregui, Bereciartu, op cit.
16. *Cambio 16*, 27/10/1986.
17. Francesc Hernandez, 'El nacionalismo catalan y la socializacion nacionalista', *Sistema*, September 1981, nos.43–4.
18. Juan Linz, *Conflicto en Euskadi*, Madrid, 1986.
19. ibid.

Chapter eight

Quebec

Michael Macmillan

After two decades of robust expansion culminating in a referendum in May 1980 on a first step on the path to independence, Quebec nationalism appears to be in active retreat. This is rather curious, if not anomalous, in that Quebec has been governed for much of the past two decades by the Parti Québécois, a party whose traditional *raison d'être* has been the goal of political independence for Quebec. In what follows, I shall attempt to account for these surprising developments, focusing on the developments since the referendum. I shall argue that these developments are a result of a series of alterations in the expectations of Québécois, some positive though others negative, which have the effect of undermining support for the nationalist cause. In particular, I shall emphasise the role of economic and linguistic factors.

Throughout the 1970s, support for independence or sovereignty-association as the referendum proposal specified, remained remarkably stable, enjoying the support of roughly 35-40 per cent of adult francophones. As is well known, the referendum result produced a support level of approximately 40 per cent for the initiation of discussions regarding greater autonomy for Quebec. Since then, there has been a virtual nosedive in public support for that option. A SORECOM poll in April 1984, reported that 19 per cent of francophones stated that they had supported independence at some time in the past, and 41 per cent, sovereignty-association. However, when asked about their current preferences, only 7 per cent favoured independence and 14 per cent, sovereignty-association. This is a strong indication of a substantial erosion of support for nationalist options. More recent opinion polls reinforce these findings. A CROP poll reported in January, 1985 that only 4 per cent of Quebec residents want independence for Quebec and only 15 per cent support sovereignty-association. Somewhat surprisingly, a majority of Quebec residents, and a plurality of Quebec francophones, want Quebec to be a province like the others (52 per cent and 48 per cent respectively).[1]

What accounts for this downturn in nationalism? I would suggest that one of the most important factors has been, somewhat paradoxically, the very success of language policies which have been inspired by and designed to achieve nationalist goals. In addition, there has been a series of economic changes which have, on the one hand, served to discourage support for political change and, on the other, to mitigate the perceived necessity for it. In fact, there is substantial overlap between both sets of factors, but each will be examined in turn.

In an early survey of the evolution of French-Canadian nationalism, Bonenfant and Falardeau noted the distinction between patriotism and nationalism, but nevertheless concluded that there was substantial overlap between the two concepts, and therefore used the term, nationalism, to refer to both phenomena. More recently, Clift has followed their lead, defining nationalism as, 'the spilling over into the realm of politics of those feelings of solidarity, patriotism, and nationality possessed by an ethnic group'.[2] This definition captures what is generally referred to as French-Canadian nationalism and shall be used in this discussion.

Language policy and nationalism

In many societies, language issues are often intimately connected to nationalist movements. This is explicable in that many issues that are the substance of nationalist demands are often related to or symbolised by particular language policies. One element of overlap concerns the manner in which language policy involves the allocation of important non-economic resources, most notably, status. The point is well illustrated in Raymond Breton's observation that,

> Indeed, in a powerful way, the language used in public affairs and institutions signified to individuals and groups 'that the society is indeed their society', and perhaps the most effective symbolic medium for asserting a mutual reflection of the public world of institutions and the private world of individuals.[3]

Historically, a prominent theme in Quebec nationalism has been the centrality of the French language to the national and cultural identity of French-Canadians. Related to it is the belief that the status and condition of the language is an important barometer of the well-being of the French 'nation'. As one keen student of Quebec history remarks, 'the state of the French language has always been regarded in Quebec as a symptom of the health of the French-Canadian nation'.[4]

Throughout the various disputes since the 1960s, there has been a close link between language issues and nationalism in Quebec. A commentator on the educational controversies of the late 1960s remarked that 'in public protests issues of independentism became confused with

French unilingualism ... a strictly educational issue was viewed in the context of cultural, economic and even political liberation'. He concluded that 'in short, French unilingualism in the schools was symbolic of economic and political and cultural liberation'.[5] The same overlap is visible in the language policy developed and implemented by the Parti Québécois (PQ). Its passage has been described as 'the high water mark of nationalist pressure'. Yet it is also identified as a significant factor in the ebbing of support for the nationalist impetus to independence. This is a puzzling combination and requires explanation.[6]

Bill 101, the Charter of the French Language, which became law in 1977, is a complex, multifaceted piece of legislation which has as its principal element the establishment of the French language as the official language of Quebec. It asserts that every person in Quebec has the right to receive government services, to work, to be educated and to obtain goods and services in French. To this end, it requires the francisation of business activity, both in terms of the language of internal communication and of collective bargaining. In addition, all governmental and quasi-governmental institutions must function in French, except where the clientele is largely of another language – though even here records and services must be available in the official language. Finally, the Charter severely restricts access to the English-language educational institutions.[7]

Bill 101 is to be understood as an explicit exercise in nation-building. Its symbolism is that of the French nation asserting its dominance over the territory of Quebec. The symbolic assertion of power is reflected in the government's white paper on language policy, where it states that what Quebec's French-speaking majority must do is reassume the power which is its by right, not in order to dominate, but to regain the status and latitude proper to its size and importance.[8] The document asserts that the use of the French language...'will accompany, symbolize and support a reconquest by the French-speaking majority in Quebec of that control over the economy which it ought to have'.[9]

The link to nationalism is explicitly drawn in Camille Laurin's address to the National Assembly on the second reading of Bill 101, where he asserted: 'Quebec owes to itself to bring into being, on every level, the nation it in fact is; to acquire the powers and resources it needs for this end;... It is in this perspective that the government's language policy is situated'.[10] He concluded that 'the Quebec that this bill prepares and heralds will be French, educated and modern – a country that will take its place side by side with countries of comparable size that have already set their mark on the world scene'.[11] Part of the purpose of the language policy, then, is to cultivate a sense of nationhood in the society which will provide a launching pad to the elevation of Quebec to the galaxy of independent states.

The symbolic significance of 'and the linkage of' nationalism with Bill 101 is clearly perceived by Quebec nationalist groups and the larger Quebec citizenry. Prominent nationalists applauded the legislation primarily as a major advance in the nationalist cause. The head of the St Jean Baptiste society exulted: 'The gesture of the affirmation of French, is before all the affirmation that we are a nation, that we have our own language, the rights of which are inalienable, with everything that follows from that'.[12]

While many nationalists applauded Bill 101 as a contribution to the cause, others were less sanguine. Bouthillier, for one, perceived the legislation as limited by the constraints of the BNA Act and concluded that the francisation of Quebec could only be achieved with the realisation of Quebec sovereignty. He shares the view of other nationalists, however, that ... 'the movement for the liberation of Quebec and that of the affirmation of French are tightly linked...'.[13]

As well, the general public perceives Bill 101 as particularly linked to nationalism. When asked to identify which groups in Quebec are likely to support Bill 101, the term 'Québécois' is much more strongly linked to support than the terms 'francophone' or 'French-Canadian'. The distinction among these terms, of course, consists of the nationalistic dimension given to the former.[14] Thus both Quebec nationalist leaders and the general public perceive Bill 101 as an expression of Quebec nationalism. In addition, there is widespread public satisfaction with the language policy. A SORECOM poll in April 1981 on public satisfaction with the PQ government performance indicated that 64 per cent were satisfied with the government's language policy, making it the most highly rated substantive policy area for the government.[15] This combination of facts would lead one to conclude that support for nationalism is waxing rather than waning. In explaining why the latter pattern coexists with these findings, we need to examine the consequences of Bill 101 somewhat more generally.

Impact on language issues

One effect of the language policy was significantly to alter the balance of the social inequality of languages in Quebec. Kloss observes that the distribution of bilingualism in a society is a very good indicator of social inequality and suggests that where it is unbalanced, this fact causes resentment.[16] As is widely recognised, the overwhelming majority of bilingual people in Canada are French-Canadians, including those in Quebec. This is a reflection of the fact that French-Canadians have historically borne the burden of language shift in 'mixed conversations'. A study of the language of work for the Gendron Commission indicated that English was used even when the person in the superior position was

French. Moreover, in their role as consumers, the Gendron Commission reported that many French-Canadians had the experience of purchasing goods with instructions in English only.[17] All these experiences have served to reinforce a sense of grievance about the unjustified subordination of their language within Quebec.

The post-Bill 101 era has witnessed a dramatic alteration in the social inequality of languages. This is evidenced by the change in the distribution of bilingualism in the province. From 1971 to 1981, bilingualism among English mother-tongue residents in Quebec rose from 37 per cent to 53 per cent. By contrast, bilingualism among French mother-tongue residents rose from 26 per cent to 29 per cent. The increase among English mother-tongue residents represents a numerical increase of 83,000 bilinguals, a fact made all the more remarkable by the simultaneous 10 per cent decrease in the total size of the English mother-tongue population in Quebec over the same period.[18] On this measure alone social inequality regarding language use has shifted sharply in favour of francophones. This evidence is reinforced by a study of language behaviour in Montreal which indicates that anglophones report more frequent use of the French language in casual encounters with francophones.[19] These results point in the direction of a marked reduction in linguistic inequality.

Another effect of Bill 101 was the remoulding of the face of Montreal. In the 1960s, the Royal Commission on Bilingualism and Biculturalism reported that French-Canadian Montrealers considered it quite unacceptable that the second-largest French city in the world should still look so English.[20] Bill 101 has contributed dramatically to rendering a Gallic facelift to Montreal, to the point where one of the most committed Quebec nationalists remarks that 'the French character of the province is strikingly apparent today'.[21] This might reasonably be expected to assuage any insecurities among francophones about the extent to which Quebec is and will remain *their* society. This expectation is consistent with the April 1984 SORECOM poll which indicated that a plurality of francophones perceived the linguistic situation to be quite favourable.[22]

This explains why Bill 101 enjoys widespread public support. This fact was clearly evidenced in February 1982 when Ted Tilden, president of the Tilden car rental firm, in a speech (delivered in English) to the Chambre de Commerce de Montréal referred to the existing language laws as 'insulting' and 'garbage'. The public reaction was swift and overwhelming. The Teachers' Union Federation, the CEQ, long a stalwart supporter of nationalism and unilingualism in Quebec, cancelled its contract with the company. Tilden's volume of business in Quebec decreased by 50 per cent within a week, prompting Tilden to issue a public statement emphasising that he had been speaking as a private citizen.[23] The incident was a strong reminder of the continuing popularity of the legislation.

One immediate consequence was virtually to eliminate language policy as a political issue. This was dramatically illustrated in the subsequent provincial election. In the months prior to the election, public opinion polls revealed that only 8 per cent of the electorate identified language issues as important in the election. Obviously, the issue had been completely defused for the bulk of the Quebec electorate. This was mirrored in the issue emphases of the provincial political parties. A study of the party press releases during the 1981 election revealed that language policy was mentioned in only 1.63 per cent of all the statements issued by the parties during the campaign – 2.44 per cent by the PQ and 0.49 per cent by the Liberals. By contrast, economic issues figured in approximately 40 per cent of all press releases.[24] While it is clear that economic issues were the focus of the 1981 election, it is none the less striking how marginal the language issue had become. It is a good illustration of the extent to which Bill 101 represents a consensus policy – at least among francophones.

While the dominance of the French language in the political and economic realms is assured for the foreseeable future, there are other areas which are potential problem areas. There remains a concern among government planners of growing cultural penetration through American culture. The popularity of American music groups, movies and television programmes is perceived as a threat to the vitality of the French language. The problem was dramatised recently in a report released by the Quebec Minister of Education, which revealed that less than half (49.8 per cent) of French-speaking senior high school students passed a test of their writing skills.[25] One sign of the times is the fact that it is now considered chic to speak English in the corridors of Quebec's most prestigious high schools.[26] In addition, a study by the Conseil de la langue Française found that 40 per cent of French-speaking adults in Quebec would like their children to study in English, double the percentage so inclined five years earlier. This may be explained by the fact that 40 per cent also believe that French will not be the language of science and technology in the future.[27] Thus, francophone parents, interested in the future career opportunities for their children, are pressuring the government for more, rather than less, access to English instruction.

Coupled with an increase of American culture is a relative decrease in French cultural expression. One telling sign is the decisions by some of Quebec's most popular music groups to record their music in English. This is being done because of the small size of the French music market. In 1983, 38 per cent fewer French-language Canadian albums were produced than in 1977. The effect is that francophones will probably be listening to even more English music. This is doubly likely in light of the Canadian Radio-Television and Telecommunications Commission decision in March 1986 to reduce the mandatory quota of French-language songs on Quebec radio stations from 65 per cent to 55 per cent. While it provoked a storm of protest from Quebec artists, the decision stands, partly because of the tremendous popular demand for American and foreign music. This simply encourages Quebec artists to follow the trend to English, or to become expatriates and pursue their careers in France. Either way, the vitality of Quebec culture suffers.[28] In light of these developments, it is hardly surprising that Quebec government officials are pondering the need for greater control over communications policy, a matter of federal jurisdiction.

Finally, demographic trends suggest some new twists to the language issue in Quebec. Demographic studies of the past decade indicate that Quebec will continue to become more French-speaking just as the rest of Canada will become more English. However, they also suggest that Quebec faces a serious long-term decline in its share of the national population, as a result of the rather ironic fact that Quebec now has one of the lowest fertility rates in the world. The 1985 rate is projected to be 1.5 children per woman, far below the simple replacement rate of 2.1, which is required for population stability.[29] In order to sustain its political strength and economic prospects, Quebec will need substantial flows of immigration. These will of necessity be mainly non-French speakers. This will pose some difficult choices for Quebec decision-makers in the future.

These various developments suggest that future language controversies in Quebec will be very different from those of the past fifteen years.

Impact on nationalism

In the light of its effects noted above, I would suggest that the very success of Bill 101 has played a significant role in the decline in support for nationalism. Its successful implementation, despite strong opposition from the anglophone minority, represented a significant demonstration that francophones control their own political institutions. It is also worth emphasising that its main components remain essentially intact, despite a series of Supreme Court decisions eliminating some of its provisions. In turn, the francisation of Quebec economic and public life has given Quebec a decidedly French look, thereby assuaging any anxieties francophones might have had about the security of their society. Moreover, Bill 101 substantially improved career prospects for the 'language professionals' of the middle class which has provided so much of the leadership of the nationalist movement, consequently reducing their economic incentives to further alterations in the socio-political status of Quebec society.

Bill 101 symbolically asserts and effectively contributes to the growing power of Québécois over Quebec society. In that regard, its traditional association with the nationalist cause leads many to perceive the achievement of language legislation as equivalent to the realisation of independence. Thus one nationalist complains that people in Quebec have confused linguistic claims with political emancipation and ceased to struggle for independence.[30] In short, the very success of Bill 101 has undercut the necessity for political change.

Evidence for this interpretation is, regrettably, suggestive rather than conclusive. The most directly relevant evidence is the Gallup polls on support for separatism in Quebec from 1977 to 1978. Throughout 1977, support for separation maintained a level of approximately 20 per cent. When Bill 101 was passed on 26 August 1977, it did not immediately influence these levels of support. However, the sections of Bill 101 requiring that public signs be in French (secs. 34, 58 and 208) did not come into force until July 1978. Obviously, these were the sections which provided the 'French face' to Quebec and were the most visible public manifestation of its impact. By September 1978, support for separation had dropped to 12 per cent.[31]

While the decline might be influenced by other factors it is not at all obvious what they might be. The decline is clearly consistent with the interpretation presented above. Other observers have also suggested that Bill 101 is responsible for the decline in nationalist sentiment, though for somewhat different reasons. Clift attributes the decline to a conservative reaction to the substantial changes accomplished by Bill 101 and an increase in psychological security among francophones. He states,

> It was as if there had been an unconscious decision that the language legislation had first to be digested before the launching of some new enterprise likely to result in fundamental transformations. It was as if the majority had turned its back on those aspects of nationalism which aim at collective isolation from English-speaking North America, and as if a genuine desire for closer contacts with English-speaking North America had come to the fore as a result of the greater security afforded by the language legislation.[32]

Clift's analysis is not accompanied by supporting evidence by which we might assess the existence of a conservative reaction, though it is quite plausible. It may well be that useful comparisons are to be drawn between the reaction to the Quiet Revolution[33] during the 1966 election and the reaction to Bill 101.

There is some indirect evidence regarding the sense of security that francophones have about their place in Quebec society. One socio-psychological study during the 1980 referendum period discovered that, whereas Quebec anglophones' view of the justice of Bill 101 varied substantially depending on the anticipated results of the referendum, francophone views were virtually unchanged. Francophones perceived the legislation as basically fair whether Quebec opted to become independent or to remain within Confederation.[34] The difference between the anglophone and francophone response patterns may be explained on the basis that Quebec anglophones believe that the anglophone majority in the Confederation entitles anglophones to more recognition within Quebec than they could justly claim as a minority within an independent Quebec. Quebec francophones, on the other hand, think that their position within Quebec is the same *as if* it were an independent country. If this interpretation is correct, then it appears that Quebec francophones have a relatively strong sense of control of Quebec political and social life. While we cannot compare these results with pre-Bill 101 attitudes, this pattern would lead one to anticipate a low level of nationalist sentiment.

As noted above, this evidence is suggestive, rather than conclusive. It is consistent with the interpretation developed here. However, it need hardly be emphasised that the language policy is not the sole factor influencing support for the nationalist cause. In the following section, another important set is explored.

Economic issues and nationalism

Much scholarly attention has been devoted to the explanation of Quebec's language controversies and nationalist upsurges of the past two decades, and these have generally emphasised economic factors as the primary basis of the conflict, whether in terms of the economic interests of particular social classes in Quebec, or in terms of the evolution of the economic structure of Quebec itself, either internally or in relation to the larger Canadian economy.[35] More recently, these macro-economic explanations have been criticised as being less informative than they initially appear, and more importantly, as being contradicted by the facts when applied in a comparative context.[36] Two elements tend to appear consistently in these analyses – the importance of the 'new middle class' and the extent of the 'cultural division of labour'. The former refers to the highly educated, professional middle class which has emerged since the Quiet Revolution; the latter to the allocation of different occupations in the economy on the basis of linguistic affiliation. Both are relevant to the discussion which follows.

In attempting to explain the decline of support for nationalism in economic terms, it is necessary to look no further than the overall stagnation of the Quebec economy in the first half of the 1980s. In particular, the statistics on unemployment are highly instructive. The evolution of the Quebec economy is depicted in Table 7.1 below. It clearly indicates the sharp decline in the overall health of the Quebec economy in the 1980s, particularly from 1982–5.

Table 8.1 Unemployment rate in Quebec, 1976–85[37]

Year	Rate (%)	Year	Rate (%)
1976	8.7	1981	10.3
1977	10.3	1982	13.8
1978	10.9	1983	13.9
1979	9.6	1984	12.3
1980	9.8	1985	11.8

It is worth noting that, similar to the experience elsewhere, there is substantial variation in these rates depending on the age categories of workers. For the unemployed youth of Quebec, their rates tend to be 50 per cent higher than these averages, registering 18.8 per cent and 18 per cent respectively for the years 1984 and 1985.

How does this relate to support for nationalism? Once again the evidence is indirect but suggestive. Relatively little is known about the impact of economic conditions on the public's political dispositions. Recent work, however, suggests some interesting findings. In general, the public is more inclined to use the unemployment rate as their barometer of the state of the economy, since it is easy to understand and highly visible. It is therefore the most useful indicator of public perceptions of the economy. In addition, a Canadian study of the effects of the economy on support for political parties indicates that bad economic times primarily reduce support for left-wing parties advocating change.[38] We might extrapolate from this that the same effect would occur in relation to support for broader political changes such as are represented by the nationalist agenda.

This is implicitly reinforced by Pinard's analysis of the 1973 Quebec election, which demonstrated clearly that the more threatening one perceived the consequence of independence to be, the less one was inclined to support the party advocating it (the PQ).[39] This pattern of responses has almost certainly influenced the fortunes of the nationalist option. Since the referendum, the Quebec economy has deteriorated significantly. A SORECOM poll in April, 1984 indicated that 66 per cent of francophones perceived the economy to be deteriorating and, more importantly, that 48 per cent believed that the economic situation of francophones would be worse in the event of independence (only 19 per cent thought it would be better). Moreover, 62 per cent of francophones agreed that the independence of Quebec would be achieved more easily if Quebec became economically strong.[40]

On this basis, it is arguable that francophones are strongly disinclined to make a bad economic situation worse, and thus the nationalist cause suffers accordingly. We might expect increased levels of support for independence if and when the economy improves. In this regard there is scant cause to anticipate increased support for independence. In the past three years, the economy has rebounded somewhat, although unemployment, has only quite recently declined to around 11.0 per cent and the short- and medium-term prospects for further improvement depend rather heavily on a strong American economy, which itself appears to be faltering. In short, the Quebec economy will continue to suppress support for the independence option.[41] It is important to emphasise that Quebec francophones continue to perceive independence as imposing economic costs, rather than benefits. This represents a persistent inhibitor to the growth of support for the independence option. Partly for that reason we must look to additional factors to understand current decreases in such support.

While the general trend of the Quebec economy has been rather negative, this has coincided with certain more positive developments which none the less have in turn attenuated the nationalist impulse. One of the consequences of Bill 101 was to alter the employment opportunities for francophones. It appears that segments of the 'new middle class' stand as beneficiaries of the language policies, but the net effects for the larger French population are mixed. Vaillancourt finds a small increase in unemployment for the general public coupled with more opportunities for upper-level administrators. He concludes that there are differential effects for different Quebec residents. In a subsequent study of effects on income differentials between English and French, Shapiro and Stelcner concluded that the benefits would be obtained primarily by highly educated francophone males. Women would at best be relatively unaffected, and at worst harmed, by the language legislation. This suggests that the positive benefits are limited to a relatively small portion of the French population. It would appear that this has had a negative impact on public support for nationalism as well. In explaining the defeat of the referendum proposal, Clift emphasises that 'distrust of nationalism rose sharply as a growing number of voters saw it as the instrument of privileged and powerful social groups'.[42]

Nevertheless these beneficiaries have been those most closely linked to the nationalist movement of the past decade, the 'new middle class'.

One disgruntled nationalist maintains that the new social class which has ascended to power in Quebec's political and economic life, and thus realised their personal ambitions, has acquired a positive disinterest in the independentist cause. Accordingly, the nationalist cause suffers from a leadership vacuum.[43] In addition, important components of this class have been stymied by the lack of growth of government employment in the past few years. Consequently, the new middle class, which was located in the public sector in large measure, has lost its dynamism and, in significant measure, its leadership role in Quebec public life.

An additional consequence of these expanded opportunities for high-level positions in the private sector has been a substantial decrease in traditional francophone economic grievances regarding income disparities between anglophones and francophones and, closely related, a decline in the cultural division of labour, whereby francophones were restricted to lower-level positions in the economy. The income gap has declined sharply and the relative under-representation of francophones at the managerial levels has been significantly reduced.[44] This both removes an important economic stimulus for support for nationalism and reduces the anticipated benefits of substantial political change.

To summarise, we can say that the Quebec economy has had a negative impact on support for nationalism by, on the one hand, increasing public concern about the state of the economy, and, on the other, distributing benefits to the professional middle classes and thereby undercutting their incentives for political change.

Political consequences and future prospects

The decline in nationalism has already had some political consequences. Noteworthy is the internal debate within the Parti Québécois over its commitment to sovereignty-association. Its decision to place it permanently 'on the back-burner' has produced an internal crisis, resulting in an exodus from the party of its most determined nationalists, who have begun the process of establishing a new independentist party. The exodus has been devastating, reducing the PQ membership from 150,319 in June 1984 (down from its peak of 302,000 in June 1981) to the current estimate of 71,000. The casualties included seven cabinet ministers and two backbenchers. This has also created a financial crisis for the PQ, which is so dependent on fund-raising by members. A new independentist group, the Rassemblement Démocratique pour l'Indépendance (RDI) has been formed by these disgruntled ex-PQ members, which poses a problem for the nationalist forces of dividing the nationalist vote, thereby improving the odds on a victory by the pro-federalist Liberal party. In fact, the 1985 election, which resulted in a resounding Liberal victory made abundantly clear that the PQ was bound for defeat quite independently of the influence of third parties.[45]

The point remains, however, that the internal divisions within the nationalist ranks ensure that, for the moment, Quebec nationalism has returned to the political wilderness of the pre-1970 era. The new leader of the PQ, Pierre Marc Johnson, has attempted to accommodate this new reality by replacing the commitment to sovereignty- association with a policy of 'national affirmation', which involves '... working within the federal system to strengthen Quebec's powers, drawing up a Quebec constitution and instituting a presidential form of government'.[46] For the present, this appears like a return to conventional Quebec-Ottawa struggles for political power.

It is much more difficult to project the future of Quebec nationalism. Clift, for one, sees it as a force in decline. While it remains the dominant ideology of Quebec, Clift nevertheless believes that '... its character becomes increasingly rhetorical and it is no longer able to give voice to the original dynamic impulses that made it into such a potent political force'.[47] Fournier, on the other hand, focusing on the longer term, argues that '... the various linguistic, cultural, demographic and economic factors which underlie the development of Quebec nationalism remained unaltered'.[48] He points to the declining demographic position of Quebec in Canada as a whole with its negative implications for 'French power' and the growing competition between the federal and provincial governments over economic policy as forces ultimately pushing Quebec towards independence. In the short term, he concludes that much will depend on the effectiveness of 'French power' in Ottawa.

The status of 'French power' has vacillated rather dramatically in the past few years. The departure of Pierre Trudeau was expected to mark the end of French influence in Ottawa. The election of a Conservative government in 1984 with a fluently bilingual prime minister from Quebec and supported by a numerically strong representation from Quebec initially lead to expectations of the extension of 'French power'. Subsequently, the resignations of Quebec ministers and dissatisfaction over the allocation of federal resources to Quebec have raised doubts about the effectiveness of Quebec's influence in the federal government. While there is some reason to believe that 'French power' has waned in the post-1985 period, it is not at all apparent that this has encouraged increased support for independence. Perhaps this requires a longer period to develop, or alternatively, the other factors suppressing nationalist enthusiasm are currently more important.

For a longer-term perspective, it may be useful to distinguish between patriotism and nationalism to describe the developments in Quebec. Bill 101 has significantly accelerated the trend towards the francisation of Quebec. Demographically, the 'two solitudes'[49] are becoming ever more solidly entrenched. This very likely contributes to an increasing sense of commitment to Quebec and decreasing commitment to Canada that has been noted in a recent analysis of Quebec political attitudes.[50] In this sense a stronger and more widespread patriotism to Quebec may be developing. This would represent an ongoing reservoir which a political nationalist might mobilise under the appropriate conditions. However, those conditions are not as likely to emerge in a Quebec that is increasingly French, in which francophones represent an increasing percentage of the population and in which francophones hold an increasing share of social and economic power. Thus, Bill 101, while expanding the base upon which a nationalist movement might ultimately mobilise, has significantly reduced the number of stimuli to inspire such a mobilisation, and has perhaps made independence that much less likely.

As a result, Bill 101 has had rather ironic consequences. As a language policy, it is very successful, enjoying broad popular support and resolving the major issues remaining from previous governments. As an exercise in nation-building, however, it has had the opposite effect of that intended. Rather than providing the springboard to a resurgent nationalism, it has removed part of the spring which is its impetus. Again, this is not entirely suprising. If the state of the language is indicative of the health of the society, then Bill 101 signifies a rather healthy situation. In that context, the status quo is not at all repugnant.

Notes

1. The results of the SORECOM poll are reported in *L'Action Nationale* 74 (1984), pp. 425–42. See especially questions 9 and 10. The CROP results are reported in 'Only 4 per cent want Independence, Quebec poll shows', *The Toronto Globe and Mail* (National Edition) 19 January 1985, p.5. The distribution of Quebec opinion on these matters throughout the decade of the 1970s is discussed in detail in Richard Hamilton and Maurice Pinard, 'The Quebec Independence Movement' in Colin H. Williams (ed.), *National Separatism*, Cardiff, 1982, pp.203–33.
2. Jean-C. Bonenfant and Jean-C. Falardeau, 'Cultural and Political Implications of French-Canadian Nationalism' in Ramsay Cook (ed.), *French Canadian Nationalism: an anthology*, Toronto, 1969, pp.18–19; Dominique Clift, *Quebec Nationalism in Crisis*, Montreal, 1982, p.viii. Ronald Lambert, in his bibliographic essay on Quebec nationalism defines it as follows: 'Nationalism.... is taken to refer broadly to personal sentiments, ideology and social movements which place a positive value on and seek to enhance the status of the French-Canadian community, the latter variously defined'. See Ronald Lambert, *The Sociology of Contemporary Quebec Nationalism: An Annotated Bibliography and Review*, New York, 1981, p.xi.

3. Raymond Breton, 'The production and allocation of symbolic resources: an analysis of the linguistic and ethnocultural fields in Canada', *Canadian Review of Sociology and Anthropology* 21 (1984), p.126.
4. Susan Mann Trofimenkoff, *Action Française: French-Canadian Nationalism in the Twenties* (Toronto, 1975), p.47.
5. Robert J. MacDonald, 'In Search of a Language Policy: Francophone Reactions to Bill 85 and 63' in John R. Mallea (ed.), *Quebec's Language Policies: Background and Responses*, Quebec, 1977, pp.221, 225.
6. Dominique Clift, op.cit., pp. 103–8.
7. Quebec, *La Charte de la Langue Française, Revised Statutes of Quebec*, 1977, C.II.
8. Government of Québec, *Quebec's Policy on the French Language*, Editeur Officiel du Québec, 1977, p.49.
9. Ibid., p.52.
10. Camille Laurin, 'Charte de la langue française/French language charter' *Canadian Review of Sociology and Anthropology* 15 (1978), p.121. This article is a reproduction of his address to the National Assembly at the second reading of Bill 101. Laurin was the cabinet minister responsible for the legislation.
11. Ibid., p.127.
12. François-Albert Angers, 'La Montée Historique vers un Québec Maître de sa Destinée' *L'Action Nationale* 68 (1978), p.33 (my translation).
13. Guy Bouthillier, 'L'an 1 de la Loi 101' *L'Action Nationale* 68 (1979), pp.423, 417 (my translation).
14. Donald M. Taylor and Lise Dubé-Simard 'Language Planning and Inter-Group Relations: Anglophone and Francophone Attitudes Toward the Charter of the French Language' in Richard Y. Bourhis, (ed.), *Conflict and Language Planning in Quebec*, Clevedon, Avon, 1984, p.153.
15. The results of the poll are reported in the Montreal Gazette, 11 April 1981.
16. Heinz Kloss, 'Bilingualism and Nationalism', *The Journal of Social Issues* 23 (1967), p.42.
17. See Raymond N. Morris and C. Michael Lanphier, *Three Scales of Inequality: Perspectives on French-English Relations*, Don Mills, 1977, pp.16–19.
18. Statistics Canada, *Language in Canada* (from the 1981 Census), Ottawa, 1985, cat. 99–935.
19. See Richard Y. Bourhis, 'The Charter of the French Language and cross-cultural communication in Montreal' in Bourhis (ed.), op.cit., pp.174–204.
20. Royal Commission on Bilingualism and Biculturalism, Preliminary Report, Ottawa, 1965, p.123.
21. Pauline Vaillancourt, 'Will Quebec Still Separate?' *Canadian Dimension* 18 (1984), p.11.

22. 'Sondage auprès des Québécois par SORECOM (mai 1984) sur la question nationale et constitutionnelle', *L'Action Nationale* 74 (1984), p.433. At the same time 51 per cent of francophones agreed that the French language is constantly threatened in Quebec (p.440). There is rather mixed evidence on the effects of Bill 101 on anxieties about the status of French. See Bourhis, 'The Charter of the French Language', and Taylor and Dubé-Simard, 'Language Planning and Intergroup Relations' in Bourhus (ed.), op.cit.,pp.186 and 155 respectively.

23. This incident is recounted in Graham Fraser, *P.Q.: René Levesque & the Parti Québécois in Power*, Toronto, 1984, pp.314–16.

24. Daniel Savas, Le discours politique et le nationalisme québécois (an unpublished MA thesis, L'Université de Laval, 1983), pp.132, 143.

25. 'Students failure rate on test of writing skills alarms Quebec official', *Globe and Mail*, 10 December 1986, pp.A5. It is noteworthy that the blame was placed on the prevalence of pop culture *per se* more so than its specifically American manifestations.

26. Mark Abley, 'The Language Effect', *Saturday Night*, June 1985, p.21.

27. 'Quebeckers show interest in English', *Globe and Mail*, 19 July 1984, p.3. It is worth recalling that one of the consequences of Bill 101 was to limit access to the English-language school system for francophones as well, a move that was not particularly popular among francophones.

28. See 'The Chanson Crisis', *Globe and Mail*, 5 April 1986, pp.C1,C3.

29. See Rejean Lachapelle and Jacques Henripin, *The Demolinguistic Situation in Canada: Past Trends and Future Prospects*, Montreal, 1982 for a sophisticated presentation of the various factors shaping future trends. For an analysis of the emerging demographic dilemma, see Gary Caldwell and Daniel Fournier, 'The Quebec question: a matter of population', *The Canadian Journal of Sociology*, 12 (1987), pp.16–41.

30. Denis Monière, 'Motivations', *L'Action Nationale* 74 (1985), p.780.

31. See the Gallup Report 13 September 1978. It should be noted that the same pattern is not apparent in relation to the levels of support for sovereignty-association. However, the difference must be assessed in light of Pinard and Hamilton's finding that the public indicated high levels of confusion regarding the meaning of sovereignty-association and their conclusion that support for independence remains the best indicator of public opinion. See Hamilton and Pinard, 'The Quebec Independence Movements' in C.H. Williams (ed.), op.cit., pp.203–33.

32. Clift, op.cit., p.104.

33. The post-war period of modernisation in Quebec which transformed a rural, highly church-dominated society into a modern, secular and technologically advanced community is generally called the Quiet Revolution.

34. Taylor and Dubé-Simard in Bourhis, *Conflict and Language Planning in Quebec*, pp.162–7.

35. See, for example, Kenneth McRoberts and Dale Postgate, *Quebec: Social Change and Political Crisis* (revised ed.), Toronto, 1980, chapter 7; William D. Coleman, 'The Class Bases of Language Policy in Quebec, 1949–1975', *Studies in Political Economy* 3 (1980), pp.93–117.

36. See, for example, Mary Beth Montcalm, 'Quebec Nationalism in a Comparative Perspective' in Alain G. Gagnon, (ed.), *Quebec: State and Society*, Toronto, 1984, pp.45–58; Kenneth McRoberts, 'The sources of neo-nationalism in Quebec', *Ethnic and Racial Studies* 7 (1984), pp.55–85.

37. These figures were compiled from the following sources: *Canada Year Book*, 1985, p.173 Table 5.7; *Canada Year Book*, 1980–81, p.270, Table 7.3; Statistics Canada, *The Labour Force*, Dec. 1985, p.87, Table 57 (cat. 71-001); *The Labour Force*, 1984, p.93, Table 61, (cat. 71-001).

38. The importance of the unemployment rate in the American context is discussed in Pamela Johnston Conover and Stanley Feldman and Kathleen Knight, 'Judging Inflation and Unemployment: The Origins of Retrospective Evaluations', *The Journal of Politics* 48 (1986), pp.565–88. The impact of the economy on Canadian political parties is treated in Kristen Monroe and Lynda Erickson, 'The Economy and Political Support: The Canadian Case', *The Journal of Politics* 48 (1986), pp.616–47.

39. Maurice Pinard and Richard Hamilton, 'The Independence Issue and the Polarization of the Electorate: The 1973 Quebec Election', *Canadian Journal of Political Science* 10 (1977), pp.215–60. For an examination of this factor in the ensuing period, see their 'The Quebec Independence Movement'.

40. SORECOM poll, *L'Action Nationale*, 74, pp.439–41.

41. See 'Report on Quebec', *Globe and Mail*, 18 September 1986, section C.

42. Clift, op.cit., p.120.

43. Denis Monière 'Motivations', *L'Action Nationale* 74 (1985), p.780.

44. This point is emphasised in Peter M. Leslie, 'Canada as a Bicommunal Polity' in Clare Beckton and Wayne MacKay (res. coords.) *Recurring Issues in Canadian Federalism*, Toronto, 1986, vol.57 of the Royal Commission on Economic Union and Development Prospects for Canada, pp. 113–44.

45. See Harold M. Angell, 'The Decline of the Parti Québécois: A Mass Party, The Polls and Political Financing' (unpublished paper presented at the Political Finance panel of the XIII Congress of the International Political Science Association, Paris, 15–20 July 1985); Lise Bissonette, 'Wanted by the PQ: An important issue for the Eighties', *Globe and Mail*, 13 September 1986, p.D2.

46. 'PQ Striving to end sovereignty wrangle', *Globe and Mail*, 13 June 1986, p.A5.

47. Clift, op.cit., p.151. This theme is evoked more caustically by Louis Favreau, who comments of the 'orthodox' Pequistes, that 'their nationalism sounded a bit as if it had been preserved in formaldehyde since the 1960s'. See Louis Favreau, 'The PQ Crisis: burnout and revival' in Marc Raboy (ed.), *Old Passions, New Visions: Social Movements and Political Activism in Quebec*, Toronto, 1986, p.247.

48. Pierre Fournier, 'The Future of Quebec Nationalism' in K. Banting and R. Simeon (eds.), *And No One Cheered*, Toronto, 1983, p.155.

49. The phrase, 'the two solitudes', was coined to describe the *de facto* social and cultural independence of French and English Canada. Policy emphasis upon bilingualism is largely a Federal Government concern and has little impact upon political and social life within Provinces.

50. Lawrence Leduc, Harold D. Clarke, Jane Jenson and John H. Pammett, 'Sovereignty-Association 'Non' – Parti-Québécois 'Oui': Trends in Political Support in Quebec' *American Review of Canadian Studies*, no.12, 1982, p.64.

Chapter nine

The Afrikaners

John Dreijmanis

Origins

Without the Imperial spur the Afrikaans-speaking section would in
all probability have been absorbed gradually into the English stream,
and Afrikaans-Dutch would probably have disappeared, as had been
the case with the Dutch language in America.

F.A. van Jaarsveld

By the end of the eighteenth century, the Afrikaners possessed all of the
characteristics that were to weld them into a separate group. As a result
of the British annexation of the Transvaal in 1877 and the First War of
Independence (1880–1), group consciousness became *volk*
consciousness. The annexation also led to the idea of a single nation
within a single state.[1] The *volk* was becoming a nation with a common
life, descent, tradition, language, religion and social organisation.[2] Like
most nationalisms, there was a standard demand 'for a government of
the same ethnic complexion as the majority'.[3] In short, political
self-determination was the goal.

The characteristic features of Afrikaner nationalism in this period
were the following: (1) resistance to the loss of independence and
absorption in the British Empire and the English cultural stream, (2) an
emphasis on nation and fatherland, (3) a major concern for the nation's
past, the content of which was interpreted as a struggle between Boer
and Briton. In the words of Van Jaarsveld: 'The struggle of the past was
the struggle of the present, and the struggle of the present the same as
that of the past'.[4] (4) There was also the usual belief of having been
'called' and 'chosen'.[5] The rediscovery of the past and its
reinterpretation created the belief that, in the words of Dr D.F. Malan,
the 'history of the Afrikaner reveals a will and a determination which
makes one feel that Afrikanerdom is not the work of men but the
creation of God'.[6]

Recently this has been challenged by André du Toit who maintains
that the 'theory of an authentic Calvinist tradition going back to a

135

primitive Calvinism nurtured in the isolated *trekboer* society on the open frontier, and ultimately derived from the golden age of "seventeenth century Calvinism" is an historical myth'.[7] Perhaps it is a moot point as to whether or not the original Dutch immigrants regarded themselves as 'called' and 'chosen'. What is beyond dispute is that they were in South Africa 'truly alone, facing possible annihilation. For them self-preservation referred not to individuals or regiments or armies but national preservation – the preservation of the species'.[8]

What really made Afrikaner nationalism different was that it came quite late by European standards. It was a case of *verspätete* (delayed) nationalism[9], the same as in the German and the Italian cases, and that it developed in a multi-ethnic and multi-racial state. Such nationalisms tend to be more strident and militant than those which developed earlier. Moreover, if a nation and state do not coincide, then there are numerous difficulties.

Differing conceptions

There was a time when we Afrikaners were divided into groups and parties and were in conflict with one another.

H.F. Verwoerd

After the Second War of Independence (1899–1902), also known as the Anglo-Boer War, the 'Afrikaner people emerged from the war proud of the republics' resistance to overwhelming odds and more determined than ever to retain their corporate identity'.[10] The Union of South Africa was created in 1910 as a compromise between the anglophone desire to maintain the British connection and the Afrikaner desire for complete independence, which was finally achieved with the creation of a republic in 1961. Until then the main political conflicts were between the two white population groups, centring on the questions of equality between them and the achievement of republican status.

There never was a monolithic Afrikaner nationalism and thus differing conceptions of it soon became evident. To use the terminology of Hans Kohn, it was a conflict between a 'closed' nationalism stressing the nation's original character, common origins (race and blood), and ancestral soil and an 'open' nationalism which upholds the belief in a nation of fellow citizens irrespective of ethnic or racial descent.[11] General J.B.M. Hertzog supported a closed or two-stream nationalism: 'Community life in South Africa flows in two streams – the English-speaking stream and the Dutch-speaking stream, each with its own language, its own way of life, its own great men, heroic deeds and noble characters'.[12] At times, however, he was ambiguous and used the term Afrikaner to refer to all whites who put South Africa first and at other times to Afrikaans-speaking and also the coloureds. There was also a third group consisting of those not yet South Africans, the *uitlanders* (foreigners). This two-stream nationalism would exist until the Afrikaner had developed to the same level as the anglophone.[13] General L. Botha in 1911 at the time of the formation of the South African and National Party advocated an open white nationalism in order to achieve 'co-operation and the formation of a single South African nationality of the White population of our country'.[14] So did General J.C. Smuts: 'We are going to create a nation – a nation which will be of a composite character, including Dutch, German, English and Jew, and whatever white nationality seeks refuge in this land – all can combine. All will be welcome'.[15]

Botha and Hertzog split in 1913 as a result of the latter's two-stream nationalism. Hertzog formed in 1914 the *Nasionale Party* (National Party). In 1934 he split with Dr Malan and the latter created the *Gesuiwerde Nasionale Party* (Purified National Party). The South African and National Parties then fused to form the United South African National Party or the United Party for short. The more militant anglophones created the Dominion Party. In 1939 Hertzog joined the Purified National Party and the following year it was renamed the *Herenigde Nasionale of Volksparty* (Reunited National or People's Party) and retained this name until 1951. The same year the *Ossewa-Brandwag* (literally the Oxwagon Fire Guard) was created as a rival organisation. Being influenced by National Socialist ideas, it was for one *volk*, one land. The pattern in this period was for the more militant and nationalistic right wing to split off and eventually to become victorious. The Transvaal and the Orange Free State party leaders increasingly upheld a closed nationalism and thus defined Afrikanerdom as consisting of white Afrikaans-speaking persons only.

In 1941 Dr Malan could already view the Reunited National or People's Party as a *volksorganisasie* (people's organisation): 'We are no ordinary party political organisation. We occupy a central position in Afrikaner ethnic life'.[16] This despite the emergence the same year of a rival political party when Hertzog and N.C. Havenga formed the *Afrikanerparty*, which advocated equal rights for both white population groups. In 1951 it merged with the National Party and thus came the long-awaited united front of Afrikanerdom.

In the interwar period there were also many efforts to promote Afrikaner socio-economic and cultural needs by the creation of parallel organisations, from the *Voortrekkers* (scouts) to business organisations, resembling the situation in Belgium and the Netherlands with their *verzuiling* (pillarisation). The *Afrikaner-Broederbond* (literally the Afrikaner Brother Association) was founded in 1918 by a small group of intellectuals. Among its goals were the following:

(a) To accomplish a healthy and progressive unity amongst all Afrikaners who actively seek the welfare of the Afrikaner.

(b) To arouse Afrikaner national self-consciousness and to inspire love of the Afrikaans language, religion, traditions, country and People.

(c) To further every concern of the Afrikaner nation.[17]

Soon it became a secret organisation, evolving in time into a mainly political one. In 1929 under its auspices was created the *Federasie van Afrikaanse Kultuurvereniginge* (Federation of Afrikaans Cultural Organisations). It in turn created in 1939 the *Reddingsdaadbond* (Rescue Action Association).

In the 1920s and 1930s many Afrikaners were impoverished, but also becoming increasingly urbanised and industrialised. The urban–rural cleavage largely coincided with the anglophone–Afrikaner cleavage. A 'poor white' problem developed when the Afrikaners had to compete for work in the cities with the non-whites (the terms non-white and non-black are used without any derogatory connotations), especially the blacks.

In the years 1924–9 there was a National Party–Labour Party coalition government which intervened in the economy to provide jobs for the poor whites; it also started industrial development.

Occupationally the Afrikaner position improved as a result of these efforts and their coming to power in 1948. In 1966, 71 per cent of the whites in the public service and 87 per cent in the police were Afrikaans-speaking. In the professions in 1946, as a proportion of 1,000 employed 43.2 were Afrikaans-speaking and in 1960, 68.1; in administrative posts their numbers rose from 30.7 to 42.4, respectively. Those in farming, however, declined from 349.6 to 198.5, respectively.[18]

A 1968 survey of incumbents of top posts revealed that Afrikaans-speakers were in the majority in the legislative (61 per cent) and the judicial (52 per cent) branches of the government, and in the public service (72 per cent).

The anglophones were in the majority in the press (68 per cent), the professions (70 per cent), the economy (63 per cent), and local government (68 per cent).[19]

According to the 1980 census data, Afrikaans was the dominant language of those earning up to R15,000 a year, but the ratio was almost exactly that of the composition of the population. The anglophones were in the majority of those earning between R15,000 and R40,000 a year and Afrikaans was the majority language of those earning more than R40,000 a year.[20]

Victory of the Nationalists in 1948

> Afrikaner nationalism and the Afrikaner's approach to ethnic differentiation were thus the two deciding determinants not only in the 1948 election but also in the subsequent unfolding of the apartheid policy.
>
> N.J. Rhoodie

The 1948 victory symbolised increasing Afrikaner solidarity. Ethnic unity was developing across class lines. *Volk* and party became closely linked; it was not much of an exaggeration for the National Party to claim that '*die party is die volk en die volk is die party*' (the party is the people and the people are the party). The National and Afrikaner Parties had become primarily of Afrikaans-speakers and the United Party of the anglophones. Once in power the central concern was that of restructuring race and social relations in an Afrikaner dominated state.

Already in the 1652–1830 period there emerged among the whites a widespread feeling that colour was a mark of inferiority, much the same as in the case of colonial America, Canada, Australia and New Zealand. Contrary to popular belief, however, the antecedents of apartheid or separate development 'are to be found in Natal [where the majority of the whites are anglophones] rather than in any of the other provinces. A long line of segregationist writers and politicians from Natal did much to create the climate of opinion in which segregation became acceptable to white electorates'.[21] In the 1910–48 period the government policy was a compromise between integration and segregation.

The fear of black domination, absorption, or annihilation (*die swart gevaar*, the black danger) has been ever present in the political consciousness of the whites, especially of the Afrikaners. In the words of J.G. Strijdom: 'Either the white man dominates or the black man takes over'.[22] Verwoerd was even blunter when he said in 1948: 'Indeed, it is not the Native whose future is being threatened, it is that of the Europeans'.[23] The question became how to reconcile white 'survival with the rightful political interests of the Bantu'.[24] In the words of Hermann Giliomee: 'without a privileged position a 'pure' and separate white race could not survive; without a 'pure' and separate white race a privileged position could not be maintained'.[25]

Complicating the multi-racial situation is the fact that socio-economic differences largely coincide with a particular race's boundaries. Sociologically speaking, the white-black 'polarisation of interests is therefore of a natural dissociative and grouping process simultaneously activated by the selective function of racial as well as socio-cultural, political and economic differences'.[26] There was a consensus among the whites that continued integration could not be limited to economic, cultural, social and political levels, but would lead to bio-genetical assimilation.

Apartheid or separate development thus became for Afrikaner nationalism the answer to the dilemma. It may be divided into three phases. The 1948–58 period was one of protecting and entrenching white political authority and reducing socio-economic and political contacts in order to avoid further integration. This was an ideologically doctrinaire, 'negative apartheid'.[27]

The 1958–66 period was one of 'positive apartheid' or the granting of independence to the black homelands.[28] There was fear of the developing Pan-Africanism if the ten major black ethnic groups were not granted separate national development. This was also in line with Afrikaner experience. In the words of Dr N. Diederichs, Minister of Economic Affairs: 'To the man who cherishes nationalism there can be only one solution to the question: Grant to others what you yourself demand'.[29] The Afrikaners were content to have a smaller white South Africa rather than be submerged into a larger black-controlled South Africa. This was well expressed by Prime Minister Verwoerd on 20 May 1959:

> In the end I would rather be content with a smaller state in South Africa, that is White ... and which will stand as a bulwark for White civilisation ... in other words rather a White nation that can fight here for its survival than a larger state which has been handed over to Bantu domination.[30]

In the period beginning in 1966 attempts were made to establish dialogue with the emerging black African states, the internal black leaders, as well as to share authority. South Africa was increasingly viewed as an African state, instead of as a 'bulwark of the West'. Instead of 'segregate or perish', the new slogan became 'adjust or perish'.[31] This involved authority-sharing with the other population groups, such as with the coloureds and the Indians under the 1983 constitution. Moreover, the Prohibition of Mixed Marriages Act, No. 55 of 1949 and Section 16 of the Immorality Act, No. 23 of 1957, job reservation, 'pass laws', and influx control, among other measures, were abolished. Freehold property rights have been granted in the national and independent states and the black townships, but the tribal system still inhibits private land ownership. When F.W. de Klerk became state president in 1989 he promised to create 'a totally changed South Africa'.[32] Since then he has released eight African National Congress (ANC) leaders from prison, permitted protest demonstrations, opened all beaches to all races, and pledged to repeal the Reservation of Separate Amenities Act, No. 49 of 1953 when Parliament reconvenes in 1990. His cabinet ministers have also indicated that the Population Registration Act No. 30 of 1950 and the Group Areas Act No. 41 of 1950 will be repealed as soon as there is negotiated alternative legislation that protects group rights without discrimination.

Responses to socio-economic and political developments

For quite some time Afrikaners have been growing apart: the interests of Afrikaner workers and Afrikaner businessmen, like those of farmers and consumers, are increasingly in conflict.

André du Toit

Under Verwoerd Afrikaner nationalism reached its zenith. There was confidence in the Verwoerdian solution. Afrikaner–anglophone relations were also improving. On becoming prime minister, Verwoerd expressed the hope that he could look 'forward to the happy day when all of us will be so joined together by a common patriotism into one people with two languages that political differences that might exist will no longer be based on sentiment but purely on differences of opinion on social and economic problems'.[33] Once a republic had been created it acted as a unifying symbol between the Afrikaners and the anglophones, as Verwoerd had expected. Since the late 1960s the term 'European' ceased to be generally used and replaced by the term 'white'. Ethnic identifications became slowly replaced by white or racial identification. A white South African patriotism emerged.

Yet problems loomed on the horizon. The efforts to remove blacks from the white urban areas were falling far short of the original expectations, with the potential that as long as the blacks enjoy a numerical superiority over the whites in the urban areas, they have the right to demand black majority government. Already in 1963, sixteen out of thirty randomly selected National Party members of Parliament answered in the affirmative the following question: 'Do you agree that as long as the permanently settled Bantu in White South Africa enjoy a numerical superiority over the whites, they have potentially the moral right to demand a Black majority government at some or other stage in the future'.[34] The urban blacks were becoming detribalised and losing their ethnic nationalisms and transforming themselves into black or Pan-African nationalists.

Since the early 1960s a right-wing reaction developed within the National Party on the question of white supremacy and authority-sharing.[35] Some right-wingers left the party in 1969 and established the *Herstigte Nasionale Party* (HNP, Reconstituted National Party). The HNP declared that it wanted a South Africa 'in which the truth is accepted that parliamentary democracy has not sufficient tolerance to

141

accommodate Whites, Coloureds, Indians (and Blacks), and that only separate political structures for each group, without any form of political power sharing, can ensure permanent order...'.[36] In 1982 there was another split in the party on the issue of authority-sharing under the new constitution, this time between the *verkramptes* (narrow-minded ones) and the *verligtes* (enlightened ones). This led to the creation of the *Konserwatiewe Party* (CP, Conservative Party). In the 1981 election the National Party got only 60 per cent of the Afrikaner vote as compared to between 83 per cent and 85 per cent in the 1970, 1974 and 1977 elections.[37] Many working-class Afrikaners deserted it for the HNP. In 1985 the National Party retained four of the five seats in the by-elections, (while the HNP won its first seat) but in two of the constituencies it got only a plurality of the votes and in the other two less than 55 per cent of the votes.[38] In the 1987 and 1989 House of Assembly elections the movement to the right continued, with the CP replacing the Progressive Federal Party (PFP) as the official opposition. This may be seen from the election results.[39]

Table 9.1 South African House of Assembly election results, 1987–9

Party	Popular vote %		Direct seats		Total seats	
	1987	*1989*	*1987*	*1989*	*1987*	*1989*
HNP	3.0	0.3				
CP	26.6	31.4	22	39	23	41
NP	52.3	48.0	123	94	133	103
NRP	2.0		1		1	
PFP	14.0		19		20	
DP		19.9		33		34
Independents	1.3		1		1	
Spoiled	0.8	0.4				
Totals			166	166	178	178

The 1989 election results were the worst ones for the NP since 1953. The CP has become a factor to be reckoned with in the Transvaal and the Orange Free State, the traditional provinces of Afrikanerdom. If it had not been for the HNP–CP rivalry, the CP would have secured an additional eight seats in 1987 and two in 1989.[40] A resurgence of a closed Afrikaner nationalism is evident, but unlike in the pre-1945 period this is within the context of increasing black or Pan-African nationalism.

On the left of the NP, the New Republic Party (NRP) disbanded in 1988. In 1989 the PFP merged with the Independent Party and the National Democratic Movement to form the Democratic Party (DP). The DP was able to improve upon the combined left's performance in the 1987 election by 2.6 per cent, but this is still well below the left's 1981 support of 26.1 per cent.[41] Much of the DP's support is soft and may be recaptured by the NP.

Basically, the policies of the HNP and the CP are similar, but there are certain differences. The HNP does not regard the Indians as an indigenous group and thus they would not be granted an independent state, unlike the coloureds.[42] The CP would do this for both of them. The HNP sees no merit in the CP's proposed Southern African State Council. It is for real bilingualism throughout the country and after this has been achieved a decision is to be made about which one of the two official languages will become the single one. The CP admits the *Afrikaner Weerstandsbeweging* (AWB, Afrikaner Resistance Movement) members, but not the HNP. It is more eager for a merger with the HNP than is the HNP, being in 'favour of taking steps which would result in the democratic unification between the CP and the HNP'.[43] The CP leader, Dr A.P. Treurnicht, has put forward the view that this could take place in the near future.

It is also necessary to include some closely allied right-wing organisations, such as the AWB, founded in 1973, and the *Afrikanervolkswag* (AV, literally the Afrikaner People's Guardian), created in 1984. There is considerable splintering and regrouping. Only the largest ones are considered. The AWB would like to create a white *volkstaat* (people's state), consisting essentially of the old Boer republics.[44] It also favours the returning of the Indians to India. The AWB takes an anti-Semitic position as well.[45] In 1989 some senior leaders broke away from it and established the *Boere Vryheidsbeweging* (BVB, Farmers' Freedom Movement). The AV aims at uniting Afrikaners in a new cultural organisation.[46] Finally, in 1987 the *Afrikaanse Protestante Kerk* (APK, Afrikaans Protestant Church) was created for Afrikaners only as a result of a split in the largest of the three Dutch churches, the *Nederduits Gereformeerde Kerk* (NGK, Dutch Reformed Church). This split was a direct result of the 1986 NGK general synod's decision to declare apartheid an error, open in principle church services to all races, regard racially mixed marriages as no longer undesirable, and proclaim racism a sin.

The National Party has evolved into one dominated by the Afrikaner bourgeoisie, with substantial support from the anglophones as well.[47] It is now a centre party, with the CP and the HNP on its right and the DP on its left. A survey of how Afrikaners voted in the 1987 election revealed the following results: 58.6 per cent NP, 32.0 per cent CP, 4.6

per cent HNP, 4.3 per cent PFP, 0.2 per cent NRP and 0.2 per cent Independents.[48]

Afrikaners' views on important issues have become significantly divergent from those of the government. In 1984, for instance, a year before the repeal of the Prohibition of Mixed Marriages Act, No. 55 of 1949 and Section 16 of the Immorality Act, No. 23 of 1957, 78.9 per cent were in favour of the former, 16.6 per cent opposed it, 3.8 per cent were neutral and 0.8 per cent were uncertain or did not know. On the latter's Section 16, 81.3 per cent were in favour of it, 13.4 per cent opposed it, 4.9 per cent were neutral, and 0.4 per cent were uncertain or did not know.[49] This may be interpreted as a sign that the 'tolerance threshold of many NP-inclined Afrikaners with regard to socio-political change is coming increasingly under pressure, especially as the Government's reformist initiatives are extended to Blacks'.[50]

Afrikaners may now be divided into two broad political groups. First, there are those seeing themselves as an exclusive *volk*, with a distinct cultural heritage and common cultural values. This is the closed nationalism group. Second, there are those who see the Afrikaner as part of an expanding South African nation, which includes the non-whites and is thus a completely open nationalism. (Modified division based on Adam and Giliomee).[51] Party politically, the first group consists mainly of the HNP and the CP supporters and the second group of many of the NP followers and nearly all of the DP supporters.

From the usual economic and demographic points of view, the amazing phenomenon is that the National Party government has not suffered even more loss of support. Inflation has been running at an annual rate of more than 10 per cent since 1974. The purchasing power of the 1970 rand had declined to 12 cents in 1988. The consumer price index grew in the 1970–88 period by an annual compound rate of 12.7 per cent. For the whites the average compound growth rate in salaries and wages was 12.5 per cent in the 1970–87 period.[52] Moreover, the value of the rand in relation to the United States dollar declined from $1.147 on 24 June 1976 to $.395 on 12 January 1990. Demographically, the proportion of the whites has declined from 19.1 per cent in 1945 to 13.9 per cent in 1985 in the republic and the independent states of Transkei, Bophuthatswana, Ciskei and Venda.[53] Yet, the economic position of the whites is still substantially better than that of most of the non-whites. Thus, to preserve an even declining situation requires retention of much of their authority. This does not mean, however, that there are no limits to their willingness to withstand economic losses.

At about the same time that a white South African patriotism was beginning to emerge in the late 1960s the behaviour of the blacks became more militant and violent. Already in 1958 at the founding of the Pan-Africanist Congress (PAC) the cry was 'Africa for the

Africans'. ANC violent acts have increased from 4 in 1976 to 136 in 1985.[54] Since the latest unrest began in September 1984, political violence as well as intimidation of blacks by other blacks, especially of community councillors and policemen, has escalated, including some fatal clashes.[55] During the state of emergency in thirty-six magisterial districts from 21 July 1985 to 7 March 1986, 787 people were killed as compared to 575 in the 1976–7 unrest situation.[56] On 12 June 1986, another state of emergency was imposed on the whole country; it was extended for another year on 10 June 1987, and again a year later in 1988 and in 1989.

Survey data of blacks have shown an increasing willingness to accept political violence and unrest as the means of improving their situation. In 1985 and 1986 blacks in the Pretoria–Witwatersrand–Vereeniging area gave the following responses to the question: 'What do you think will achieve more for Blacks in South Africa in the long run: Violence or negotiation?'[57]

Table 9.2 Survey of black attitudes to political violence, 1985–6

	May 1985 %	March 1986 %
Violence	22.3	20.2
Negotiation	66.2	65.9
Both	5.2	10.1
Uncertain or do not know	6.3	3.8
To the question: 'Have blacks gained anything from the unrest *up to now*?'		
Yes	7.3	20.1
No	87.7	75.4
Uncertain or do not know	5.0	4.6
To the question: 'Will blacks gain anything from the unrest *in the future*?'		
Yes	16.1	39.3
No	72.5	43.9
Uncertain or do not know	11.3	16.8

There was a stronger tendency among younger blacks, those with higher education, and in the higher-income categories to believe that blacks would benefit from unrest in the future than among the older, less educated, and those in the lower-income categories.[58]

These findings helped confirm earlier evidence presented by the Buthelezi Commission, from a 1981 survey of the blacks on the Witwatersrand. Of these, 31 per cent said 'nothing will work/only bloodshed', but of those with Standard 10 education or higher 49 per cent answered this statement in the affirmative, and 70 per cent did the same with a university degree.[59]

However the reaction of the other ethnic groups to the possibility of black majority rule has been negative. In 1981 Natalians were asked the following question: 'If all blacks were given the vote in South Africa, what do you think would happen?' (More than one answer possible.)[60]

Table 9.3 Survey of Natalian attitudes to black majority rule, 1981

Responses	Afrikaners %	Anglophones %	Coloureds %	Indians %
Positive image	0	3	36	35
Unrest/instability	24	27	18	15
Deterioration of standards	41	52	27	20
Political domination	100	89	74	65
Lack of democracy	11	20	15	3

The Buthelezi Commission correctly concluded that there is 'considerable basic attitudinal resistance to the idea of an open system and that this represents a hard political reality which is not likely to be altered by any development in Africa, southern Africa or South Africa in the near future'.[61]

A 1986 survey of the non-blacks in the Pretoria–Witwatersrand–Vereeniging area supported the above conclusion, with a black-dominated government being rated as bad to very bad (one of the three forms possible) by 88 per cent of whites, 67 per cent of coloureds and 73.6 per cent of Indians.[62]

Future prospects

But the problem for the present leadership remains one of risking too much change too quickly, for what is now required of the Afrikaner is that he abandon an ideology which has given him a sense of supremacy and security for self-doubt and self-examination at a time when he knows the survival of his nation is once again threatened.

C.F.B. Naudé

Predictions in human affairs are sometimes notoriously off the mark. Only short-range (one to five years) and medium-range predictions (six to fifteen years) have much chance of being reasonably accurate. Even then there may be unforeseen developments of major proportions which negate the best projections. Nevertheless there are some apparent trends.

Afrikaner nationalism has been evolving from a closed one into a predominantly open one, but since the late 1960s a reaction to this movement has started. White or racial identification is replacing ethnic identification. However, at about the same time as a white South African patriotism was appearing a militant and violent black or Pan-African nationalism began to emerge. Like Afrikaner nationalism at the turn of the century, it also wants political self-determination and control of the state.

Party politically, the Conservative Party will probably gain votes in the next election, but whether or not this will lead to more seats will depend upon the expected new delimitation of constituencies. The new delimitation will most likely result in a reduction of the *platteland* (rural) over-representation and thus work to the disadvantage of the CP. Since the National Party is in the centre, it can afford to lose some seats on its right as long as there is a party on its left from which it can recoup at least some of its losses.

Economically, the high rates of inflation will probably continue in the short range at least and thus lead to a further erosion of the whites' standard of living. This might create fears of proletarianisation on the part of the middle class and further weaken its support for the National Party. Despite the government's privatisation measures in a number of areas, more increases in government expenditures for education, welfare and employment creation may be expected in the medium range. If there are ever more comprehensive economic sanctions against the country, this could cause even more loss of support for the National Party and strengthen the Conservative Party.

Demographically, the minorisation of the whites will continue. Even under low fertility assumptions, by the year 2000 blacks will constitute 80.1 per cent, whites 10.4 per cent, coloureds 7.4 per cent and Indians 2.1 per cent of the total population.[63]

Politically, negotiations for a new constitution and black representation at the national level will lead to a new political system in the medium range at the latest. The new polity will be a consociational system with mutual veto for groups on key issues, such as educational and linguistic rights, and group autonomy through regional or federal division of authority. Its challenge will be to create an overriding patriotism above the existing nationalisms and tribal loyalties, an inclusive South African patriotism, to keep the state together. In short, giving a new meaning to putting 'South Africa first'.

The basic conflict is no longer between the anglophones and the Afrikaners. Unlike in the struggle against Britain, the country's independence is not in question. There is little fear of absorption within the English cultural stream. The political, socio-economic, cultural and religious divisions within Afrikaner nationalism are in response to *die swart gevaar* and how to deal with it. The dread of total incorporation within the Third World socio-economic, cultural, and political streams is strong. Like most nationalisms, Afrikaner nationalism has relied upon the state for its success. It is fearful that if its dominant position were to be destroyed it would then be reduced to merely another ethnic minority nationalism in a country with many ethnic, racial, and minority nationalisms. As long as there is increasing militancy, violence, and to a certain extent unity of purpose within black or Pan-African nationalism, which seems almost certain in the short-run at least, Afrikaner nationalism will remain divided and substantially closed.

The situation is not only complex, but has also elements of the tragic. This concept has not received much attention by political scientists. Robert Dahl sees the South African situation as a political tragedy 'fated by history, by an historical past from which those struggling in the present cannot break free'.[64]

There are undoubtedly those who fit this description. Dahl also notes, however, that in a classical tragedy the outcome is pre-determined by the gods and their laws. It may be that the South African case resembles a classical Greek tragedy, not in the sense of any gods or their laws, but in the sense that, in the words of Wilhelm Röpke, 'there may be no satisfactory solution at all',[65] only an unavoidable zero-sum conflict.

Acknowledgement

I would like to thank Drs D.J. van Vuuren, J.J.N. Cloete and J.J. van Tonder for comments on an earlier draft of the paper and Professor F.A. van Jaarsveld for his willingness to discuss a number of issues.

Notes

1. Van Jaarsveld, F.A., *The Awakening of Afrikaner Nationalism, 1868–1881*, Cape Town, 1961, p.187.
2. Degenaar, J., *Afrikaner Nationalism*, University of Cape Town, 1978, Occasional Paper No.1, Centre for Intergroup Studies, pp.11–12.
3. Kohn, H., 'Nationalism' in *International Encyclopaedia of the Social Sciences*, vol.II, pp.63–70.
4. Van Jaarsveld, op. cit., p.224.
5. Ibid., pp.221–3.
6. Quoted in Moodie, T.D., *The Rise of Afrikanerdom: Power, Apartheid and Afrikaner Civil Religion*, Berkeley, 1975, p.1.

7. Du Toit, A., 'Puritans in Africa? Afrikaner "Calvinism" and Kuyperian Neo-Calvinism in Late Nineteenth Century South Africa', *Contemporary Studies in Society and History*, Vol.27, no.2, 1985, p.234.
8. Moerane, M.T., 'Afrikaners as seen by Africans' in Van der Merwe, H.W. (ed.), *Looking at the Afrikaner Today*, Cape Town, 1975, p.69.
.9. Van Jaarsveld, F.A., 'Die Afrikanerdom: 'n Histories vertraagde volk-weg en selfbegrip', *Historia*, Vol.30, no.2, 1985, p.6.
10. Thompson, L., 'The Compromise of Union', in Wilson, M. and Thompson (eds.), *The Oxford History of South Africa*, Vol. II, Oxford, 1971, p.333.
11. Kohn, op. cit., p.66.
12. Quoted in Moodie, op. cit., p.75.
13. Adam, H. and Giliomee, H., *The Rise and Crisis of Afrikaner Power*, Cape Town, 1979, p.106.
14. Botha, L., 'Gen. Louis Botha, 1911', in Krüger, D.W. (ed.), *South African Parties and Policies, 1910–1960: A Select Source Book*, Cape Town, 1960, p.51.
15. Quoted in Moodie, op. cit., p.75.
16. Ibid., p.217.
17. Ibid., p.50.
18. Buitendag, J.J. and Van der Merwe, H.W., 'The Movement of Afrikaners into Higher Occupational Levels', *Humanitas*, Vol.1, no.4, 1971–2, p.298.
19. Ibid., p.299.
20. *South African Digest*, 17 May 1985, p.429.
21. Welsh, D., 'Natal Racial Policy and the Institutions of Traditional African Society: 1845 to 1910', Ph.D. thesis, University of Cape Town, 1969, p.353.
22. Quoted in Doorin, E.P., *Racial Separation in South Africa: An Analysis of Apartheid Theory*, Chicago, 1952, p.210.
23. Quoted in Pelzer, A.N. (ed.), *Verwoerd Speaks*, Johannesburg, 1966, p.18.
24. Rhoodie, N.J., *Apartheid and Racial Partnership in Southern Africa*, 2nd rev. ed., Pretória, 1969, p.42.
25. Giliomee, H., 'The Development of the Afrikaner's Self-Concept,' in Van der Merwe, op. cit., p.29.
26. Rhoodie, op. cit., p.31.
27. Van Jaarsveld, F.A., 'Von der Apartheid zu den Anfängen eines demokratischen Pluralismus', *Zeitschrift für Politik*, Vol.29, no.1, 1982, p.91.
28. Ibid., p.101.
29. 'The Doctrine of *Apartheid*', *Round Table*, Vol.XXXIX, no. 153, 1948, p.33.
30. Quoted in Rhoodie, op. cit., p.358.
31. Van Jaarsveld, op. cit., 1982, p.105.
32. De Klerk, F.W., 'Address by Mr F.W. de Klerk, DMS, at his Inauguration as State President, Pretoria, September 20, 1989', p.1.
33. Quoted in Pelzer (ed.), op. cit., p.162.

34. Rhoodie, op. cit., pp.80–1.
35. Worrall, D.J., 'Afrikaner Nationalism: A Contemporary Analysis', in Potholm, C.P. and Dale, R. (eds.), *Southern Africa in Perspective: Essays in Regional Politics*, New York, 1972, p.23.
36. 'Election 1981: The HNP Policy,' *Die Afrikaner*, 27 March 1981, p.10.
37. Giliomee, H., *The Parting of the Ways: South African Politics 1976–1982*, Cape Town, 1982, pp.113 and 140.
38. *South African Digest*, 1 November 1985, p.995.
39. Department of Foreign Affairs, *South Africa 1987–1988*, Pretoria, 1988, pp.164 and 166; *The Star*, international air mail weekly, 13 September 1989, pp.12–13; *Business Day*, 6 October 1989, p.1.
40. Department of Foreign Affairs, op. cit., p.164; *The Star*, op. cit., p.13.
41. Ibid., p.166.
42. Information on the HNP in this paragraph was secured from an interview with J. Marais on 4 September 1986, in Pretoria and on the CP from a letter from Dr Treurnicht on 9 September 1986.
43. *CP View Points*, no.1, 1986, p.2.
44. 'Wie en wat is die AWB?', *Quo Vadis*, Vol.1, no.1, 1986, p.16.
45. 'Dit ruik na Hitler', *Rapport*, 23 Februarie 1986, p.5.
46. Van Vuuren, D.J., 'Political Reform in South Africa', in Van Vuuren *et al.* (eds.), *South Africa: A Plural Society in Transition*, Durban, 1985, p.41.
47. Charney, C., 'Class Conflict and the National Party Split', *Journal of Southern African Studies*, Vol.10, no.2, 1984, p.269.
48. Schlemmer, L., 'Assessment: The 1987 Election in the South African Political Process', in Van Vuuren *et al.* (eds.), *South African Election 1987: Context, Process and Prospect*, Pinetown, 1987, p.322.
49. Rhoodie, N.J., De Kock, C.P. and Couper, M.P., 'White Perceptions of Socio-Political Change in South Africa', in Van Vuuren, *et al.* (eds.), op. cit., 1985, p.314.
50. Ibid., p.329.
51. Adam and Giliomee, op. cit., pp.121–3.
52. Central Statistical Services, *RSA Statistics in Brief*, Pretoria, 1989.
53. *Rand Daily Mail*, 25 June 1976, p.20; *New York Times*, 13 January 1990, p.43; Mostert, W.P., 'Demographic Trends in South Africa' in Marais, H.C. (ed.), *South Africa: Perspectives on the Future*, Pinetown, 1988, p.61.
54. Bureau for Information, *Talking with the ANC...*, Pretoria, 1986, p.25.
55. Du Toit, A., 'The Changing Patterns and Limits of Political Violence', *South Africa Foundation News*, Vol.12, no.7, 1986, p.2.
56. 'Comment on Political Violence', *South Africa Foundation News*, Vol.12, no.7, 1986, p.2.
57. Institute for Sociological and Demographic Research, 'The Perceptions of Adult Blacks in the Black Residential Areas of the PWV Complex of Various Current Issues Including Violence and Disinvestment', Pretoria, 1986, pp.2–5.
58. Ibid., pp.8–9.
59. *The Buthelezi Commission*, Vol.1, Durban, 1982, p.209.

60. Ibid., p.290.
61. Ibid., p.289.
62. Institute for Sociological and Demographic Research, op. cit., p.13; a 1987 survey based on a national sample of whites revealed similar results. See Hugo, P., 'Towards Darkness and Death: Racial Demonology in South Africa', *Journal of Modern African Studies*, Vol.26, no.4, 1988, p.585.
63. Mostert, op. cit., p.80.
64. Dahl, R. 'Citizenship: The Problem of Inclusion and Exclusion in Democratic Theory and Practice', Paper read at the Political Science Association of South Africa Congress, University of Natal, Pietermaritzburg, 19–20 September 1985, p.1.
65. Röpke, W., 'Conceptions and Misconceptions of Apartheid', *Africa Institute Bulletin*, Vol.IV, no.1, 1964, p.23.

Chapter ten

The USSR

Peter Duncan

Introduction

This chapter will outline the main features of minority nationalism in the
Soviet Union in the 1980s.[1] The relatively closed nature of the Communist political system makes it harder for nationalists in the USSR to
make their grievances known than it is for nationalists considered in
some other chapters of this book. Openly nationalist organisations
cannot be created by the Soviet minorities, and the KGB makes life
difficult for underground groups which seek to defend the rights of their
nations. The low participation in such groups should not be taken to
mean that they do not command wider support from their community as
a whole, but neither should this support be taken for granted. In the west
we are dependent for information on the nationalists themselves, often
provided by *emigré* channels which may have an interest in
exaggerating the level of support; and on Soviet sources, which until
recently at least, have portrayed the masses of the minorities as happy
with their situation in the Soviet Union. Even under the *glasnost* (openness, publicity, voicing of criticism) of 1986 on, when demonstrations
have been covered in the Soviet press, the actual demands of the
participants and the numbers involved have not always been accurately
reported.

The USSR is unlike all the other states examined in this book in that
it was consciously created in order to accommodate the political
aspirations of a large number of constituent nationalities. Lenin
conceived the Soviet Union as a response to the nationalism of the
Ukrainian, Georgian, Armenian and other minorities. By granting
statehood to the principal nations of what had been the Russian Empire,
the Bolsheviks hoped to undercut minority nationalism and encourage
the nationalities to co-operate within the federal framework of the
USSR. In the Soviet Union today, there are over 100 nationalities, each
with their own language. Some fifty of these have their own republican
or local political structures which are intended to give them political

integrity. Normally the leading officials of these territories are from the nationality after whom the territory is named (the eponymous nationality), and the local language is used in some of the schools and in part of the press. The most important of these territories are the fifteen Union Republics which together make up the Soviet Union. The largest is the Russian Soviet Federative Socialist Republic (RSFSR) which includes 52 per cent of the whole Soviet population. According to the Soviet Constitution, the Union Republics are sovereign states with the right to secede from the USSR. This right is nullified in practice, however, by the centralised nature of the Communist Party of the Soviet Union (CPSU), which as the same Constitution says, is the 'leading and guiding force' of political life. The Communist parties of the republics are an integral part of the CPSU and subject to control from the Central Committee Secretariat in Moscow.

The Russians are still a majority in the Soviet Union, but their share of the population has fallen from 54.6 per cent in the 1959 census to 52.4 per cent in 1979. (They are already a minority among people under 20). While most of them live in the RSFSR, there are Russians in all the non-Russian republics (i.e. the fourteen other Union Republics), but these are not expected to learn the local language. The most important nationalism in the USSR is Russian nationalism. Its development has provoked a nationalist reaction among the non-Russians, and this reaction has in turn stimulated a further nationalist backlash among the Russians. Russian nationalism is conceptually distinct from the desire of the Moscow leadership to promote the appearance of a 'new socialist person', who is bilingual in Russian and the mother tongue (if this is not Russian), and who has broken from national traditions such as religion. In fact Russian nationalism, linked with Russian Orthodoxy, is sometimes hostile to the official 'Sovietising' policies. But for the national minorities, Sovietisation is often seen as Russification, and it leads to the growth of minority nationalism.

Soviet nationality policy – historical background

To understand the emergence of minority nationalism in the Soviet Union it is necessary to say something about the nationality policy pursued by Soviet governments since 1917. Lenin, like Marx and Engels, favoured the existence of a single unitary party for the workers of a particular state, irrespective of nationality. Also like the founding fathers of Marxism, he believed that the right of nations to self-determination was subordinate to the class struggle. In 1917, many of the borderlands of Russia declared themselves independent, and anti-Bolshevik governments came to the fore. In these territories support for the Bolsheviks was mainly confined to the workers, who were

Russians, while the peasants belonged to the national minorities. During the Civil War (1918–20), the Bolsheviks reconquered most of the Russian Empire, and the Soviet federal structure was created in 1922 as a concession to the minorities. Lenin at the end of his life became very disturbed at Russian domination of the Soviet Union, and was prepared to decentralise power to the individual republics. He feared that if measures were not taken, the right of republics to secede would become 'a mere scrap of paper'.[2]

In fact, from the start, agitation for the secession of one's republic from the Soviet Union was considered counter-revolutionary. On the other hand, through the 1920s and 1930s the Communist Party went out of its way to promote the use of the local national (i.e. non-Russian) languages and of national cadres in the republics. This policy, known as *korenizatsiia* – seeking roots in the native populations – led to the dramatic expansion of publication and education in the national languages. Many nationalities were given literary languages and alphabets for the first time. The cultures of the republics were supposed to be 'national in form, socialist in content'. But in this process, which was conceived in order to undermine nationalism, there arose a new national consciousness among many of the non-Russian nationalities, who now had their own republics, party committees and native elites.

The process of industrialisation in the 1920s and 1930s was accompanied by the migration of Russian specialists, managers and skilled workers to assist the development of the borderlands. One aim of this industrial development was, in line with *korenizatsiia*, to bring into being native working classes among the non-Russians, and train them to assume leading managerial positions. Even in the 1930s, however, the emphasis on the native cultures began to disappear. Stalin and the central party leadership moved towards using Russian national themes, and purged the non-Russian elites on accusations of 'bourgeois nationalism'. Russians were put into leading positions in the non-Russian republics. In 1938, the Russian language was made a compulsory subject in all Soviet schools, for the first time since the revolution. These moves may have reflected a fear in Moscow that central control over the republics was becoming too weak. The national languages had flourished to the extent that in some schools there was no Russian taught at all.[3] As the war danger faced the USSR, Stalin increasingly tried to rely on traditional Russian patriotism to mobilise support. Meanwhile the police terror and the atomisation of the later Stalin period prevented the appearance of cohesive opposition from the non-Russians. Exceptions to this were some of the territories incorporated in the Soviet Union during and after the Second World War: the Western Ukraine, which had been part of Poland between the wars, and the Baltic states of Estonia, Latvia and Lithuania which had won independence after the revolution. These regions suffered severe repression as Moscow sought to root out opposition, but armed nationalist resistance in the Ukraine continued into the 1950s.

It was after Stalin's death, and especially after Khrushchev's denunciation of him at the XX Party Congress in 1956, that the resurgence of the national minorities began. The top positions in the republics – First Secretaries of the Central Committees of the republican party organisations, republican Prime Ministers and others – were given to representatives of the eponymous nationalities. As a rule Russians from outside the republic were given the post of Second Secretary, with the aim of ensuring that Moscow's policies were implemented. Other leading cadres of local origin were regularly given Russian deputies. But the ending of mass terror allowed the non-Russian elites to articulate their own interests and demands on behalf of their own republics. Sometimes they cited Lenin's opposition to Russian chauvinism to back their claims. The literary and academic elites extolled the histories of their own nations, even when this led them into conflict with the claims of Russian historians. These patterns have continued into the 1980s. At the same time Khrushchev also promoted the use of the Russian language, giving rise to fears that he was aiming at bringing about the 'fusion' of nationalities, which Lenin had proclaimed as an aim of socialism. There were hints, too, that the federal structure of the Soviet Union would be abolished in favour of a unitary system. These fears led to resistance from the elites in some republics, especially from the writers.

The Brezhnev era

The Brezhnev era (1964–82) was a period of paradoxes in the development of the Soviet Union. On one hand, the country gained strategic parity with the USA and made substantial advances in industrial development and living standards. On the other hand, the expectations of the Soviet public grew faster than the system could cope with them, and in the latter part of the period growth rates fell significantly (to zero by some western estimates). These conditions were fertile for the growth of nationalism; the non-Russians saw the central government as mismanaging the economy or exploiting the resources of their republics, while Russians believed that the non-Russians were being subsidised at their expense. Furthermore, in the non-Russian republics, with the spread of higher education among the local nationalities, there was increased competition between Russian and natives for the better jobs. Positive discrimination in favour of the latter led to resentment among Russians. It is interesting to note that professionals and white-collar workers show more hostility to people from other nationalities than do blue-collar workers – an indication that it is only for higher-status jobs that nationality is a criterion of employment.[4]

The Brezhnev leadership abandoned references to the 'fusion' of nationalities and in the 1977 Soviet Constitution maintained the federal system. There was sloganistic talk of the 'coming together' of the national cultures, but also of their 'flourishing', and in fact over the Brezhnev era as a whole there was a significant expansion of the non-Russian press. Television programmes in the local languages were broadcast routinely. Societies were established in the republics to restore historical monuments, allowing the Central Asians, for example, to be reminded of the great days of Tamerlane. But while the indigenous elites consolidated their power in the non-Russian republics, the central all-Union authorities in Moscow became more of a Russian preserve. The Central Committee apparatus, the ministries, the army and the KGB were all staffed primarily by Russians, especially in the top positions. Priorities for economic development were no longer to be the more backward (primarily non-Russian) regions, but those which had most to offer the Soviet Union as a whole, such as Siberia and the Central Russian agricultural regions.

The language issue was the most salient factor in provoking minority nationalism in the Brezhnev era. The Ukrainians are the second largest nationality in the Soviet Union, comprising 16 per cent of the population in 1979. As early as 1965 they suffered a crackdown aimed against writers and journalists who were defending the Ukrainian language against Russian encroachment. The Ukrainian and Belorussian languages are close to Russian, and an increasing minority of Ukrainians and Belorussians have adopted Russian as their first language. In the capitals of their two republics, Kiev and Minsk, the national languages are rarely heard on the streets, and despite official talk of the equality of languages, Russian has been consistently encouraged in public life. Among the considerable Ukrainian nationalist samizdat, there stands out Ivan Dziuba's *'Internationalism' or 'Russification'?* (1965), which attacked Soviet language policy from a Leninist standpoint and led to his imprisonment.[5] Petro Shelest, the First Secretary of the Ukrainian Central Committee, who had circulated the work to leading Ukrainian officials and who was believed to favour the Ukrainian language, was himself dismissed in 1972. The Ukrainian press subsequently attacked him, claiming that a book he had written might 'stimulate nationalist illusions and prejudices'.[6]

It was in the mid-1970s that the language issue heated up in the non-Russian republics. As in the late 1930s, the central leaders became concerned at the poor state of knowledge of the Russian language among the minorities. A key role in this concern was played by demographic factors. The censuses of 1970 and 1979 showed a considerable increase in the sise of most of those nationalities which had traditionally been Muslim. The Muslim share of the population grew from 12 to 13 per cent in 1959 to about 17 per cent in 1979. Among them, the Tajiks doubled in numbers, as did the Uzbeks, who displaced the Belorussians as the third-largest nationality in the Soviet Union. Soviet policy-makers appeared to believe that knowledge of the Russian language would promote love for the Russian people among the Muslims. More pragmatically, the needs of the economy and of the Soviet armed forces, where the sole language of command is Russian, dictated a higher level of facility in Russian than existed. In 1978 the Soviet government issued a decree on improving the teaching of the Russian language, which extended the use of Russian in schools where it was not the main medium of instruction and introduced it into nursery schools as well. Similar measures were taken to expand the use of Russian in higher education.

The non-Russians responded in a variety of ways. The congresses of the official Union of Writers in Belorussia and Georgia heard delegates' speeches protesting at the curtailment of the rights of the national languages which inevitably accompanied the expansion of Russian. In Georgia in 1978 a demonstration of several thousands took place in protest against a proposal to make Russian an official language of the republic – a proposal which was soon withdrawn. A petition opposing Russification was sent to Brezhnev, bearing the signatures of 365 Georgian intellectuals. Similar developments, although not on such a scale, took place in other republics. In Estonia, several demonstrations took place which not only opposed Russification but also called for the withdrawal of non-Estonian troops. In Lithuania, the samizdat journal *Auvra* called in 1981 for a boycott of the Russian language.[7]

Outside influences also assisted the development of minority nationalism. The Jewish emigration movement, with much American support, was the most successful form of minority nationalism in the USSR. Détente and the Conference on Security and Co-operation in Europe led in the mid-1970s to the sprouting of a variety of unofficial dissident movements. In 1976 an independent group to monitor the application by the Soviet authorities of the human rights provisions of the Helsinki Final Act was established in Moscow. Similar groups were established in the Ukraine, Georgia, Lithuania and Armenia, all including dissident nationalists. The appearance of the independent Polish trade union Solidarity in 1980–1 appears to have found popular support in the Baltic republics and in Transcaucasia (Georgia, Armenia and Azerbaijan) but little elsewhere. Of greater concern for the Soviet authorities was the growth of fundamentalist Islam in Khomeini's Iran, which beamed subversive broadcasts towards Soviet Muslims.

Following the Soviet invasion of Afghanistan in 1979, fraternisation between Soviet Central Asian Muslim troops and Afghan Muslims led the Russians to withdraw the Central Asians, because of fears that they were being ideologically contaminated.

Religion and minority nationalism in the 1980s

The intensity of minority nationalism in the USSR varies widely between the different nationalities. An important factor here is whether the national culture has been historically linked with a particular religion. Since the CPSU is committed to atheism, any attachment to religion is a form of dissent, and attachment to the national religion is additionally seen as a way of preserving the national cultures. The link goes the opposite way as well; non-Russians who are devoted to religion are forced into opposition to the anti-religious policies of the Soviet state and may become involved in dissident nationalist activity. Religion is a factor strengthening nationalism in Lithuania, the Muslim areas (especially central Asia and Azerbaijan), Estonia, Georgia and Armenia. It plays a divisive role in the Ukraine and Latvia.

In the Ukraine, for example, the western part of the republic where the Uniate Church was traditionally strong is the centre of nationalist activity. The Uniates are Catholics of the eastern rite who recognise the Pope as head of the church. Eastern Ukrainians – the majority of the nation – traditionally adhered to the Russian Orthodox Church. When the Western Ukraine was incorporated into the Soviet Union, the Uniate Church was forcibly incorporated into the Russian Orthodox Church, at the insistence of the Soviet government. This move did not undermine Ukrainian nationalism, however, as the Uniate Church maintained an illegal existence. In 1982 five Uniates led by Iosyp Terelia established the 'Initiative Group for the Defence of the Rights of Believers and the Church', which sought to restore legality to the Uniates. In 1984 in the group's 'Chronicle of the Catholic Church in the Ukraine', Terelia wrote of the role of the Uniate Church in the resurrection of the Ukrainian nation.[8] Terelia was imprisoned from 1985 to 1987, but the group continued to function. While it is unclear how much support the group has in the Western Ukraine, it is unlikely that it will have many adherents in the eastern part of the republic.

The strong identification of the Lithuanian nation and the Roman Catholic Church, on the other hand, has created from the 1970s what can be described as a mass movement of religio-nationalist opposition. While some of the Lithuanian samizdat journals put more emphasis on religion and others more on the nation, the two issues are intertwined with each other and with the question of human rights. In 1979 a petition calling for the return to the believers of the church at Klaipeda, confiscated by the state, attracted 149,000 signatures – 5 per cent of all Lithuanians. This feat would be unthinkable in Russia itself. A series of appeals were ignored by the local officials (presumably acting under Moscow's instructions) until 1987 when, in the more tolerant atmosphere promoted by the Gorbachev leadership, the church was given back to the believers.

The Muslims and Soviet Central Asia

The relationship between nationalism and religion is probably most sensitive among the Muslim nationalities. Soviet Muslims are divided in several ways. Most are Sunnites, but some are Shi'ites; most speak Turkic languages, while the Tajik language belongs to the Iranian family. For some nationalities, such as the Uzbeks, Islam is central to national traditions; for the Kazakhs it is less important. In the Soviet period, Moscow has fought pan-Islamic and pan-Turkic feeling by encouraging identification with the nationality and individual Soviet republic, as well as loyalty to the Soviet Union as a whole. Instead of one big Muslim republic in Central Asia, there are five: Uzbekistan, Kazakhstan, Tajikistan, Turkmenia and Kirghizia.

The development of this form of national consciousness has not, however, displaced the Islamic consciousness but rather coexisted with it. With large numbers of Tajiks and Uzbeks living in Afghanistan, and Azerbaijanis in Iran (as well as Kazakhs living in China benefiting from the new religious tolerance there), it would not be surprising if Islamic feeling in the Soviet Union had grown in the 1980s. Certainly the local Soviet press from 1983 onwards paid considerably more attention to Islam and nationalism than it had before. This may have reflected not an increase in the problem from 1983, however, but rather the greater openness that appeared generally in the Soviet media at that time. In 1986 Gorbachev himself made a major speech in the Uzbek capital Tashkent attacking religion. This was not republished in the Moscow papers, and the implication is that it was particularly Islam which was worrying the General Secretary.

Specialists are divided about the political attitudes of Soviet Muslims. The fact that traditional Muslim circumcision and burial customs are almost universal does not mean that political nationalism or pan-Islam is widespread. Industrial development in Central Asia has benefited the population, and the status of women has improved. The indigenous republican elites have been seen as having a stake in the Soviet system and being loyal to Moscow. This perception needs to be reviewed in the light of the campaign against corruption which Andropov launched in the Soviet Union in 1982 and which Gorbachev carried on. The most striking case involved Sharaf Rashidov, the First

Secretary of the Uzbekistan Central Committee since 1959, who rose to be a candidate member of the Politburo but died suddenly in 1983. He had been an enthusiastic supporter of the use of the Russian language and appeared subservient to Moscow. After his death he was accused of tolerating corruption and theft and of hoodwinking Moscow about the republic's economic achievements. Party organisations were said to be flirting with religion. Rashidov's body was dug up from its place of honour and reburied. Between June 1984 and January 1986 forty out of sixty-five provincial party secretaries were replaced. For the first time since the Stalin period, Moscow sent in Russians to fill some of the new key vacancies, replacing locals who were considered unreliable. This process was repeated in important posts in Kazakhstan and Turkmenia.

It was the replacement of the Kazakhstan First Secretary, the Kazakh Dinmukhamed Kunaev, by a Russian, Gennady Kolbin, in December 1986 which provoked the first major nationalist demonstration of the Gorbachev period. Kunaev had held his post since 1964 and become a full Politburo member. His replacement by a Russian insulted Kazakh national feeling. Several thousand Kazakhs rioted in the capital Alma-Ata. They bore slogans such as 'Kazakhstan for the Kazakhs', 'Autonomy and a separate place in the UN for Kazakhstan', and 'Kolbin, clear off to Russia!' Several deaths occurred, and by late 1987 at least 1,380 people had been punished (ranging from expulsion from the Komdomol to a reported death sentence).[9] Accounts agreed that the slogans were purely nationalist rather than religious. *Pravda* rapidly reported the occurrence of the riots, although without full details, and the Politburo sent one of its full members to investigate and regain control.[10]

Paradoxically, this tendency to send in Russians to sort out the problems of Central Asia came when the Gorbachev leadership was making serious efforts to deconcentrate and decentralise decision-making from Moscow to the republics and the enterprises. It also roughly coincided with a decision in August 1986 to stop work on a grandiose scheme to reverse part of the flow of two Siberian rivers (which end in the Arctic) and send the water to Central Asia, which with its burgeoning population claims to be in dire need of it. The decision was taken after pressure from ecologists and Russian nationalists, especially writers, concerned about the effect of the scheme on the Russian North. Prior to the decision, Central Asian party leaders had publicly argued for the scheme, but they were quiet after *Pravda* printed the Politburo statement announcing the end of the scheme. In 1987, however, Central Asian writers began to raise the issue again.[11] The seriousness of the economic position in Central Asia was revealed by the publication of an article in a Moscow newspaper claiming that in Uzbekistan (total population 15.3 million in 1979) there were one million unemployed.[12]

It may be that Moscow was expecting dissatisfaction to develop in Central Asia, and decided to take back some power from the indigenous elites in order to ensure political stability. At the same time, the Muslim nationalities have lost their representation in the Soviet Politburo. Whereas in 1982–3 they had two full Politburo members and one candidate, at the beginning of 1988 they were unrepresented. The combination of exclusion from the centre and reduction of their power in what are seen as their own republics will inevitably increase the nationalist feelings of the Central Asian elites.

Glasnost and minority nationalism

The implementation under Gorbachev of a policy of *glasnost* allowed a freer discussion of nationality problems in the official media, and more tolerance of unofficial demonstrations. In his speech to the January 1987 Plenum of the Central Committee, Gorbachev referred to the Alma-Ata events. He spoke at some length of 'errors' in nationality policy, and warned of the dangers of (minority) nationalism and (Russian) chauvinism. 'It is especially important to protect our youth from the demoralising effects of nationalism'.[13] In his speech on the seventieth anniversary of the October Revolution (November 1987), however, when Gorbachev was making concessions to reformers less radical than himself, he was much more restrained about nationality problems. He even referred to the 'profound respect and gratitude to the great Russian people' felt by the peoples of the Soviet Union – a formulation used by Soviet leaders before him, which was not calculated to win over the non-Russians.[14]

The republican newspapers carried a number of articles, mainly by creative writers, urging the defence of the national languages against the encroachments of Russian. At the Ukrainian Writers' Union Congress in June 1986, the leading Ukrainian writer Oles Honchar (a candidate member of the CPSU Central Committee) denounced those who held the Ukrainian language in contempt.[15] The following month, at the Congress of the USSR Writers' Union, the Ukrainian poet Borys Oliinyk denounced non-Russian officials who abandoned their native language as 'the worst great-power chauvinists'.[16] In September 1986, the Estonian-language literary monthly *Looming* reported after several months' delay that the language question had been an important issue at the Estonian Writers' Union Congress the previous April. The writer Mats Traat had complained that 'Institutions and enterprises in which the Estonian language is shunned and in which Russian reigns ... violate the fundamentals of Leninist language policy'.[17] Also in September, a Belorussian literary weekly published a letter urging state protection for the Belorussian language. An accompanying article pointed out that

Belorussian was the medium of instruction for pupils over seven in no urban school in the republic.[18] There are the beginnings of a common desire among the republican cultural elites to emulate each other in the defence of the native languages. In July 1986 the Uzbek poetess Gulchera Nurullaeva suggested that her republic take 'as a model' the native-language festivals due to be held officially in Latvia.[19]

The year 1987 saw the release of a large number of political prisoners, many of whom were non-Russians holding nationalist views. The new atmosphere led to a revival of nationalist samizdat (the *Ukrainian Herald*, for example, recommenced after a fifteen-year gap) and to a spate of nationalist demonstrations, tolerated by the authorities. There is no space here to list all the groups which emerged and their publications. Small groups of Jews, seeking to emigrate in order to find cultural and religious freedom, had the largest impact with a series of demonstrations in Moscow, from February onwards. In July around 500 Crimean Tartars demonstrated in Red Square. The Crimean Tartars were deported *en masse* from the Crimea to Central Asia in 1944, after being accused of collaborating with the Nazis. Since the 1960s they have been campaigning unsuccessfully to be allowed to return to the Crimea, and for the re-establishment of the Crimean Autonomous Soviet Socialist Republic, originally created by Lenin within the RSFSR. On the demonstration they carried portraits of Lenin and Gorbachev. They were received by Soviet President Andrei Gromyko, who was later named the head of a commission to investigate their grievances. Nevertheless, they were not allowed to remain in Moscow. While the commission's work continued, the Tartars organised further demonstrations. In September 2,000 tried to march from Taman to the Crimea, but most were arrested and beaten up.[20]

Of particular significance were the series of demonstrations held in August 1987, on the 48th anniversary of the Molotov–Ribbentrop Pact, under which the Baltic states were to be joined to the USSR. In the three Baltic capitals, Tallinn (Estonia), Riga (Latvia) and Vilnius (Lithuania), demonstrators demanded the publication of the pact and its denunciation by the government. Estimates of the number of participants vary, but there appear to have been around 2,000 in Tallinn, 7,000 in Riga, organised by the 'Helsinki 86' dissident group, and 500 in Vilnius (in relative terms, a surprisingly low number).[21] The 'Helsinki 86' group had earlier appealed for a referendum to be held on Latvian self-determination, and for an examination of the problem of Russification in Latvia.[22] At these and other demonstrations in the Baltic republics in 1987–8, the cry of 'Freedom' was repeatedly raised. The participants were clearly not motivated solely by a desire to change language policy, but were questioning the continued membership of the Baltic republics in the Soviet Union. While many of the organisers of these peaceful demonstrations have been subjected to repression, including labour camp sentences, it remains the case that as recently as three or more years before they could not have taken place at all.

Finally (so far) the events of 1988–9 in the Nagorny Karabakh Autonomous Region of the Azerbaijan Republic raised the stakes for Gorbachev in relation to the nationality question to a new high point. The demand by the regional Communist Party of this predominantly Armenian area to unite with the Armenian Republic led to demonstrations and strikes around Armenia itself involving over one million people. Moscow's response was to say that no change could take place without the agreement of the Azerbaijan Republican authorities. Thus an unprecedented situation arose where the parties of the two Republics were in a state bordering on civil war. The refusal in Armenia to accept the status quo made it likely that Moscow would have to reconsider the situation; but Moscow also knew that to transfer the territory against Azerbaijan's wishes could provoke a backlash capable of spreading to the other Muslim republics. With violent confrontation growing, its direct intervention became almost inevitable.

Conclusions

Our knowledge of minority nationalism in the contemporary Soviet Union remains uneven. The creation of the formally federal system, designed to undermine nationalist opposition, promoted the growth of national consciousness in the non-Russian republics. The Andropov–Gorbachev anti-corruption campaign has intensified nationalist feeling in the strategically important region of Central Asia.

Meanwhile, throughout the Soviet Union, the spirit of *glasnost* has made it easier for the minorities to articulate their grievances, whether through official channels or through samizdat literature and demonstrations. Generally, these appeals relate to language, religious freedoms and basic human rights. Only in the Baltic republics has the question of secession from the USSR become a live issue. On the whole, the federal system combined with the power of the KGB has proved adequate to meet and keep in check the aspirations of the major Soviet nations. The struggle for greater republic autonomy and a larger slice of the cake takes place within the official party and state framework. None the less, the events in Alma-Ata and most recently in Armenia and Azerbaijan have shown that conflict within the elites can spill out to the streets, in a populist challenge, as problems develop, while, as in the Baltic states, parties and parliaments can now become mobilised behind nationalist aspirations.

Notes

I gratefully acknowledge the financial support of the Economic and Social Research Council, grant no. E 00 22 2011.

1. Among the general studies of minority nationalism in the USSR, see *Nationalism in the USSR and Eastern Europe in the Era of Brezhnev and Kosygin*, ed. George W. Simmonds, Detroit, Mich., 1977; Hélène Carrere d'Encausse, *Decline of an Empire: The Soviet Socialist Republics in Revolt*, trans. M. Sokolinsky and H.A. LaFarge, New York, 1979; *Soviet Nationality Policies and Practices*, ed. Jeremy R. Azrael, New York, 1978; Walker Connor, *The National Question in Marxist-Leninist Theory and Strategy*, Princeton, N.J., 1984; Rasma Karklins, *Ethnic Relations in the USSR: The Perspective from Below*, Boston, Mass., 1986; *The Last Empire: Nationality and the Soviet Future*, ed. Robert Conquest, Stanford, Cal., 1986. For studies of particular regions see, e.g. Alexandre Bennigsen and Marie Broxup, *The Islamic Threat to the Soviet State*, London, 1983; Michael Rywkin, *Moscow's Muslim Challenge: Soviet Central Asia*, London, 1982; Kenneth C. Farmer, *Ukrainian Nationalism in the Post-Stalin Era: Myth, Symbols & Ideology in Soviet Nationalities Policy*, The Hague, 1980; Thomas Remeikis, *Opposition to Soviet Rule in Lithuania 1945–1980*, Chicago, 1980.
2. Lenin, Polnoe sobranie sochinenii, 5th edn., M. Politizdat, 1958–1965, XLV, pp.356–62.
3. Isabelle Kreindler, 'The Changing Status of Russian in the Soviet Union', *International Journal of the Sociology of Language*, No.33, 1982, pp.10–11.
4. R. Karklins, op.cit., pp.140–8; A. Surokolov, 'Vliianie razlichii v urovne obrazovaniia i chislennosti kontaktiruiushchikh etnicheskikh grupp na mezhetnicheskie otnosheniia (po materialam perepisei naseleniia SSSR 1959 i 1970 hh.)', *Sovetskaia etnografiia*, 1976, No.1, p.110.
5. Ivan Dzuiba, *Internationalism or Russification? A Study in the Soviet Nationalities Problem*, New York, 1974.
6. As cited in Teresa Rakowska-Harmstone, 'The Dialectics of Nationalism in the USSR', *Problems of Communism*, XXIII, No.3, May–June 1974, p.13.
7. Roman Solchanyk, 'Russian Language and Soviet Politics', *Soviet Studies*, XXXIV, No.1 January 1982, pp.23–42.
8. Andrew Sorokowski, 'The Chronicle of the Catholic Church in Ukraine', *Religion in Communist Lands*, XIII, No.3, Winter 1985, pp.292–7.
9. *USSR News Brief*, 31 December 1986, item 24-23, and ibid., 31 October 1987, 19/20-6, and the daily reports from 21 to 26 December on the reasons for the riots.
10. *Pravda*, 19 December 1986 and the daily reports from 21 to 26 December on the reasons for the riots.

11. Sergei Voronitsyn, 'Renewed Debate over Canceled River Diversion Project', RL 205/87 (27 May 1987). RL refers to the document number in the *Radio Liberty Research Bulletin.*

12. *Sel'skaia zhizn'*, 24 March 1987, in *Current Digest of the Soviet Press,* XXIX, No.14, 1987, p.4.

13. M.S. Gorbachev, *Reorganisation and the Party's Personnel Policy,* Moscow, Novosti, 1987, pp.41–43.

14. *Soviet News*, 4 November 1987, p.400.

15. *Literaturna Ukraina* (in Ukrainian), 12 June 1986, cited in Roman Solchanyk, 'The Ukrainian Writers' Congress: A Spirited Defense of the Native Language', RL 247/86 (24 June 1986).

16. *Literaturna Ukraina* (in Ukrainian), 3 July 1986, cited in Roman Solchanyk, 'Ukrainian Writer Lambastes "Great-Power Chauvinism" and "Home-Grown Russifiers"', RL 270/86 (8 July 1986).

17. Cited in Toomas Ilves, 'Estonia: What the Writers' Union Congress Really Talked About', *Radio Free Europe Baltic Area* SR/6 (25 September 1986), p.4.

18. *Literatura i mastatsva* (in Belorussian), 19 September 1986, cited in Roman Solchanyk, 'Criticism of the Status of the Native Language in Belorussia's Schools', RL 365/86 (28 September 1986).

19. *Ozbekistan adabiyati va sanati* (in Uzbek), 18 July 1986, cited in Joseph Seagram, 'Central Asian Reaction to Writers' Congress', RL 337/86 (8 August 1986).

20. *USSR News Brief*, 31 July 1987, 14-4, 31 August 1987, 15/16-4, 30 September 1987, 17/18-3 and 31 October 1987, 19/20-4.

21. *USSR News Brief*, 31 August 1987, 15/16-3.

22. *USSR News Brief*, 31 January 1987, 1/2-1.

Chapter eleven

Rights and minority nationalism

Howard Williams

The object of this chapter is to examine the proposition that members of established minority nationalities within larger states have a right to be treated by the rest of the community and the state in a manner which allows them to preserve their cultural identity and practice. This analysis deals, I believe, with the situation of such minority nationalities as the Basques in Spain, the French in Canada, the Bretons in France, the Welsh in Britain and several countries more. I cannot testify to its universal applicability but I can testify to its particular relevance in the Welsh context.

In his novel the *Best of Friends*, which concerns two young girls who become students in a University College of Wales in the early 1920s, Emyr Humphreys describes how Enid and Amy are one night caught in a fearful storm in their seafront hall of residence. The hall of residence is in the charge of a fearsome anglicised woman academic who has little sympathy with the Welsh language and its culture. The hall of residence, which unremarkably bears a close resemblance to the present Alexandra Hall at Aberystwyth, is violently rocked by the extraordinary storm and because of the threat of flooding and subsidence it is decided to evacuate the building. Whilst Amy (who hitherto has been portrayed as the most politically conscious of the two friends) is preparing to leave the building with some of her fellow-residents she suddenly remembers Enid. She has not seen Enid since the beginning of the storm. She returns to Enid's room to find her hunched in a corner. Enid although terrified by the storm, which has in the meantime become more threatening, is refusing to leave the building since the evacuation order has not been addressed to her in Welsh. Amy understands immediately that her friend is insisting on her right to be addressed in her own language in her own country. The right seems more pressing to both since it is being insisted upon in what purports to be a national educational establishment. Amy, more pragmatic than her friend, is prepared to insist on her right at a more appropriate moment. However, Enid is not moved by any of her utilitarian arguments. Enid is not prepared to move even if her own life is endangered as a consequence.

Amy returns downstairs to explain the position to the warden of the hall who is becoming increasingly more anxious and impatient. The warden greets Amy's story with incredulity. The warden sees no case for the Welsh language being employed formally within the institution. Her unexpressed view is that English is the language of the majority and also the true language of learning. Even if she were to admit some legitimacy to Enid's standpoint, now is not the time to insist upon it. She accompanies Amy back upstairs to put these points to Enid. Enid refuses to acknowledge her presence. The warden's arguments fall on deaf ears. The situation reaches an impasse because Enid is determined that her assumed rights be respected.

We can learn a great deal about our theme from this allegorical scene which Humphreys describes. Enid is claiming the very kind of minority right we intend to examine. Humphreys is sympathetic to the case of Welsh-language speakers and portrays their predicament with great skill and fidelity. We can hazard a guess that the uncontrollable storm welling up outside on the promenade represents the great tide of Englishness which threatens to overwhelm the small Welsh nation. We can also perhaps surmise that Humphreys sees Enid's response to the tide which threatens to engulf and destroy her as representing the only effective path of saving the language. The minority have to act unreasonably to attain their rights, but this unreasonableness should not threaten the lives and interests of the opposed majority. To win the majority over, the unreasonableness must threaten only the well-being of the minority. The threat of the Welsh nationalist leader Gwynfor Evans in 1979–80 to fast to death unless the Welsh-medium television channel was granted appears to fall in with the scene of stubborn, self-denying defiance Humphreys depicts.

But Gwynfor Evans and Enid seem to be making extraordinarily heavy weather of insisting on their rights. Surely rights that are rights are uncontroversial and are recognised as such by all members of a civilised community. So confident did a large number of the world states feel about the self-evident nature of human rights that in 1948 they joined together to produce a universal declaration of human rights. This declaration has remained a yardstick by which to measure human progress ever since. Thus not only is it now taken for granted that we can enjoy certain rights, such as the life, liberty and security of person (Article 3) within states, but also that we can enjoy these rights wherever we are in virtue of being human. Article 15 of the Declaration, which states that 'everyone has the right to a nationality' would appear to provide helpful support for the kind of right which Enid demands. The whole presumption of the document is, as the Preamble states, that there is 'a common standard of achievement for all peoples and all nations'.

However, this optimistic picture does not tell us everything that there is to be known about rights. We have to return to Humphreys's allegory to gain a firmer grasp of the full picture. Under normal circumstances the warden of the seafront hall would not grant nor respect Enid's right to be addressed in her own language. The warden cannot even speak Welsh and her deputy, who can, has already escaped to a nearby hall. In the warden's eyes Enid's right has no standing. In normal circumstances the right has no stannding, first, because it is not enshrined in the country's law, second, because it is not a right insisted upon and recognised by a large section of the population and, finally (most crucially) it is not a right that the minority have the power to enforce.

This final point is central to our theme. Rights do not exist where the power to enforce those rights is absent. This is why the UN document on human rights is merely a declaration. Ideally I may, for instance, believe that every adult in Britain has the right to enjoy a minimum wage of £120 a week. But the right does not exist merely by virtue of my stating it. For the right to become real requires positive legislation by the government, and even then it may turn out difficult to enforce.

Kant goes straight to the heart of the matter when he says: 'Nothing seems more natural than if the people have rights then they also have a power; however, simply for the reason that they cannot establish any lawful power the people likewise have no strict rights only ideal rights'.[1] People believe they enjoy rights independently of the ability of their state's power to enforce their rights. Paine embodied this belief in his enthusiatic defence of the Rights of Man.[2] In a moral sense no one can dispute that certain rights such as the right to freedom of conscience, the right to our personal possessions and the right to the freedom of association are ours in virtue of our being human. The moral case that we should enjoy some such rights in one form or other in order that we can properly develop as human beings seems incontrovertible. As Article 29 of the UN Declaration puts it: everyone has duties to the community in which alone the free and full development of his personality is possible. But, as Kant points out, we must recognise there is a hiatus between what the morally mature individual may wish to insist upon and what authorities actually do, and have to do, to maintain their ascendancy. Political authority is necessary to enforce rights, but the recognition of rights is not wholly essential to the maintenance of political authority. Governments can and do ride roughshod over the rights of their people. For rights actually to exist first of all requires the creation of a morally sensitive political authority. But where I would differ from Kant is in his pessimism about the ability of people to bring about such a morally sensitive political authority. Since the people have so much to gain from bringing about such an authority I am inclined to the view that they must eventually create such an authority.

In Kant's terms Enid has chosen to take her stand under propitious circumstances. Normally Enid would not wield sufficient power to insist that her right to be addressed in her own language be observed. Lacking law and custom behind her the right would remain an ideal. But in the circumstances of the storm (and the known insecurity of the hall of residence) the warden is becoming increasingly more agitated. She screams at Enid to leave her room. She attempts to exercise in full her authority as warden. However, Enid simply screams inaudibly back at her. The warden's impulse is to leave Enid to her fate. But a fatality amongst those in her charge cannot be contemplated. She knows Enid is not bluffing. The scene ends extraordinarily with the warden eventually agreeing to transmit her order in Welsh to Enid through Amy acting as interpreter. This ploy satisfies Enid who then submits to her rescuers and quits her room. For once her (assumed) right to be addressed in her own language in her national university has been respected. However, Enid's triumph is short lived. For her insubordination she is suspended by the College and, unlike Amy, she ultimately gives up her studies.

What is interesting here is that Enid's right to be addressed in her own language ceased to be an actual right once she lost the power to enforce it. Once saved from herself the College was free to enforce the usual position on the rights of Welsh-language speakers. Without an authority sensitive to her claim her right lapsed. This argument appears to suggest that the only successful way for minorities to realise their rights is through the use of force. After all, Enid's right was actual only whilst she had the power to insist upon it. This is, of course, a conclusion that very many minority nationalists have drawn. Many Palestinians, Basques and Irish people in Northern Ireland, for instance, have come to this conclusion. The conclusion appears to be that there are no rights without political power. Following Machiavelli, they seem to have concluded there can in their circumstances be 'no good laws without good arms'.[3]

The situation is not, though, as bleak as this. That the power to enforce is essential to the existence of a right is but one side of the coin. Rights to be rights have also to enjoy the consent of the people amongst whom they are enforced. Rights which are enforced without the consent of the people: for instance, the supposed right of the members of a governing party to enjoy a higher standard of life than their fellow-citizens, cease to be rights and become instead privileges. A right which is seen as unfair by the majority of citizens is inherently contradictory. All rights have of necessity to be enjoyed equally by all full members of a community. The UN declaration is, for instance, universal and put forward as 'a common standard of achievement for all peoples and nations'. A football association which allowed some of its members the 'right' to count away goals as double and excluded most of its members from this privilege would soon cease to function as an association. To be excluded from rights enjoyed by others is to be excluded from proper membership of an association or society.

This demonstrates the reciprocity of rights. As T.H. Green stressed, to claim a right of any form is not only to demand recognition of certain advantages for myself but is also to recognise that all others who form the community must enjoy that right. 'No one therefore can have a right except (1) as a member of a society, and (2) of a society in which some common good is recognised by the members of society as their own ideal good, as that which should be for each of them'.[4] This is a point that is astutely brought out in Kant's account of property. Kant was conscious that most people regarded their property rights in the same light as they are depicted in the political theory of John Locke, namely, as natural rights growing out from the individual's labour and mastery of nature. We generally see our property as the reward for the work we or our ancestors have done. We insist on this right without regard to the circumstances of others and wherever we find ourselves. But for Kant this commonsense point of view overlooks the reciprocity of rights. We cannot always individually insist upon and enforce our rights. Since the crucial thing is that others respect our right to our property their consent must be won. To gain such consent Kant thinks we have to suppose ourselves enjoying with others an original community of ownership over the earth and all its fruits. It is only this moral notion of an original community that can justify our present ownership rights.[5] We own what we do because the community has consented to our being employed in a particular way in earning a living for ourselves and enjoying the produce of our labour. Our rewards are ours not only because they are the outcome of our hard work, but also because the community consents to such a reward. Without this moral, reciprocal foundation, property rights would cease to exist. No society could hope to enforce property rights without such consent. Thus, for instance, in a society where theft enjoyed an equal moral standing with supposed property rights, no amount of power would be sufficient to prevent the demise of property.

Thus for rights to exist a sense of community (embodied in a generally accepted notion of the reciprocity of rights) is as essential as the political authority to enforce those rights. This suggests that there may be two fronts on which minorities might tackle the problem of attempting to establish and enforce their rights. First, there is the direct political course through which they can seek to establish a measure of political authority for themselves and, second, there is the indirect moral course through which they can seek to establish the consent of the larger community for the recognition of the minority's right. The moral course represents an indirect battle of ideas which mirrors the direct political battle. But the situation of the minority communities we have been looking at would seem to rule out outright success on the political front. The communities are too small, too weak and too internally divided to force the larger nations to grant them independence. My suggestion is, however, that this should not lead to a sense of defeat and despair within the minority nation. They might draw strength from the reciprocity of rights. If members of the majority community enjoy the right to live their lives in the way they best see fit, and can insist on being addressed in their own language, and can ensure that their national institutions are respected and that their cultural heritage is preserved then it would be morally and politically inconsistent for them always to refuse such rights to members of the minority community within their midst. This would be true even though it might be difficult for them to have experienced the problems of such a situation themselves.

Political realists will dismiss such conclusions as wishful thinking. Relying on the good will of the members of the majority community cannot, in their view, in the end realise the goals of the minority. Members of the majority will always have more important priorities than the recognition and acceptance of the rights of minorities. Force, the political realist may say, is the only answer for the minority party. But the facts are not all on the realists' side. If the issue is left solely to force, the majority – unless it is hopelessly divided – will always win. Indeed the excessive and indiscriminate use of force may succeed only in putting off the truly sympathetic in the majority community. Political realism may therefore dictate the more cautious path of persuasion and non-violent forms of protest.

I want now to examine the possibility that this kind of 'moral' and 'cultural' pursuit of minority rights within the larger community may, in the end, run counter to the claims of nationalism. The nationalist tries to establish the minority's right through the creation of a separate nation. Despairing of achieving true recognition for his/her culture in the majority community he/she concludes that the only proper solution is for the minority to have its own state. This view might be reinforced by the conviction that there can be no true nation without its own state. Whether or not this is the case is not a question I intend to answer here. What can be said, though, is that the person who wishes to see minority rights established in this way gives greater priority to the achievement of a goal other than the goal of the realisation of minority rights. Independence is seen as a greater value than the goals for which independence is sought. This is a possible position but it is not the position of an individual who is wholly committed to the achievement of minority rights. An individual who pursues independence at all costs may well have no interest in persuading the majority of the legitimacy of the minority's claims. Indeed it is possible for the out-and-out nationalist to applaud the majority's steadfastness in the defence of its own national identity, and only wish that his own compatriots were as single-minded and intolerant.

Enid's insistence on her own cultural identity in Humphrey's novel need not therefore be the stance of an out-and-out nationalist. Humphreys might argue that there is even a strain of internationalism in the position Enid so epically defends. Enid is wholly conscious of the reciprocity of rights. She wants from her English warden the recognition and respect she is wholeheartedly prepared to give her. It is interesting that Enid leaves the threatened role not when her English warden has herself learnt to say in Welsh what Enid wants to hear, but when the warden secures the means of transferring the message from her own native language to Enid's native language. Enid's protest comes to an end not when her territorial rights within Wales are respected but rather when her rights as a human being in her own society are respected. All of Enid's demands might be met without the creation of a Welsh national state.

The implication of our analysis so far would seem to be that the position of minority nations is not a hopeless one. Although the pressures will all be on the members of the minority nation to conform to the customs and culture of the majority, if members of the majority enjoy rights and, in particular, cultural and linguistic rights, then there exists a toe-hold or purchase for the minority nation to claim rights on its own behalf. There is, of course, no absolute necessity for the majority to yield to the minority's demands. But, as we have seen, the existence of all rights depends on the prior creation of a community of interests. A minority permanently excluded from the enjoyment of equal rights will not only threaten this sense of community from without but, because for many purposes they have to be counted as part of the whole (e.g. taxation, work, social security and defence), also from within. By excluding the minority from the rights enjoyed by itself, the majority will be at odds with itself. This is an inherently unstable situation which, because the necessary element of consent does not exist, can only be resolved by force. Minority nations should therefore persist in their fight for the realisation of their rights as the members of a distinct cultural group because this will improve the lives of their members and, through the greater tolerance it enforces on the members of the majority and the peace this brings in its wake, it will improve their lives as well.

Notes

1. I. Kant, Reflections on the Philosophy of Right, *Gesammelte Schriften*, vol. xlx Akademie-Ausgabe, Berlin, p.504.

2. T. Paine, *Rights of Man*, London, 1969, p.44.
3. N. Machiavelli, *The Prince*, London, 1968, p.77.
4. T.H. Green, *Lectures on the Principles of Political Obligation*, Cambridge, 1986, p.25.
5. H. Williams, *Kant's Political Philosophy*, Oxford, 1983, ch.3.

Chapter twelve

Minority nationalism and the state: the European case

Michael Keating

The growth of minority nationalism – confounding the predictions of integration theory – has been one of the striking features of post-war western European politics. Perhaps equally striking from the perspective of the 1980s is the resilience of the state in the face of this challenge. Much of the work on the growth of minority nationalism has suffered from a number of defects. Often, it has been merely taxonomic, categorising 'types' of minority nationalism with too little consideration of the specific political, social and economic circumstances in which each had its birth. Other work has erred in the other direction, confining itself to individual case studies. In many cases work has been under-theorised and in others explanations have been over-determined. There has, in consequence, been little success in explaining why minority nationalism and political regionalism should advance at some times in some places and, in other circumstances, fall back. In the 1950s and early 1960s, the future, it seemed, was with the 'nation state'. In the 1970s, the trend to disintegration seemed inexorable. Where do we stand in the 1980s? These are large issues which force us to examine the phenomenon of minority nationalism in all its complexity, adopting a comparative approach yet recognising that each case must be located in its peculiar historical, cultural, economic and political circumstances. One view sometimes expressed in the literature is that nationalism and, perhaps, other territorial issues, are not negotiable as are run-of-the-mill matters of social and economic policy where compromise and splitting the difference are possible. My view is very different. Minority nationalism and regionalism are complex phenomena combining a diversity of elements most of which are quite amenable to negotiation and it is this very fact which largely accounts for the failure of minority nationalist movements in contemporary western Europe. It is for this reason, too, that my analysis does not start off with a rigorous definition of the terms 'nationalism' or indeed 'minority'. Such a predetermined framework would defeat the purposes of the analysis which are to explore the content and meaning of the political demands posed by territorial political movements and the extent to which they can in practice be accommodated within the existing state structures (including the political parties). The ultimate explicandum is the creation of territorial autonomist movements able to sustain a credible challenge to the contemporary nation state; but this process is complex, nowhere complete, and subject to territorial management techniques on the part of existing political and bureaucratic elites aimed at ensuring that the process is not completed. So while in some regions, movements have developed which have moved from the politics of territorial defence to pushing for autonomy and even separation, in others territorial politics are limited to lobbying activity.

It is to the ambitious task of analysing these processes that my present research is dedicated. The cases examined here are Britain, France and Spain, all of which have experienced peripheral pressure and attempted with varying degrees of success to establish devolved government in the post-war period. Within these states, I draw on the examples of Scotland, Wales, Brittany, Languedoc, Catalonia and the Basque country, though other cases are brought in from time to time. The elements of the analysis are the process of state building in each case; the persistence of regional diversity; the politics of territorial management; the politics of regional development; the mobilisation of the periphery and the success or otherwise of nationalist movements in sythesising cultural, economic and constitutional demands into a politically viable programme.

State building

The process of state building took rather different forms in our three cases, though there are important points in common. France is often taken as the prototype of the 'nation state'. Built from the top by the monarchy over a period of centuries, it retained a remarkable degree of cultural and institutional diversity up to the revolution.[1] It was the revolution which really established the notion of French nationality by giving it a popular and democratic base, while under the Third Republic the ideology of French nationalism was imparted to the masses through the spread of education and military service.[2] Minority cultures were suppressed in the name of progress and enlightenment and minority elites, to participate in the system, had to become culturally assimilated and support the centralised regime. As long as they played by these rules, however, there was scope for them to derive benefits for their localities; so there developed the *notable* system, a mode of territorial politics which, by allowing individualised and localised benefits to be derived from the regime, defused the potential for broader challenges. Democracy and progress were associated with the centralised 'Jacobin' state while the provinces were seen as hiding places for clerical, monarchical and reactionary forces. The French example is important not only in its own right but also as a model for developments in Spain (as well as Italy).

The United Kingdom was always a more informal union, proceeding over the centuries for military and economic reasons without acquiring a guiding ideology. It depended all along on collaborators in the periphery who were allowed to maintain certain privileges in return. This is most clearly seen in the 1707 Act of Union with Scotland, a rather half-baked attempt to enshrine this type of bargain in constitutional form. Scots law, the separate established Church, the burghs and other institutions were not to be assimilated – as a *quid pro quo* the Scots surrendered their Parliament, the only mechanism which could have ensured that the bargain was kept. On the other hand, there was a degree of cultural assimilation though the pressures were more diffuse than in France, not the driving force of a monolithic state but a series of pressures in the schools, universities, civil service and professions to conform to the more prestigious southern English cultural norms. Parliament itself came to be seen as the descendant of the English Parliament (it even celebrates anniversaries of its foundation in 1254 rather than 1707) and took on attributes such as parliamentary sovereignty unknown in Scotland. This principle of parliamentary sovereignty substituted for the popular sovereignty found in other systems and, as long as this principle was respected, a variety of systems of government could be developed on the periphery to manage the affairs of the respective territories. The pragmatic development of governing arrangements in the United Kingdom has led some observers to deny that there is such a thing as a state here or to claim complacently that the British genius for compromise has accommodated territorial and cultural differences without conflict. Yet, in the case of Ireland there is a historical failure of integration. Ireland threatened the stability of the parliamentary regime from the late nineteenth century and for much of the twentieth century was managed only by granting independence to the larger part and marginalising the smaller part from the affairs of the state by a combination of devolution and parliamentary under-representation.

Spain, for a large part of its history, was the most informal union of all. The catholic kings had created no more than a dynastic union, with the kingdoms of Castille and Aragon retaining their separate institutions, while within the Castillian territories there were special privileges for Navarre and the Basque provinces and, within the Crown of Aragon, separate parliamentary institutions for Aragon, Catalonia, Valencia and Mallorca. Differing fiscal regimes in the various territories accentuated economic disparities. It was the Bourbon victory in the War of the Spanish Succession which led to the first attempt at a truly unitary state on the model of the French monarchy after 1714.[3] During the nineteenth century, liberal-monarchist governments pursued the same line as their French and Italian counterparts, promoting the Castilian language, suppressing or subordinating local institutions and denying the possibility of intermediary institutions between the sovereign state and the individual citizen. As in France and Italy, the reality was that the localities were managed by caciques, extracting individualised favours in return for supporting the parliamentary majority of the moment.[4] Meanwhile, support for a federalised system remained among the reactionary right of the Carlist movement and the radical liberals on the left, gaining brief recognition in the First Republic of 1869–75.

The survival of identity

Assimilationist policies in the four states had varied degrees of success by the late nineteenth century. Minority languages survived in Wales, the Scottish islands, the west of Ireland, Catalonia, the Basque country, Brittany while in Occitanie and lowland Scotland they had been driven down to the status of patois and widely regarded as no more than dialect or 'incorrect' forms of the state language. A substantial degree of institutional uniformity prevailed in each state, with no parliamentary institutions below the state level and customary and legal differences under pressure where they survived, as in Scotland and Catalonia. Yet this period saw a marked revival of minority nationalism in response to the expanded scope of the modern state. In all cases, the movements had a cultural element, an economic element and a political/constitutional element, though these were integrated with varying degrees of success.

In France, cultural regionalism was associated with conservative forces opposed to the centralising tendencies of the 'godless' Third Republic. In Occitanie, the Provencal poet Mistral and his colleagues in the Felibrige, an organisation dedicated to reviving the culture and language of the south, emphasised romantic, traditionalist and anti-modernist themes and identified politically with the monarchists and the right. There was a smaller and weaker tendency to the left, the Felibrige Rouge but by and large the regionalists avoided identification with popular struggles such as those of the peasant wine producers which culminated in the revolt of 1907.[5] So the identification of the clerical right with regionalism and the republican left with centralism was merely reinforced. In Brittany, too, regionalism and the Breton language were seen as a defence for the Church against the godless state but widely regarded in radical circles as a means of keeping the masses in ignorance. So in nineteenth-century France, regionalist movements failed to synthesise their demands into a political programme or movement challenging the Jacobin, French-nationalist view of the state which itself was pushed even more strongly after 1870. The practical outcome of the regionalist revival was negligible, with the traditional pattern of territorial representation through the unitary state remaining in place.

In Ireland, the Gaelic revival had limited success on the linguistic front but did provide an intellectual underpinning for the nationalist movement which was fuelled by economic grievances, notably over the land question. The movement was essentially conservative, catholic and rural, albeit with a weaker liberal-progressive element, but the political conditions were quite different. There was no prospect of Irish catholic interests gaining a preponderant influence in the UK state, nor, with the development of two-party politics in Britain, could the Irish hope to extract favours for coalition support, so the only viable strategy was Home Rule. In Scotland and Wales, nationalism similarly drew upon both cultural and economic concerns, though in these cases the political association was with the left. In Scotland, the prospect of incorporation into the English education system by the 1870 Act provoked an outcry which gave Scotland its own Act, its own education department and, from 1885, the Scottish Office. Radical Liberals were not satisfied with this and called for Home Rule to effect Church disestablishment, temperance legislation and land reform. Similarly, in Wales, early nationalist agitation was associated with the threat to Welsh culture as represented by the language, with the struggle against control of the schools by the Anglican Church and for the disestablishment of the Church itself and with a general resentment at the social and economic dominance of the Anglicised elite. In both Scotland and Wales, nationalist feeling was carried over from radical Liberalism to the Labour Party but in the event neither Liberals nor Labour was prepared to give Home Rule priority.[6] Rather, it had to be subordinated to the parties' wider UK concerns and, given the choice, generations of Scottish and Welsh leaders opted for the chance to rise in UK politics rather than leading Home Rule movements in their own countries. In any case, the changing agenda of politics soon pushed the issues fuelling the Home Rule agitation aside, while the economic dependence of the periphery discouraged autonomist aspirations.

In Spain, the late nineteenth century saw the rise of nationalist movements in Catalonia and the Basque country, again inspired by cultural as well as economic concerns. Again, there are reactionary and progressive elements, notably in the Catalan case.[7] There was a romantic Catalan nationalism stemming from the cultural Renaixenca and linked to the Felibrige in southern France. There was, especially in the late nineteenth century, a reactionary-clerical nationalism opposed to the secularising state and looking back to the order hierarchy of the middle ages based on family, language and religion. There was also a sense of economic grievance among the middle classes who saw Catalonia, with its advanced industry, as subsidising the rest of Spain. These elements coalesced in the Lliga Regionalista of Prat dela Riba which from 1901 to 1923 was the dominant element in Catalan politics. Yet the Lliga was riddled with contradictions. The alliance between the rural clerical-reactionary elements and the urban bourgoisie was a little unnatural and the Lliga's attitude towards the Spanish state was ambiguous. On the one hand, there was resentment at prosperous, industrialised Catalonia having to subsidise the rest of Spain. On the other, there was the knowledge that, in international terms, Catalan industry was not competitive and depended on its privileged access to the protected Spanish market. So, while playing for a limited range of Home Rule, the Lliga set itself the aim of transforming and modernising the Spanish state itself, a project which, given the interests represented in the state, proved impossible. There was a left-wing Catalan nationalism, alto-gether weaker, while the labour movement was dominated by anarcho-syndicalism which disdained all forms of political activity and the classic left-Jacobin line was pushed in the form of Lerrouxisme. After the Lliga had discredited itself by its attitude to the dictatorship of Primo de Rivera[8] the leadership of the Catalan movement was taken by the Esquerra Republicana de Catalunya, a left-of-centre movement with support among the lower middle classes. It was the turbulent circum-stances of the 1930s which were to push the left into adopting nationalist positions, more from tactical necessity than nationalist conviction.

In the Basque country, early nationalism was also traditionalist, catholic and conservative where not reactionary. There was a limited cultural revival in the late nineteenth century but not on the same scale as in Catalonia and mainly in the Castillian language. In 1894 was formed the Partido Nacionalist Vasco with most support in the rural areas and the more traditional sectors of the community. The Spanish left as a whole, as it developed, tended to Jacobin centralisation and under the Second Republic only grudgingly conceded rights of autonomy to Catalonia, Galicia and the Basque country.

The phase of minority nationalism which we have been considering lasted from the late nineteenth century until the aftermath of the First World War, except in the case of Spain where it was to be an important element in the turbulent politics and civil war of the 1930s. It was, as we have seen, a diverse phenomenon, associated in different countries with differing social and economic ideologies and interests. There are, on the other hand, common elements. Nationalism was in this phase essentially defensive, concerned with the protection of existing interests against the expansion of the modern state and changing social and economic conditions. In some cases, this linked it with political conservatism or even reaction, and with traditionalist catholicism threatened by the modern secular state. In other cases, as in Scotland and Wales, it took on a more progressive aspect, linked with popular struggles but associated with the political agenda of the late nineteenth century rather than the issues which were to be of importance in the twentieth. The attitude of the left and the working-class movement tended to indifference or hostility accentuated by the economic dependence of many regions and, after the early 1920s, except in the case of Spain where the issue was inextricably entwined with wider political concerns, the question faded in importance. These points are important for it has often been said that the nineteenth century was the age of nationalism, a phenomenon which was associated with capitalist development, economic progress and social change; but this was the nationalism of the big states, nationalism which denied and opposed that of the minority nationalities.

The politics of territorial management

For some years after the Second World War, it was widely believed that, in the states we are considering, regionalism and minority nationalism were fading, that regional identity itself was weakening and confined to small pockets while economic and cultural homogenisation were undermining the basis for territorial politics. In fact, there was a complex of political forces at work, serving to manage territorial politics with greater or lesser degrees of success.

In France, the role of the notables as territorial managers has been analysed many times, notably by Gremion[9], who also makes the important point that twentieth-century notables are not the traditional social and economic elites of the nineteenth century but are essentially political entrepreneurs, playing on the machinery of the state to obtain favours. In Languedoc, for example, their main concern was to maintain state support for viticulture in the face of recurrent crises of disease and overproduction. While the notable, of right or left, will declaim against centralisation and demand greater autonomy, in reality his relationship with the state is symbiotic. It is the centralised system of government which provides the basis for his power and in practice he will shy away from the direct responsibility which goes with genuine devolution. Nor were any of the political parties in the post-war era interested in decentralisation. The clauses in the 1946 Constitution giving executive power to the presidents of the conseils généraux remained a dead letter for fear of Communist influence while the Socialists of the SFIO (Section Française de l'Internationale Ouvrière) preached a rhetorical Jacobinism while in practice becoming increasingly dependent on their network of notables.

In Britain, too, the post-war years were ones of centralisation, with Northern Ireland largely ignored by the centre and Scotland and Wales managed through systems of administrative decentralisation. The nationalisation programme of the Attlee government was highly centralist and the Labour Party as a whole was committed to centralised economic planning, if decidedly ambiguous about just what this meant. The Conservatives briefly tried to exploit Labour's centralism before 1951 but had no real interest in the issue and on their return to government showed no great interest in territorial government. In Scotland and, to some extent, Wales, a conscious trade-off was made by politicians between local autonomy and the need to support a centralised system of government as the only means of channeling resources to the poorer parts of Britain. The articulation of this choice, which might otherwise have remained implicit, was necessary because of competing visions both from the nationalist parties and the Labour Party's own Home Rule past. The outcome was a system in which economic policy was centralised but with privileged access by Scottish (and later Welsh) interests to central decision-making through guaranteed cabinet seats, with their corresponding bureaucratic links, and parliamentary over-representation. A limited amount of informal devolution was allowed on social and environmental policies through the Scottish and Welsh Secretaries of State, classic examples of 'territorial managers'. Scottish MPs, too, fell into this mode of territorial politics, most of them concentrating on purely Scottish matters and venturing into the UK arena only where matters of economic interest to Scotland were concerned.[10] It is only at first sight paradoxical that it was these 'Scottish-orientated' MPs who were most hostile to devolution, while the 'UK-oriented' minority tended to be more open to the idea; for, with an elected Scottish Assembly, it was the 'Scottish-oriented' members who would find their role as territorial representatives under challenge. This role sometimes produced hilarious results as on the occasion when an anti-devolution Conservative helped filibuster a proposal to change the Scottish divorce law, having himself recently obtained a divorce under the more liberal English legislation by virtue of his London domicile or the equally anti-devolution Labour member who insisted that only Scottish members should be allowed to vote on the issue.

In Spain under Franco, all expressions of regionalism were brutally suppressed, the leaders of Basque and Catalan nationalism executed or driven into exile. Initially, there were fines for anyone overheard speaking Basque or Catalan and, while this type of vigilance was relaxed in the 1950s, education, public administration and business were conducted exclusively in Castillian. The result was to drive into the opposition to the regime not only the left but large sections of the catholic and conservative population in Catalonia and the Basque country and to create a firm association between democracy and the return of autonomous self-government. The very lack of effective territorial representation drove the democratic opposition into support for Home Rule and prevented the state from managing territorial relationships through political measures. The fact that all manifestations of regional identity were illegal drove elements of regional movements together in common interest where, in our other cases, they would have been divided.

The politics of regional development

The growth years of the 1950s and 1960s saw governments in all three countries converted to economic planning and the promotion of industrial development. This soon took on a territorial dimension, as governments saw the need to diversify regional economies, to bring into use unemployed resources in the periphery and promote balanced national development, avoiding overheating in the boom areas as well as depression in the declining ones. There were common elements in all three cases – the development of infrastructure, investment grants, large-scale projects as the focus of 'growth poles'. While the political circumstances differed from one state to another, in all cases regional policies were centralised, bypassing existing territorial representatives and destabilising the existing networks. There were, in any case, major social and economic changes afoot in several of our peripheries, with the emergence in some regions of what the French call *forces vives* (such as those forming the CELIB (Committee for the Study and Liaison of Breton Interests) in Brittany or the founders of the Banca Catalana in Catalonia), pressing for modernisation and development policies under regional control. In other cases, such as Languedoc, Scotland, Wales and Northern Ireland development remained in the hands of the state or outside capital, reinforcing political as well as economic dependence. In all the cases, the state was forced to establish machinery for planning and delivering regional development policies but in all cases attempted to keep control of the development process in its own hands, reducing regional economic and political actors to a subordinate role.

In France, large-scale regional development policies delivered through the DATAR (Delegation for Regional Development and Planning) and centralised regional missions outflanked the notables who had no say in their elaboration or the distribution of resources. Great reliance was placed on large-scale works which did not have to be inserted into delicate existing economic networks but could spark off their own complementary industries (the growth pole theory). This strategy suited the Gaullist regime well, freeing it from dependence on the territorial network (which was, however, to have its revenge in 1969). It also suited the notables, able to observe the 'manna' showered down upon them without any effort on their own part, until it became apparent that not only was the strategy bypassing their roles as channels to the centre but the economic change resulting was undermining their political base. In the case of Languedoc, for example, economic diversification meant the end of the viticultural monopoly and of the notables' role in defending it. The subordination of the *forces vives* was achieved through the CODER established in 1964 as nominated, advisory bodies subordinate to the regional prefect. De Gaulle's defeat in 1969 on a measure to reform regional administration and the Senate to the disadvantage of the notables was followed by Pompidou's legislation of 1972 establishing weak regional councils, indirectly elected and including all the existing territorial representatives but with little role in the process of regional economic development. Because of the fear of encouraging autonomist sentiment in the regions, their boundaries, following those of the CODER (Committees of Regional Economic Development), were artificially constructed to cut across traditional provinces and regions; nor did they always correspond to contemporary social and economic geography. It was another way of bypassing the existing pattern of representation.[11] Yet the state's tactical victory may have meant a strategic defeat, for by promoting the ideology of regional development and encouraging people to articulate their demands in regional terms, it put the issue of control of regional development on the agenda, as did the efforts of more enterprising councils, within the tight limits of their resources.

In Britain, there was a similar process, of promoting regional development and planning but keeping it under central control. Regional industrial policies were the exclusive affair of central government, though subject to intensive lobbying through political and bureaucratic channels. The Labour government's Regional (and Scottish and Welsh) Economic Planning Councils and Boards of 1964 were very similar to the French arrangements, as an attempt to establish a network of reliable collaborators in the regions, with nominated representation from local government and industry on the councils, while the boards consisted of central civil servants. There was intense ambiguity about whether they were there to channel regional demands to the centre or central policies to the regions. Some ministers in their sponsoring department, the DEA (Department of Economic Affairs), saw them as regional governments in embryo but for most departments they were clearly a subordinate, if not irrelevant, part of the planning machinery; while local authorities, with the support of the Ministry of Housing and Local Government, were equally keen to put them in their place[12], though without themselves aspiring to a role in the economic and regional planning process. This powerlessness, combined with the failure of the National Plan, produced intense disillusion and many Council members resigned after a short time, though the Councils themselves lingered on until their euthanasia at the hands of Sir Keith Joseph in 1979.[13] Local government reform betrayed a similar ambiguity. Central government clearly saw the need to modernise the system of local administration to cope with the demands of economic and physical development but at the same time had no intention of producing genuinely autonomous local or regional authorities with a capacity to challenge central economic and social management. Again, the attempt to bring into being reliable and capable collaborators on the periphery, replacing the old local elites, castigated as of 'poor calibre', failed, leading eventually to the present crisis in central-local relations. As for the delicate autonomy-access trade-off which characterised Scottish management, this was vulnerable to changes in economic circumstances which could alter the balance. With the existing territorial representatives increasingly justifying both their value and their opposition to Home Rule in terms of their ability to bring back the pork barrel, they were open to outflanking by any competing political grouping which could claim plausibly the ability to deliver both autonomy and economic advantage. This was the real significance of North Sea oil, not that it converted a generation of Scots from staunch unionists to ardent nationalists at the sight of an extra bauble but that it altered the terms of the political bargain by which Scotland had been governed, allowing a widespread aspiration to Home Rule (revealed in every opinion poll since the 1930s) to be expressed.[14]

Even in Franco's Spain the state felt the need in the 1960s to take in hand economic planning and regional development. If the British and French states were suspicious and fearful of regionalism, the Franco regime was quite paranoid. Early Francoist development plans were on a grandiose scale and involved large-scale hydraulic engineering works planned by engineers with little consideration of the social and economic costs and benefits. This was a pre-Francoist tradition in Spain[15] but suited the regime well, freeing it from the need to engage in any detailed regional planning or dialogue with local representatives. In the 1950s a plan was produced for the Badajoz area but its earlier promises of social and economic reform were dropped for fear of eroding the regime's powerful supporters and only the technical, engineering works completed. The same fate overtook a later plan for Ja'n. After a highly critical report from the World Bank, a National Plan was produced in 1964, promising action to correct the economic inequalities among the regions of the country[16], but the ensuing programme did not recognise the concept of regions, trying to tie its interventions to smaller units. The Second Plan of 1968 recognised that the provinces might be too small for effective planning but did not dare take this logic further; the same was true of the Third Plan of 1972. The prime role in local implementation was given to municipalities and provincial councils linked to the Francoist Movimiento and, though there were later some power struggles with the central technocrats of the Comisaria del Plan, there was a complete exclusion of locally-based economic actors. This had different implications in different regions.

In all three states then, there was a phase of centrally-directed regional policy. In all cases, a central element of this was the creation of large, one-off industrial developments, justified in terms of the 'growth-pole' theory but having the political advantage of being easily managed, requiring minimum co-operation from local elites and little attention to the intricacies of local and regional economies. As regional policies became more elaborate, an increasing need for coherent planning was accepted to manage the business of economic transition and modernisation. This in turn required local partners but, in the search for these, all the states sought to avoid the creation of strong regional governments which could challenge the centre's view of priorities or even act as equal partners in framing development strategies. This political difficulty was exacerbated in the 1970s with the world economic crisis, hitting vulnerable peripheral economies particularly hard, and the Europeanisation and internationalisation of the economy, which increased competition and reduced the capacity of national governments to engage in diversionary regional policies. Many of the large one-off developments were revealed to be 'cathedrals in the desert', failing, for want of detailed regional planning and analysis, to produce the spin-offs which had been assumed to follow more or less automatically. In Scotland, nearly all the large manufacturing plants brought in by this method in the 1960s had closed by the mid-1980s. An example common to all three countries is the steel industry, used in the 1960s as an instrument of regional industrial policy which would enable the regions to contribute to national modernisation, a classic case of the identity between the needs of national and regional development assumed at the time.

The political crisis

The societies into which these centrally-directed regional policy initiatives were inserted differed considerably in political traditions and in the extent to which there was an organised civil society and economic elite. In all cases, there had been a centralisation of economic, industrial and financial decision-making, but the process was more complete in some cases than others while in some regions there had been a reaction and the emergence of new economic actors. In southern Spain and Languedoc, there was a lack of native entrepreneurship and an increasing dependence on the state as an agent of economic development. The same is largely true of Scotland and Wales, despite efforts by

185

bodies like the Scottish Council (Development and Industry) and worries on the part of the Conservative Party that its historically strong position in Scotland was being undermined. On the other hand, in Brittany and Catalonia, there emerged new local economic forces, committed to a more autonomous and more balanced mode of development. On the cultural front, too, there was a resilience of local traditions in some areas and a revival in others. Movements for language revival developed in the 1960s and 1970s in Catalonia, the Basque country, Wales, Brittany and Languedoc, while folk music, revived and politicised, broke out of the quaint 'folklore' status to which it had been reduced in much of western Europe. Culture is an important part of my general argument but beyond the limited scope of this paper. Suffice it to say here that, as well as a mobilising force, it can be a divisive one in places like Wales and Brittany, reducing the appeal of nationalist movements. Other aspects of civil society had been preserved and developed to a greater or lesser extent in various territories. In Scotland, the law and education systems had preserved their identities and helped to frame a continued Scottish identity but, enjoying a degree of autonomy not only from the wider UK system but also, due to the arrangements for handling Scottish government, from other elements of Scottish society, they were not at the forefront of demands for Home Rule. In Brittany, the strong catholic culture provided a counterpoint to the state while in Catalonia a network of Catalan groups developed in all areas which could be presented as 'non-political' and therefore legal – sport, culture, etc.

In some regions, the crisis of economic transformation of the 1960s and 1970s and of recession of the 1970s and 1980s coincided with a realignment of the party system at the national level. In Britain, the crisis of the two-party system from the late 1960s created a political opening as did the more profound changes in the French party system – the expansion of Gaullist influence from 1962 to 1974, the collapse of the Socialist SFIO, the decline of the Communists and the squeezing of the political centre. In Spain, the break in the party system was complete, with new political forces seeking to establish their positions in clandestinity from the late 1960s in anticipation of the demise of Francoism.

We have, then, in different societies, a crisis of economic transformation and a crisis of political representation caused by the breakup of old party systems and the inability of the existing territorial representatives to manage the process of social and economic change or to deliver the goods to their constituents. This provided the basis for territorial political movements, exploiting disillusion with the central state and advocating a more autonomous mode of development. The dynamics of the process by which regional interests coalesce behind programmes for regional autonomy and progress to mature 'nationalism' will be one of the concerns of my wider work. Here I must limit myself to pointing out some of the difficulties in the way of such mobilisation. Regionalist and minority nationalist movements, of course, have taken a wide variety of forms in differing national contexts but there are common themes which are worth exploring. One is the tension between defence of the traditional economic and social structures and modernisation. Some regionalist movements, for example the CELIB in Brittany and the Catalan movement led by Jordi Pujol, have been modernising, seeking a transformation of the region guided by local interests in place of the destabilising interventions of the central state. On the other hand, much of the support for regional movements comes from sectors in irreversible decline or threatened by state modernisation policies or the opening of the international market, such as viticulture in Languedoc. The conflict between defence of the old and transformation to the new is not an irresolvable contradiction but a challenge to political skills and one with which regionalist movements have coped with varying degrees of success. In the mobilising phase, they can accommodate both types of complaint, blaming the central state for all their ills but when it comes to framing programmes the problem becomes acute.

A well-documented problem is that of economically weak peripheral regions dependent on state transfers. Regional discontent may be directed at the inadequacy of these transfers, a complaint which implicitly calls for stronger central government regional policies rather than autonomy. This point is insistently and effectively made by opponents of separatism in Scotland and Wales. Of course, the validity of this argument depends on the potential of the regional economy and whether a more autonomous development strategy would be viable. In Scotland, nationalists have always claimed that it would and, with North Sea oil their case was strengthened, but their heterogeneous make-up has prevented them ever developing a coherent economic policy (beyond the claim that oil would allow them to do everything) and the obvious weakness of Scottish business and industrial leadership and consequent dependence on the state has undermined their credibility. In Catalonia, by contrast, autonomy would seem to have obvious economic advantages, given the net outflows in inter-regional transfers, but this is misleading. Catalonia has historically depended on the protected Spanish market for outlets for its products so, while autonomy has great attractions, there has never been much support for separatism.

We come here to the difficult problem for regionalist movements of constitutional objectives. At one extreme there are mere territorial lobbies, seeking to persuade the state to be more generous in transfers and regional policy measures. This is found in all states but particularly in Britain where much of territorial politics is limited to this. In some cases, demands have gone beyond this to pressing for more coherent regional planning, associating with it local and regional actors, without making explicit the political implications or even trying to avoid becoming entangled in 'politics', seen as a diversion from the needs of economic development. This attitude characterises at least the early phase of the CELIB as well as some of the proposals in Francoist Spain.[17] There is a similar tradition in Scotland going back to the 1930s and reinforced under Secretary of State Tom Johnston during the war, advocating a political consensus planning to modernise the Scottish economy. Of course, this is unrealistic, since the process of modernisation necessarily involves political choices and must confront varying interests in the regional population. So we come to the question of regional autonomy and here too there is a variety of positions, from limited self-government to separatism. Both pose severe problems of definition and practice. The regional autonomy with which all three states have experimented with greater or lesser success is an entirely new constitutional creature, if we leave aside federal systems which have quite different characteristics. Dividing powers in social and environmental policy matters is relatively unproblematic – not that states are always keen to surrender these powers. Dividing economic responsibilities, however, is extremely difficult, given the nationalisation and internationalisation of the economy and the needs of inter-regional balance. So movements for regional autonomy have found difficulty in presenting a totally convincing formula and have frequently merely asserted the need for regional self-government and national solidarity equally loudly.

Nor does separatism provide an easy answer. Some regionalist movements are overtly separatist, aiming to create a new state. The Scottish National Party is of this type, though like nearly all nationalist movements they deplore the use of the word 'separatist'. This seems to be related to a conviction that, once independence is achieved, they will not be responsible for putting up barriers with the rest of the world. There will, we are assured, be no customs posts at Gretna. Yet the ability to impose barriers to the movement of people, goods and capital has hitherto been one of the marks of the nation state and an indispensable set of tools for independent economic management. The confusion in SNP thinking over what would happen to a Scottish exchange rate if it became a petro-currency and the effects on Scottish industry is typical of the failure to think the issue through. Most peripheral nationalist movements, however, have not aimed at the creation of a new nation state on the lines of the old one but at the transformation of the new state system, a breaking down of international barriers. This is a strong theme in the Occitan movement, in Wales and to some degree in Catalonia which sees itself as more 'European' than the rest of Spain. So we have an idealistic internationalist nationalism which is able to portray the big states of Europee as parochial and inward-looking and seize back the universalistic values previously appropriated by the larger units. Of course, this is an immensely difficult strategy to pursue. Not only are the large European states remarkably resilient in the face of both regionalist and European challenges but much of the support base for regionalism is derived from the very sectors which find themselves under challenge from international competition and the opening of the market. Here again there is the dilemma between going for a protectionist, autarkic strategy or supporting a modernisation of the region which would permit its insertion into the competitive world economy but at a heavy political cost to any government which had to achieve it. This was a crucial factor in the breakup of the Occitan regionalist alliance, with a populist wing insisting on protection of the viticultural interest and opposing Spanish entry into the European Community and an internationalist wing wishing to create a united Europe and seeing the entry of Spain into the EC as positive, allowing them to make common cause with the Catalans in undermining both French and Spanish states.

Linking cultural to economic concerns is by no means impossible but it can create difficulties for regional and nationalist movements. In many cases, local languages – Breton, Welsh, Occitan, Basque – are spoken only by minorities in their respective regions and, while there have been revival efforts, these often appear irrelevant to the main economic struggles. Indeed, language revivals are often the affair of the professional middle classes rather than the traditional rural sectors or the industrial working class, who find themselves in the midst of regional economic conflicts. So a stress on language and cultural affairs may appear elitist and an obstacle to large-scale mobilisation.

Finally, there is the problem of the relationship of regionalist movements to class issues and ideological matters on the left–right spectrum. Ideally, the nationalist wants to unite the population against the state in which they find themselves; but in practice nationalist and regionalist movements must address the political, social and economic divisions within their societies. One, too glib, answer from the nationalist, is that divisive issues must be postponed until after independence when it will be possible to form left wing, right wing, centrist or any other form of party. This does not address the immediate question and for the regionalist who is not aiming at complete separation but the mobilisation of the population on a territorial basis it does not provide an answer at all since regional mobilisation will presumably be a continuing necessity in whatever new constitutional order he wishes to create. Earlier, it was noted that nineteenth-century political nationalism tended politically to the right, though with a radical wing. In the last two decades, it has tended to the left, though with conservative examples still existing. As the territorial organisation of government is not something inherently related to the left–right divide, this is the result of circumstances in the societies concerned, as we note below.

We have so far been considering regionalism and minority nationalism in the abstract, but in practice they must take the form of concrete social and political movements operating in conditions of political competition. The articulation of regionalism and nationalism in the form of political movements varies greatly. In some cases, such as Scotland and Wales in the early twentieth century, we are talking of movements operating within the mainstream political parties. In other cases, we are talking of separate political parties. Given the conflicts and dilemmas outlined above, it is not surprising that nationalist and regionalist parties show a tendency to fragmentation rivalling that of the extreme left. In some circumstances, co-operation among competing nationalist/regionalist tendencies may be easier. For example, in Francoist Catalonia, with all normal political activity driven underground, there was some sense of common purpose in the need to replace the dictatorship and in the need to re-establish Catalan self-government as part of democratisation; but even here there were serious left–right divisions and divisions over the meaning and degree of Catalan self-government which were to emerge after 1975.

What all this amounts to is that regionalists and minority nationalists in the three states in question have failed to develop a convincing alternative paradigm to the contemporary nation state. This, together with the tendency to fragmentation and the difficulty of breaking into existing party systems even at times of political turbulence, has made it possible for the nationalist/regionalist perspective to be unpicked, with mainstream parties taking on board elements of their demands. This has been achieved largely through the parties of the left taking up the themes of regionalism and decentralisation. In France, the new Socialist Party of the early 1970s was less tied to the old notables who had dominated the SFIO and had received an influx of members raised in the regionalist struggles of the time and schooled in the autogestion ideas of the 1968 generation. In local election victories a new generation of councillors emerged committed to decentralisation while the activities of the Gaullist state and the social and economic failures of centralised regional policies convinced many in the party that the central state was not inevitably an instrument of good purpose. During the long right-wing dominance of the Fifth Republic, territorial government became a substitute for alternation at the centre, with Socialist local governments seeking to make the most of their powers and convincing themselves in the process of the merits of decentralisation. In Britain, the Labour Party retained its traditional centralist approach until 1974 when electoral competition forced it into conceding Scottish and Welsh devolution. This was not quite as cynical a policy reversal as it has often been portrayed since large elements in the party had been edging slowly in this direction for some time[18], but the timing of the change owed everything to expediency. The devolution proposals as they emerged represented more an attempt to retain the old system of territorial government than to break it, since the assemblies were to be confined to social and environmental matters under central supervision while all taxation, economic and industrial matters would remain with the centre where Scotland and Wales would continue to have their Secretaries of State and parliamentary over-representation. In time, though, Labour came to convince itself of the merits of its own policy, at least for Scotland, particularly after the 1979 election defeat and the repeal of the Scotland Act. Since 1979 there have also been very significant developments at local level, with a new generation of council leaders committed to decentralisation and a more expansive view of the role of local government, particularly in the economic sphere, and serious consideration being given to regionalism and regional government in England. During the 1979–83 Parliament, local government leaders gained additional status from their position in the front line of opposition to the Thatcher government, while the parliamentary party and NEC were divided and ineffectual. In Spain, too, the left came to adopt decentralisation and the rights of self-determination of the 'nationalities' (Catalans, Galicians and Basques), with both the Socialists and the Communists committed to a federal republic by the early 1970s. This was largely a reaction to the centralisation of Franco, together with the need to compete with nationalist forces in Catalonia and the Basque country.

There have been big changes on the left and to a striking degree they have succeeded in defusing the potential of regionalist and nationalist movements. This is clearly the case in Brittany and Languedoc, where explicit choices were made by nationalist groups to co-operate with the Socialist Party in the hope of achieving at least some of their objectives. In Britain, Labour's adoption of a policy of Scottish devolution appeared to stem the advance of the SNP, though in Wales nationalism was halted by the cultural division of the country and the policy may have damaged Labour. In Spain, the acceptance of the PSOE (Spanish Socialist Workers' Party) of regional government has been a political necessity to sustain its own position, though it has certainly not succeeded in stemming nationalist advances in Catalonia and the Basque country.

Yet, despite these changes, the left in all three countries retains strong centralist elements. In opposition, it is relatively easy to take on board decentralist demands but, on the approach to government, these have to confront the centralist bent of economic thinking on the European left and the reluctance to allow powers to remain in the hands of their political opponents. In France, the Socialists' programme was a compromise between the new regionalists, the remaining Jacobins and the notables. In government, it was the municipalities and, above all, the departments, which gained in power while the regions had to wait five years for direct elections and the status of *collectivités territoriales* that went with it.[19] Nor did a redrawing of regional boundaries to correspond with regional sentiment and functional needs prove possible, while there has been no effective regionalisation of economic powers. In Britain, the Labour Party is torn between its commitment to Scottish devolution and a regional solution for England, and the continued centralist bias of its economic strategy. It is also unprepared for the idea that decentralisation could leave large areas of England under permanent Conservative control.[20] In Spain, the limited commitment of the left to regional autonomy became apparent during the transition to democracy[21]; while in 1982 the Socialists supported the LOAPA, an attempt to limit the extent of regional autonomy.

It may in fact be the very ambiguity of the left's commitment to regionalism which is the secret of its success in managing the issue, for in the three states in question, the left parties are able to offer the promise of regional autonomy together with the assurance of centralised economic policies to look after the interests of needy regions. In practical terms, this means devolving social and environmental policies while retaining economy policy at the centre. Centralised economic management is further defended in terms of the need to ensure international competitiveness. The formula does not address the problem raised in the first part of the paper, of the inability of regions to master the process of their own social and economic development but might at least help to make these processes more manageable politically by controlling their social and environmental effects. In a period of recession, however, none of this is particularly relevant since energies are focused on essentially defensive battles to retain economic activities under threat (including some of the 'cathedrals in the desert'). In the longer run, though, the left has a lot of thinking to do on the relationship of centralised and decentralised economic power.

The problems arise not just at the regional level but at the national level too. I have criticised the regionalist and nationalist movements for their failure to develop an alternative model to the traditional 'nation state'. Yet this form too is under threat and with it many of the assumptions of the left about economic and territorial management. In a relatively closed economy, with strong instruments of policy at the national level, it was possible to defend the strong state as an instrument of economic management. It was also possible to engage in strong centralised regional policies, diverting industrial investment and subsidising investment in favoured regions. Now the internationalisation of the economy, the practical impossibility of exchange controls, the difficulties of unilateral reflation and the growth of multinational firms have all greatly restricted the capacity of states to manage their economies in ways which the left has traditionally favoured. At the same time, the mobility of capital and the need to minimise costs to meet international competition have reduced the scope for diversionary regional policies. Economic policy must now be conducted in a framework quite different from that of the past and in which national governments have lost their dominant position. Increasingly it will become a question of seeking to master the effect of causes beyond national control, the very problem faced by regional interests in the past. In these circumstances, a regional approach to managing change may appear as realistic as a national one. It is too early to say. The left may deepen its regional commitment and build up its support; or it may swing back to support for state-level solutions and open the way to a new wave of regionalist/nationalist movements.

Notes

1. F. Braudel, *L'Identité de la France*, Paris, 1986.
2. B. Weber, *Peasants into Frenchmen. The Modernisation of Rural France 1870–1914*, London, 1977.
3. V. Vasquez de Prada, 'La Epoca Moderna : Los Siglos XVI a XIX' in R. Acosta Espana (ed.), *La Espana de las Autonomias*, Madrid, 1981.
4. I. Gortazar 'La Cuestion regional en Espana, 1808–1939', in R. Acosta Espana, op. cit.
5. G. Cholvy, *Histoire du Languedoc de 1900 à Nos Jours*, Toulouse, 1980.
6. M. Keating and D. Bleiman, *Labour and Scottish Nationalism*, London, 1979.
7. B. Oltra, F. Mercade and F. Hernandez, *La Ideologia Nacional Catalona*, Barcelona, 1981.
8. G. Gispert and J. Prato, *Espana : un estado plurinacional*, Barcelona, 1978.
9. P. Grémion, *Le Pouvoir Periphique*, Paris, 1976.
10. M. Keating, 'The Role of the Scottish MP', Ph.D. Thesis, CNAA, 1975.
11. P. Grémion, op. cit.
12. P. Lindley, 'The Framework of Regional Planning, 1964–80' in B. Hogwood and M. Keating (eds.), *Regional Government in England*, Oxford, 1982.
13. M. Keating, 'Whatever Happened to Regional Government', *Local Government Studies*, Vol.11, no.6, 1985.
14. V. Miller, *The End of British Politics?* Oxford, 1981.
15. M. Gonzalez, 'El Desarrollo Regional Frustrado Durante Treinte Anos de Dirigismo 1928–58' in R. Acosta Espana (ed.), op.cit.

16. J. Roura, 'La Politica Regional en Los Planes de desarrollo, 1944–75', in R. Acosta Espana, op. cit.
17. A. Barbancho, *Disparidades Regionales Y Ordenacion del Territorio*, Barcelona, 1979.
18. M. Keating and D. Bleiman, op.cit.
19. M. Keating and P. Hainsworth, *Decentralisation and Change in Contemporary France*, Aldershot, 1986.
20. B. Jones and M. Keating, *Labour and the British State*, Oxford, 1985.
21. Guerrero, A. (1978), 'El problema nacional-regional en los programmas del PSOE y PCE'. *Revista de Estudios Politicos*, 4.

Chapter thirteen

Conclusion: the 1970s, 1980s and beyond

Michael Watson

The assessment of minority nationalism's resurgence

The upsurge of minority nationalism in the 1960s and 1970s was generally greeted with surprise: it had seemed an anachronistic relic in the process of being consigned 'to the dustheap of history'. For, 'homogeneity [was] imposed by the objective, inescapable imperative' of industrial civilisation, of which the major state nationalisms were the expression and vehicle, with minority national groups 'dissolving into the wider culture'[1]; state and culture had to be one on a large scale, as required by the industrial society based on economic growth to which mankind was irreversibly committed.

But it now appeared that a considerable number of national minorities were not ready to 'go meekly to their doom'.[2] Such refusal was strongly expressed in party and electoral, and at times violent, assertion of political and cultural demands, summed up in the need for self-determination (whether requiring outright independence or a 'home-rule' type of autonomy). This unexpected phenomenon led to analyses couched in terms of 'ethnic resurgence'[3], 'peripheral politicisation'[4], *la poussée régionaliste: l'Etat-nation en question*[5], or more specifically 'the breakup of Britain'.[6] The 1945–60 period in which the assimilation and integration of these minorities into their 'host' states had been considered to have reached an advanced stage was now seen as an 'aberration'; the earlier dismissal of minority nationalism as a political phenomenon was replaced by the prominence accorded it.[7] Indeed, far from being moribund, it could be viewed as an 'ascendant ideology'.[8] 'National separatism'[9] was back on the political agenda, posing a fundamental challenge to the legitimacy of long and well-established states.

With its importance and significance acknowledged, attention was focused on explaining the resurgence and its explosive potential for existing states. It was widely accepted that the 'modern' theories of a progressive integration of peoples, of cultural assimilation, driven largely by the process of economic development and modernisation, were seriously flawed. While there was such development and modernisation, it threw up its own contradictions and divergent elements, of which national minorities were a principal expression. On the whole, their resurgence was considered to be prompted by general problems and conditions. Yet their very capacity for reaction and reassertion pointed to the fact that 'cultural and ethnic loyalties are durable'.[10]

General conditions which were identified as fertilising minority nationalism concerned the state, the economy and society. There was a 'failure of the state'[11] along a number of axes, of which perhaps the main one was its increasingly bureaucratic and impersonal character. This was closely related to its centralisation and the Jacobin attitudes of central politicians and civil servants ('the centre knows best', 'only the centre is in a position to resolve basic economic and social problems', 'only the centre can serve the public interest'). Thus there was a lack of political participation, which particularly affected non-economic, non-sectional groups like national minorities; they were not represented as such in the political and governmental institutions. The major, state-wide parties for their part operated principally on class or confessional lines, and even if tending electorally to present 'catch-all' images found it difficult to include minority nationalist themes: for a state-wide party this could be counter-productive as well as ideologically foreign. In fact, the major parties were incapable of integrating national minorities into the political system.[12] Minority nationalism was, therefore, a natural vehicle for the expression of dissatisfaction with the politically and bureaucratically centralised state wherever minority cultural and ethnic loyalties were territorially well defined.

The emphasis in the above explanation was on what could be termed the need for participatory justice rather than distributive justice. The latter was, however, given an important place as a motivation factor in the success of minority nationalism. The post-1945 world had experienced unprecedented economic growth, but it was unevenly distributed, not just socially but in particular geographically. More broadly, the development or modernisation process gave rise to spatially differentiated results.[13] Where negative results coincided with a national minority, the potential for a political movement was very likely to be activated; it was noted that the grievances articulated by the minority nationalism were often to do with economic and social disadvantage or exploitation.

One explanation combined the various types of disadvantage associated with uneven development and specifically related them to one cause – basic cultural or ethnic differences. As in a colonial situation, various forms of discrimination and exploitation were directed at the cultural and ethnic minority in their territory. The situation was thus viewed as one of 'internal colonialism',[14] based essentially on a cultural (culturally-determined) division of labour, producing both social and economic consequences: exclusion of the minority nationality from top positions and roles in the community; along with a truncated economic development, one confined to basic, low-value-added sectors. However, the very fact of this discrimination helped to keep alive a distinctive ethnic or cultural consciousness, most importantly spilling over into the political culture, providing the basis for minority nationalist mobilisation. As awareness of the reasons for the deprivation grew, and as the gap widened economically between the 'internal colony' and the 'metropolitan power', so the minority nationalism would grow to challenge the status quo – as was apparently happening.

Already by the late 1970s, the 'internal colonial' explanation was being seriously questioned by such as Professor A.H. Birch, as not fitting in a number of respects the different cases of the minority nationalist upsurge. In particular, economic exploitation did not seem to occur in all cases, most notably not in that of the Basques or of the Catalans, whose regions were after all the richest in Spain; Jean Grugel confirms in this book that economic dissatisfaction has not been significant in the development of Basque nationalism, in recent years or earlier. Nor was the evidence for a cultural division of labour conclusive. Professor Birch himself offered an alternative explanation.[15] In the first place, ethnic and cultural loyalties and identity were primordial, not dependent on other, political or economic, facors for their importance. Whether national minorities accepted a *modus vivendi* with the larger state in which they were located depended on the balance of advantages during any particular period. Since 1945, the balance of advantage in being part of a 'sizeable state' as against being a small one had shifted in favour of the latter, largely through changes in the international system and the threat of mass television to cultural minorities in larger states. This line of reasoning tied in with Orridge's point that formerly dominant imperial states had lost power and prestige as a result of decolonisation and this inevitably had the effect of weakening the attachment of the national minorities existing within their boundaries.[16] In addition, in these circumstances, the task of minority nationalist activism was facilitated by technological developments, which made propaganda and disruption easier, more effective and with greater impact on public opinion; it was also facilitated by the tendency of Western states, at least, to be ready to make concessions in the climate of post-war consensus politics.

Governments were certainly made aware of regional disparities in the 1950s and 1960s and responded by devising regional development policies. A range of territorial management techniques, as discussed by

Keating in Chapter 12, were progressively set in place. Politically the aim was to remove the sting from protests at insufficient economic development, both by accommodating demands through welfare state social provision and by tackling the problems retarding regional economies. In the 1960s there was a move to regional planning and this involved new co-ordinating and consultative institutions at regional level, in which local interests could play a part. However, such administrative decentralisation left the state's structures and political decision-making processes essentially untouched.[17]

During the 1970s regional policy and planning interventions came increasingly to be viewed as encouraging minority nationalism's development. Various aspects were identified in this. In the first place such interventions reinforced the belief that economic growth should be balanced in a territorial sense, that all 'regions' had an equal right to it, while at the same time being in effect an official corroboration that certain areas and communities were indeed disadvantaged economically. Furthermore, the interventions raised expectations concerning the rectification of geographical disparities; but in practice, disappointment soon surfaced concerning their effectiveness and nature. The failings of the policies and the planning process provided ammunition for minority nationalism and encouraged anti-central government sentiment. In particular, there was insufficient attention paid to the variety and specificity of local conditions and needs, linked to over-centralised and bureaucratic policy-making procedures. Devolution and democratisation, going hand in hand, seemed the obvious and logical answer. Minority nationalism was the most powerful vehicle for such change and appeared in keeping with the tide of contemporary political history towards decentralisation and greater democratic control of planning and decision-making. Moreover, purely in terms of pressure-group politics, minority nationalism was the most effective articulator of a national minority's (or region's) demands.

For Rokkan and Urwin, in a major study in the late 1970s[18], there was a 'cultural and territorial identity syndrome' underlying the whole minority nationalist-cum-regionalist phenomenon. Crucially linked to this syndrome was the key characteristic of 'peripherality', deriving from three basic factors: distance, difference and dependence *vis-à-vis* the central state and its dominant political culture. Out of this conjunction of subjective and objective conditions had arisen an enduring situation of peripheral predicaments; these involved a dialectic of integration and resistance of peripheral communities in relation to the state. There were historically two basic sorts of territorial strain which promoted a politicisation of peripheral predicaments. Traditionally, culture had been the battleground and the original motivation of minority nationalism. Peripherality meant a cultural distance and distinctiveness that was to be defended. The latest upsurge, however, was fuelled primarily by economic discrepancies and problems. This was reflected in the disparate nature of contemporary minority nationalism, which articulated a variety of specific demands according to its location and lacked any ideological world view of society – identity with a territory was the only common element.

Nevertheless, minority nationalisms were also a reflection of broader and deeper concerns in modern society, such as disquiet at standardisation, an intensifying identity crisis, and growing general dissatisfaction with government and the major parties. Greater mobility and the decline of class in a more atomised society were widely regarded as making people more available for the appeal of minority nationalism. Social changes of this nature brought the spotlight to focus on the right to roots, as a source of continuity, identity and difference, in contradistinction to the right to options of an individualist materialistic sort which characterised liberal market society. Ideologically, minority nationalism offered a combination of older themes to do with community, common inheritance and culture along with newer ones relating to economic development and democratic control. Important in the growth of this challenge to the established order was the role of the new middle classes – professional, technical, administrative/managerial – which had emerged since 1945, notably in the expanded public sector.[19] These had progressively replaced the traditional leadership of cultural-cum-territorial minorities, both a reflection and cause of their greater preoccupation with economic and social issues.

It was generally agreed that, without the new economic and socio-logical admixture, minority nationalism would not have achieved the significant success it had. Yet, as already mentioned, central government's role was also invoked. Some emphasised its difficulties in meeting the needs expressed through minority nationalism. The phenomenon of rising expectations in society was seen as a general one to which governments had to respond, and expectations – certainly middle-class ones – were hardly less high in those regions that were lagging behind in economic development. Responding was one thing, however, keeping pace with and satisfying demands was another. Moreover, in the harsher economic climate that emerged during the 1970s, it became more difficult as Rokkan and Urwin observed, to budget for the resolution of problems through the liberal application of funds. The idea of the 'economic contradictions of democracy' began to be applied to the case of minority nationalism. Guthrie and McLean wrote in 1978: 'The new parties benefitted from the failure of politicians to deliver on promises which were inherently unfulfillable because liberal democracies generate excessive expectations and cannot restrain the "disruptive effects of the pursuit of group self interest"'.[20] Were government actions, such as regional policy, to some extent the source, then, of nationalist protest? Might the 'fundamental failure of the older democracies' be not so much in centralised bureaucracy, economic discrepancies, inadequate participation and party systems irrelevant to ethnic needs[21], as in their encouragement of demands by their readiness to assume responsibility for solutions? For such interventionism was unlikely, as it increasingly appeared, to meet with significant substantive success, certainly in the short to medium term.

Yet observers tended to draw the conclusion from the various failings of government action that the nationalist challenge could, therefore, hardly be resisted. Thus devolution, at the least, was being forced towards the top of the political agenda wherever minority nationalism was active. Urwin stressed the importance of resolving territorial strains. There were two ways, basically, of accommodating (or defusing) territorial demands: either through forms of power-sharing in existing government structures; or through forms of federalism.[22] When the protagonists viewed the conflict as overwhelmingly territorial, then some devolution of power was indicated. This seemed to apply in the case of minority nationalism. Of course, moves in that direction could be seen as a 'slippery slope' leading to a separatist solution. Yet there appeared to be no alternative. As McIver argued, central governments had assumed responsibilities in regional policy for higher living standards everywhere and for greater participation that were incompatible (since the former pointed to increased central co-ordination).[23] Failure for that if for no other reason was inevitable, enhancing hostility towards central government by those in the regions whose expectations had been previously raised. Professor Birch hoped that government leaders would become more relaxed in respect of autonomy or even secession, as independence and sovereignty were in reality becoming less significant in today's world. Thus the nationalist question could be treated with more equanimity.[24]

In the mid-to-late 1970s the current was thus generally viewed as running strongly in favour of minority nationalism, with central governments not being able, ultimately, to stem it or at best only partially and probably temporarily by accepting some measure of devolution. This was so, in particular, because the motivation behind the upsurge co-joined factors specific to minority nationalism, notably ethnic or cultural identity, along with factors associated with wider concerns and problems – indeed for some a general malaise – affecting modern capitalist and/or advanced industrial society.

In itself minority nationalism was rather variously evaluated by those who studied it. For some it tended to be backward looking, in still being concerned with historical questions which often seemed obscure and generally irrelevant to today's problems. Its preoccupation with statehood, or even political autonomy, was also viewed as having archaic undertones, given the growing interdependence of countries, communities and economic organisations: as Birch put it, the 'Woodrow Wilson model' of the sovereign nation-state was on the road to obsolescence.[25] On the other hand, those who believed that the traditional state still had a predominant place and role in society were not inclined to accept that this could be made more effective by breaking it down into smaller versions ('Balkanising'). The nationalists could themselves be caught in an apparently contradictory position of criticising shortfalls in state aid while calling for independence.

However, nationalists were seen as becoming more aware of potential economic and social problems stemming from secession and turning in reality towards autonomist solutions. Beneath the rhetoric, minority nationalism's real nature was becoming essentially regionalist. Yet there remained a more radical interpretation which insisted on its special political qualities, as essentially alien to the existing political system and an irreconcilable opponent of the established state. Tactics and even its manifestations might vary, but it was not to be confounded with other political forces or reduced to an expression of economic or social forces. It was the working out of the nationalist impulse to political self-determination where a people still retained an ethnic, cultural and/or institutional identity – generally as a result of discrimination imposed by the irreducible structural inequalities inherent in the existing system of power. This power structure, therefore, lay in the direct line of historical development for being overthrown and broken up.

Perspectives on minority nationalism in the 1980s

If for the 1970s (as for the 1960s) the balance sheet of minority nationalism was proclaimed positive, the 1980s have proved less successful. Most notably, the political challenge marked time or even faded. Moreover, it could be said that an uglier face has come to the fore, not in all or even most cases, but with a prominence that has brought home the traits potentially shared with majority or state nationalism, including those of the most xenophobic and authoritarian kind. Any parallel with the bigger, imperialistic state nationalisms of the nineteenth and first half of the twentieth centuries seemed ruled out in the 1960s and 1970s by the nature and situation of minority nationalism's resurgence. In this book Jean Grugel does this specifically for Basque nationalism from its earliest days; yet it too has its xenophobic, fanatical, aggressive element, increasingly exemplified during the 1980s by ETA-m (the nationalist rather than Marxist hard core). Breton nationalism, as Rogers states, has had to live down its relatively recent past when it succumbed to the temptation of the fascist road.

In the conditions of liberal democracy's success in the west after 1945 ('thirty glorious years' as Jean Fourastier has called them), minority nationalism had few problems in pursuing the parliamentary path. Even in Northern Ireland's special circumstances this seemed to be becoming true in the 1960s and early 1970s. In Spain the break-down of Francoism in the 1970s paved the way for the re-assertion of democratic Basque politics. Liberal democracy's overall success opened the way for minority nationalism's progress, providing the opportunity for a further political option to stake its claim as well as holding out the promise of minorities' self-realisation, politically and culturally, as part of a widening and deepening of the pluralist, polyarchical[26] political society. At the same time, there was, as we have seen, a cluster of problems which minority nationalism could exploit and to which it seemed particularly relevant as an answer or at least as the means, the motor to bring appropriate policies.

However, the 1980s have brought other pressures and other responses which have found out minority nationalism's weaknesses and highlighted its previously ignored faults, including notably its extremist expressions. In particular, the growing challenge to the South African government has brought home the dark, illiberal, repressive streak that can emerge and become predominant in minority nationalism. Afrikaner nationalism has become particularly beleaguered, of course; but others, too, have been put on the defensive and momentum and direction have been lost. In these circumstances, the violent aspect has frequently become more pronounced. Overlapping with this there has been an enhanced bifurcation of many movements into extremists and moderates, or hard-liners and pragmatists.

External factors and events, international and global, political and economic, have impinged with greater force in the 1980s on the situation of minority nationalisms, sometimes directly, sometimes mediated through the 'host' states. The Afrikaners have revealed, in reaction, the lengths to which a minority nationalism usurping majority power will go in defence of its privileged and dominant position, previously acquired through a Machiavellian determination sustained by a belief in its own sanctity and destiny. The Afrikaner majority has moved away from a fundamentalist, purist conception of its interests to one embracing shared interests with other minority nationalities (notably the anglophone white South Africans) over and against the black majority. This development has increasingly and significantly divided Afrikaner nationalism, with the (as yet) minority, the 'narrow-minded', clinging to a backward-looking and uncompromising view of the nation, against all-comers (the laager mentality). Thus the 1980s have strikingly reminded us that minority nationalism as much as any major one can harbour the Nietzschean virus of belief in its rightful and necessary superiority within a certain territory, giving it the justification for the subordination if not exploitation of other peoples within its boundaries. Moreover, the virus is especially activated when the nationalism is threatened, whether in its dominance or current purpose or very *raison d'être*. If Afrikaner nationalism is the best exemplification of the virus's strength in these circumstances, it is not the only manifestation: one can also look to Northern Ireland in the 1980s, or Euskadi, or Corsica, in descending order of intensity.

Side by side with the recourse to extremism with its frequent concomitant of violence, one can also see the growth of divisiveness and disorientation in minority nationalism in the face of the difficulties of the 1980s. Problems have stemmed from certain successes which the 1960s and 1970s advance gave rise to. This applies particularly to the case of Quebec nationalism where, as Dr Macmillan shows in Chapter 8, the achievement of language reform (to favour French) has removed a principal spur to nationalist success. French Canadians have also been reassured, by the reform, of their power in Quebec, and in being legitimised in this way, nationalism has taken on a less mobilised, more diffuse patriotic nature. This has left the Parti Québécois in a weakened condition, searching for a new strategy as the independentist option recedes in practical political terms, but with a hard-core of unrepentant separatists and the consequent threat from schism.

We have already seen the destructive seeds buried within Afrikaner nationalism's successful appropriation of power; and it may be asked if there is not some similarity, albeit on the whole in much milder form, in the case of Basque nationalism. Success came in 1977 in achieving the devolution of political power to Euskadi as an autonomous region and then in occupying that power. However, the problem of extremism has not been resolved, with ETA violence in pursuit of independence undiminished and continuing to find support in the population. In fact, the political wing of separatism has increased its vote in the 1980s. There are undoubtedly significant 'purist', fundamentalist elements who brook no compromise with 'foreigners' and see the current autonomy status as little or even no improvement: only sovereign statehood will satisfy their exclusive notion of Euskadi, with its distinctive interests and character to be recuperated from external control or influences. On the other hand, increasingly contrasted with these elements are those nationalists, and notably the original Nationalist Party, who in practice accept the autonomist solution and indeed are ready to work with Spanish parties; they increasingly align on the side of authority, Spanish or not, against ETA (which finds a parallel in Ireland in the struggle against the IRA, which has become to an increasing extent in the 1980s a matter *within* nationalism).

In Corsica, too, the 1980s have seen earlier success, with the granting of regional devolution, giving way to disillusion and division in the nationalist and autonomist camp. For moderates supporting the Corsican and Basque causes the achievement of regional government has given rise to a basic satisfaction and to participation in the new institutions. For the hard-line separatists this has meant increasing isolation and frustration, which may account for the violence. However, for the moderates, acceptance of the centre's devolution formula has brought the problem not only of increased division and the challenge of extremism but also of where they go now in political and policy-programme terms. Further reform may be advocated in a devolutionary sense; but the establishment of regional government is bound to stand as the major, crucial achievement in the eyes of the moderate nationalist electorate; beyond that, further measures inevitably appear of less significance and concern. In addition, if as has happened in the 1980s regional government does not in practice appear to make a lot of difference to how things are economically, socially or even politically (notably in Corsica, but also in Brittany), then support for more change in that direction can fall away in disillusion or dissipate itself to some extent on a widening political front within nationalism, as in Euskadi.

It is also clear that moderate Basque nationalism, in acceding to power in a pluralistic and federalistic political structure, has had to adopt and adjust to various cross-pressures. Not for the first time, of course, a movement radically at variance in major ways with the established order, but adopting a reformist approach, has become increasingly tactical and pragmatic in its behaviour as progress has been made and in particular governmental responsibility exercised. Why indeed should it be thought otherwise where minority nationalism is concerned? Even where the resurgence did not lead to regional devolution or the achievement of a governing role, the 1980s have seen a pragmatic shift to greater emphasis by moderates on immediate economic and social issues rather than constitutional transformation. This has reflected major set-backs around the turn of the decade in pursuit of political change (Scotland, Wales, Quebec; and Northern Ireland from the mid-1970s). These set-backs dashed strong expectations and lowered confidence, to which the response was either to turn inward to a sectarian dogmatism or, what emerged as predominant, to compete on the same policy ground as state-wide political forces.

However, explanation of the reversal of fortune, of the loss of momentum and coherence and what it signifies (not to say of boos replacing cheers) needs to be set in a wider and more general context. One factor that has become more evident is the weight of inertia in existing structures and attitudes whose roots are deep in historical experience. This inertia has affected minority nationalism itself, hampering its adaptation and development, as well as being a greater road-block to its progress than was generally expected. The former is especially true of the Afrikaners and Northern Irish who remain resolutely over-determined by the past in their current behaviour. As regards the latter, governmental and party systems have after all shown considerable resistance to the minority nationalist challenge; in general, state-wide parties have not been weakened in nationalist 'homelands'. Where violence has been a feature, attitudes have hardened still further against nationalist political aspirations. Established political structures are clearly more deeply embedded than was often assumed in the first flush or two of the nationalist upsurge. It can also be put in a more positive way, that the centre and its supporters have fought back and re-asserted their power and political will.

However, the major source of minority nationalism's difficulties in the 1980s has been economic. 'Stagflation', world recession, unemployment, have brought a growing concentration in all countries on economics; it came to dominate policy preoccupations, prescriptions and yardsticks. But even more important than the simple concentration on economics has been the nature of it, namely the return to an anti-state market-dominant conception of the economy associated with the rise to power of the New Right and the even wider spread of the ideology of neo-liberalism. This political turn around is certainly uncongenial to minority nationalism. For a start, the new orthodoxy is opposed to the extension of the political sphere, which the creation of new governmental structures is taken to signify. Politics is viewed as inimical to economic progress. The philosophy of 'economics first' means giving the market free rein (the only reins being the rules of the market game) so prima facie the fewer political powers the better; it means concentrating on wealth creation and not distribution; and it means that social and political considerations in policy content come a poor second. Application of these principles produces a very different approach to the problems that were identified in the 1970s as giving encouragement to minority nationalism. In a sense, the earlier analysis is stood on its head.

Regional development exemplifies the new approach. Rather than disparities being seen as the cause of significant nationalist or regionalist politicisation, this is considered to flow from the ideology and practice of intervention, on which regional policy and planning was based. The failings of such interventions were inevitable, and increasingly costly, since they incessantly raised expectations while being fundamentally counter-economic. The answer, therefore, to the 'failure of the state' was not to look to other political solutions, but to pull back from government involvement and clear the way for market incentives for private initiative. It can now be seen that this is a logical response in its way to some of the diagnoses of the 1970s (pp.196–9). For minority nationalism the consequence has been threefold. First, the emasculation of regional policy has removed something that minority nationalism could feed on; it can still protest, but now it has little to show for it in substantive terms: the time of concessionary consensus politics is over, the dialectic of demand and response has been broken by the public expenditure retrenchment. Second, minority nationalism is inherently about political means and political answers, but these are now in disrepute: economic forces are seen as holding the key and politics can do little about them, except to get out of their way. In this way the claim to effectiveness of a movement such as minority nationalism is diminished. Its marginalisation as an irrelevant solution in contemporary world conditions is further increased by the political fatalism that is bred by neo-liberal ideology regarding economic outcomes (e.g. uneven development).

The 1980s belief in the impotence of politics or even its negative effects has certainly rubbed off badly on minority nationalism. A significant example of this is the retreat of public opinion from the separatist option in Quebec. In general there is a lack of enthusiasm, and in some instances (Corsica, Spain, Northern Ireland, South Africa) growing or intensifying opposition, in respect of institutional innovation. There may, as in South Africa, be specific political reasons for this. But a more negative, defensive attitude has become widespread in the face of the growth of externally generated difficulties and pressures, characterised as beyond the control of individual states. The New Right has of course made much of this state of affairs and played to the political fatalism that it inspires. Behind it lies the loss of confidence in economic well-being which interventionism, i.e. 'politics', seemed unable to ensure (and the New Right offered a different, radical strong remedy in this respect). In these circumstances, arguments about the economic costs of separatism, or even of extending autonomy, have come to overshadow the whole question, being widely viewed as significantly increasing the risks associated with the nationalist project of political reorganisation. Minority nationalism's experience in the 1980s exemplifies the thesis that economic difficulties of an enduring nature call forth the belief in public opinion and government that the situation is not propitious for political and especially constitutional change.

Third, the response of minority nationalism to the predominance of economic themes and of neo-liberalism has been to focus its political actions and policy proposals much more in the economic and social sphere, and to move to the left – in other words, to compete increasingly in terms of the conventional political spectrum and its agenda. Perhaps this is not surprising – it is part of the conventional wisdom of electoral competition – but it does diminish the specificity (except in name, of course) and originality of minority nationalism. There are dangers in this of being marginalised by being absorbed into the established party game, i.e. as simply a minor party like any other. Of course, where there are political structures apart from those of the central state, these can provide a 'protected' area for nationalist party expression. The Basque case illustrates this; yet the fate of the Parti Québécois equally shows that it is not in itself a guarantee of continued strength. It is probably no coincidence that Basque nationalism's undiminished support is in a newly democratic state in which politics retains its appeal and the New Right has made little headway as yet. However, a leftward move is occurring there, too, and signals widening divisions in the movement.

In terms of the general political and economic tendencies and climate of the decade, minority nationalism has been in a more conventional 'oppositional' position in the 1980s. The political dynamics of this situation have pushed it to a more left-wing alignment on policy matters. This is not to deny the independent role of ideological evolution, which in some instances was making its mark in the 1970s (though on the more extreme expressions of movements, Brittany being the main exception, where the principal party, the Union Démocratique Bretonne, was clearly on the left). But in the 1960s and 1970s things seemed to be moving in the direction that nationalism in its own right desired, without any particular socialist implications; it could be, and was, in opposition to left- and right-wing governments. In Brittany, the alignment, in particular the alliance, with the left in the 1970s was spurred by the existence of a right-wing government. Rogers in Chapter 5 brings out the problems this gave rise to for the UDB in the 1980s. This was especially so after the Socialists, having won power in 1981, revised their policies in 1983–4 in a more neo-liberal direction. Should the UDB stick with its alliance or take again a more independent line – but if so, which? (Some UDB, including leading figures, drew perhaps the logical conclusion from their left-wing stance, especially with the right threatening, and joined the Socialists).

On the whole, minority nationalisms are more at ease opposing right-wing governments, since these are generally the arch-defenders of the constitutional and political status quo. But when politics polarises, as in the 1970s and especially the 1980s, it becomes increasingly difficult in practice to avoid taking up a more identifiable and conventional stance in terms of the left–right spectrum. Thus opposition for moderate, mainstream European minority nationalism has meant a closer alignment with a centre-left or broadly social democratic position. In this, it tends to merge as an element into the parliamentary resistance to neo-liberalism (of course, in Spain this is to some extent from within the occupancy of power, at regional level).

When minority nationalism moves into closer alignment or support for social democracy, it tends also to be drawn into a more 'centrist', pragmatic sort of political behaviour, especially if the left is in power. This was true of the SNP and Plaid Cymru in the latter part of the 1970s, the UDB from the mid-1970s to mid-1980s, and the PNB since the early to mid-1980s. The movement then comes under centrifugal pressures and division can be provoked. A further consequence, ultimately perhaps more serious, of a social democratic alignment is ideological assimilation and/or subordination. The parliamentary left has shown in the past decade in Western Europe a readiness, especially in opposition, to accept, not to say exploit, themes from minority nationalism. This has been probably most evident in France. Of course, it would be unlikely that the tail would wag the dog and in practice what was central to nationalism has tended to become an adjunct to socialism – something which in office could fairly readily be put on the backburner, if not jettisoned. Some of the ideas which the interpreters of the upsurge identified as spearheading it have thus, in the 1980s, been absorbed and often diluted in left-wing political culture; while at the same time, the New Right has either simply ignored them or stood them on their head, e.g. answering the call for development 'from below' and autonomy by the 'small business' enterprise culture, or the critique of bureaucratic centralisation by 'rolling back' the state.

Ideologically and politically, then, minority nationalism has lost something of its force, distinctiveness and *élan*. In the former respect, the New Right in government has proved a tough and unaccommodating opponent, certainly compared with the responsiveness that was previously assumed to be a necessary and inevitable feature of liberal democratic government; of course, this has also reflected a hardening of 'metropolitan' public opinion against minorities' demands in the harsher economic and social climate of the 1980s. Distinctiveness has, in a sense, been traded for a position and role in the opposition to the new neo-liberal order and, on the other hand, as part of a distancing from the more violent extremism by the ultras in the movement. But the increasingly 'mainstream' centrist or centre-left posture and the focus on economic and social issues amounts to a political practice defensive of welfare statism, the mixed economy and government intervention (e.g. protests at plant closures, at health and education service cuts, at the run-down of regional policy, etc.).

The danger in the longer run for the nationalist movement of this social democratisation seems very real (remembering, also, that the state-wide centre left, particularly in its 'branches' in the nationalist homelands, has become more regionalist and autonomist in outlook). This alignment comes when social democratic ideology has shown growing signs of being unable to develop a new dynamic with which to reply to the onslaught of neo-liberalism; apparently, it is stuck with protecting its post-war creations and so of offering mainly a return to the status quo ante along with a more humane managerialism and more attractive and caring leaders. It is unlikely that minority nationalism will find renewed impetus in these themes, or in being pulled along in their wake. Whether it has had any choice in the matter, given the left–right polarisation, or will have henceforth, is another question. None the less, lack of a more radical, alternative prospectus is likely to mean it remains confined to an essentially defensive and rather indistinct, amorphous position in a '*cartel des nons*' to neo-liberalism.

The way forward: the need and role for minority nationalism

Can minority nationalism in the western democracies extricate itself from the actual or looming impasse into which it has been pushed in the 1980s? Does it matter? Do democratic systems benefit from the presence of dynamic minority nationalist movements, as these have been experienced since their 1960s resurgence? What is in it for the minority peoples themselves? One of the principle dilemmas for nationalist movements is whether to reach some understanding or even alliance with other political forces, at least for electoral purposes. This, of course, depends on the particular circumstances, including possible 'partners', political culture, electoral system, etc. In any event, there are pitfalls, of the sort already discussed above, which lie in the way of an alliance strategy with one of the major state-wide parties, as the experience of the UDB testifies. Though the SNP and Plaid Cymru have made some recovery in the course of the 1980s with a generally centre-left stand, they have played second fiddle to the British parties and especially Labour as the vehicle of mounting opposition in Scotland and Wales to Thatcherism.

In 1978 Guthrie and McLean asked if Labour or nationalism would in Britain be the voice of the 'subject-periphery'[27]: in the face of the New Right's triumph, it has clearly been Labour, seen as the stronger and more natural defender against the depredations of neo-liberal economic and social policy (including its anti-regionalism). After the disillusionment with the 1981–6 Socialist government, the same is basically true of France: social democracy is the recourse for those fearing even worse from neo-liberalism, i.e. in particular in the periphery (and it should be said the periphery is right to be the most fearful of neo-liberalism, for the latter's economic philosophy has belief in uneven development at its heart, while its political strategy is to base its appeal unashamedly on the immediate self-interest of those in the regions, no less than social classes, which are *not* in the economic tail). Only in Spain has nationalism not been trailing behind as the voice of national minorities. But this is in a situation where neo-liberalism has not yet made significant progress, with social democracy remaining in power; in any case, Basque concerns (like Catalan ones) focus less on economic and social grievances, which is socialism's forte, and more on political and cultural demands for which nationalism is better equipped.

Indeed, as the Parti Québécois has also shown, minority nationalism can more readily achieve a leading role when political and/or cultural rights are a central issue; events in the Soviet Union further substantiate that nationalist activity is stimulated when rights concerns come to the fore in political consciousness, for whatever reason. It is true that achievement of such rights, as in Quebec, readily appears as a once and for all matter – and so has a demobilising effect – unlike economic and social demands which are constantly renewed as the target shifts. Nevertheless, it must be concluded that minority nationalism has greater affinity, and therefore success, with rights concerns (and Dr Williams's chapter brings out the link in political theory). A major question, then, for minority nationalist movements is how to raise consciousness in this respect, and then articulate it effectively. The Northern Ireland Civil Rights Association achieved this in circumstances when discrimination and denial of equal rights were a daily reality. But it is more often outside the western world that suppression of a minority nation's rights is glaringly obvious and the problem is how to throw off the yoke or at least bring effective pressure to bear on an oppressive central power to permit some expression of a minority's identity and rights. In this, as Duncan explains in respect of the USSR, religion can be a significant ally and additionally so if it can look for support to co-religionists in neighbouring states. Indeed, minority nations represent one of the least monolithic aspects of the Soviet system, with the main ones at least maintaining their presence and distinctiveness. Though there have been fluctuations in official policy, a *modus vivendi* has characterised the state's relationship with these over the longer term; even so, rights can be seen as the continuing focus of minority nationalist concern in the USSR.

In the west, however, minority nationalism is today faced with the primacy of economic and social concerns, thus a key aspect of the challenge to it is to link such concerns to the question of rights, and these in turn to that of institutions. It calls for an ideological prospectus which places emphasis on the specificity and diversity of policy requirements, on indigenous resources and resourcefulness, on pluralism (*droite à la différence*) and roots – the latter referring to a combination of the traditions, the natural and cultural patrimony, and the sense of place and territorial community (the familiar and stable milieu) to which a person subscribes; and, moreover, whose continuing availability is also a touchstone of pluralism's reality. Minority nationalism's special task is to personify these themes, with their contemporary appeal to a range of positions across the conventional political spectrum[28], and put them across as rights which can only be secured by embodiment in and through political, social, economic and cultural structures. The crucial message is that as rights they require, if they are not to have just an abstract, shadowy existence, to be provided with institutional homes – and defences. Such defences can be mobilised in a range of institutions, organisations and groups of an intermediate status, i.e. between the individual and the macro-society or state, from provincial parliaments through local authorities, educational and cultural organisations, development agencies to churches, trade unions and professional associations. Where these structures are lacking at the level of the national minority as a whole, effort evidently needs to be directed to securing their creation, including not least of course, governmental institutions through which the nation's identity, inheritance, culture, resources and specific problems can find full expression and priviliged treatment. The recognition of the case for a more differentiated and decentralised approach to problems has become more widespread in political, governmental and public opinion, certainly in Western Europe.[29] The at least relative failure of the centre's territorial management techniques – that is, in resolving regional problems at acceptable cost – certainly enabled neo-liberalism's *laissez-faire* solution to make more converts. The right's adoption of it, and they could hardly be expected freely to adopt autonomist solutions, meant that it was the only effective alternative when the pendulum swung rightwards as it did in the west in the 1980s. This outcome can also be viewed as having led to minority nationalism's bluff being called (and indeed all regionalisms); Spain, as an exception to this, is only relatively so: the debate there has been conducted much less on and in nationalist/ regionalist terms (for example, *Ley para la armonizacion del processo autonomico*, see pp.107 and 192).

Yet as the 1990s approach it becomes increasingly evident that a decade of neo-liberalism has not removed the minority nationalism question from the political agenda – rather it has infused it with a greater relevance and even urgency; neither, more generally, has the centre-periphery problem been disposed of in its material aspect: the gap between richer and poorer regions has widened. The sources for improvement in minority nationalism's fortunes remain: where there is need there is opportunity. But its relevance is less in relation specifically to the economic gap between centre and periphery than to the general socio-cultural process that Gellner conceptualised as 'entropy'.[30] By analogy with the process of energy transformation (second law of thermodynamics), this refers to the dissolving of social and cultural differences of a group nature (class, ethnic or religion-based), into a wider, increasingly homogeneous society as the necessary accompaniment of industrial development; this is the essence of the modernisation and secularisation process. The historic task of the major state nationalisms has been to further this, notably through a common education system (exo-socialisation) and facilitate it by widening the bounds for the unimpeded operation of the economic system (the European Community is, in its contemporary expression, an exemplification of this, through the pooling and limiting of sovereignty in the interest of the bigger market). Hence minority cultures and societies are called on imperiously by history to wither away. This whole social 'entropy' business is considered beneficial and Gellner is concerned about 'entropy-resistant' traits, in particular in respect of their capacity for 'fissure-generation'. Certainly, as the cases of Northern Ireland, South Africa, and in some respects the Soviet Union have shown, minority nationalism can produce deeply entrenched 'fissures' in politics and society with tragic consequences in terms of violence, discrimination and lack of civil and human rights.

Gellner recognised that 'entropy-resistance' based on nationality or ethnicity and/or religion, may have qualities of great endurance (more so than class). This is not surprising since it is the expression of a deep and fundamental motivation in human life as manifested publicly in the themes already referred to (a sense of lived and not abstract community, of inherited identity associated with historical and cultural continuity and contiguity, of stability, of difference, of roots). In practice, the question of scale is a key variable in the concrete embodiment of these themes in everyday existence. They are less easily and naturally sustainable on a large-scale basis. In this respect, 'entropy-resistance' of national minorities is not irrational for human existence and well-being. The themes generally come into what Peter Berger has called the 'calculus of meaning'[31] (in essence, 'Man does not live by bread alone'), which the homogenisation and anonymity of already affluent industrial societies pose more acutely. Homogenisation, rationalisation, mobility may indeed be imperatives of such societies justified in terms of economic growth as Gellner says, but ultimately no less of an imperative is what may be summed up as the need for roots. This is so in two main ways: in relation, of course, to the 'calculus of meaning' and the avoidance of collective disorientation and shifting fashions in beliefs and values, with their eventual dangers of dissipation of the social bond ('entropy' can be applied here in its true, negative sense); but imperative also in respect of the maintenance of human cultural diversity, itself desirable for its enhancement of the quality of life and necessary to avoid damage to the cultural ecology of humanity through a process of over-simplification or syncretism.

To conserve a range of cultures, each with their particular wisdom and evolving traditions, is of vital importance for the human race as a whole. Such differences are comparable to the rich genetic inheritance of the multiplicity of plant and animal species which have emerged through the evolutionary process; today they rest above all, both in their major embodiment and actual and potential value, on distinctions of religion and nationality associated with language and literature, history, art, customs, myths as well as specific cosmological and ontological beliefs, 'mind-sets' and *Weltanschauung*. The ecological analogy strongly suggests that their loss could be as limiting and damaging for humanity and its future prospects in responding to necessarily unforeseen challenges and demands as the precipitate loss of species and shrinking of the gene pool as a result of man's activities would be for the evolution of the world's eco-system (including the 'domesticated' plants and animals managed directly by man, where commercial and technological 'imperatives' are reducing the number of varieties being maintained).

The principal threat to cultural pluralism based on nationality and religion comes from the ideology of economic growth, with the deracinating tendencies of its imperatives. Everything becomes subordinated to the criterion of economic efficiency as measured by profitability for the purposes of accumulation and a yet bigger 'cake' *ad infinitum*. It may be pursued through market and/or statist procedures, involving incremental, *ad hoc* decision-making or planning (which seeks essentially to replicate market norms of efficiency[32]) and associated with private or public ownership (it is true that 'free enterprise' is in the main more efficient in these terms). Increasingly the ideology and its operation takes on a technocratic guise, which can shelter a convergence in these matters between east and west. What is sought is ever greater mobility, redeployment, restructuring, 'flexibility', etc., and priority in education to science and the technical over the humanities and religion. Statists (nationalists and socialists), cosmopolitan liberals or economic individualists can share much in respect of this commitment. The ultimate justification resides in ever greater consumption. The upshot of it is the diminishing of intermediate structures except of a functional nature, viz. companies operating solely to maximise accumulation and growth.

Society has become increasingly stretched between a more and more atomistic base (the individual producer, citizen or especially consumer) and an enlarging over-arching, macro level – economic, administrative and even political (multi-national corporations, international financial and commercial markets, supra-national economic 'communities', international agencies). The classic distinction between the individual and the state has itself become sharper. For as the ethos of materialistic individualism at the heart of the growth process under market capitalism has advanced, so the intermediate structures of community have been weakened and central government has become solicited to provide the resulting 'deficit' of solidarity, security and collective 'goods' generally – some of which, notably a common education system, are equally required for the growth process (hence for Gellner nationalism is essentially functional to this 'state-building' necessary for economic growth; not least, it integrates or kills off smaller nationalities). In addition, this whole process has encouraged the erosion of the moral capital inherited from Christianity, in particular in respect of people's sense of social obligation and responsibility. This has made central management of the economy or of provision of collective goods (e.g. public services) more difficult, by weakening the legitimacy accorded to government and public action generally.[33] The state may, anyway, become over-solicited as far as maximising economic efficiency in pursuit of growth is concerned. The New Right has, of course, derived considerable political benefit from these problems. Yet its answer hardly provides for a restoration of intermediate structures, only a tightening of the structural support (a tougher legal framework, more 'vocational' education) via central government for the promotion of growth based on the self-interest motive. Neither the social fabric nor the environment are assured any respite from the 'entropic' degenerative action of the growth process and commercialisation bias[34] (unfortunately, this points to further directive, even coercive, state action in its restricted range of functions).

In the light of the above analysis, the political vocation of minority nationalism in 'advanced' countries in the 1990s and beyond should be, I believe, to contribute to shifting change and development away from its 'entropic' excesses (in that sense to be a political and social factor in 'entropy-resistance') towards a more balanced politico-economic system in which the 'right to roots' and a more socially and environmentally benign economic process and technology have a leading place. Rokkan and Urwin recognised two basic rights, which impinged particularly on the situation of national minorities and peripheral regionalisms, the one to 'roots' the other to 'options', that is the sphere of individual choice (for most, in contemporary society, of material consumption).[35] They saw the advantages and disadvantages of both; but this was rather from a theoretical perspective. In practice, in western society, 'options' is the right greatly privileged by the economic system, and mostly by governments – it is a *leitmotif*, after all, of neo-liberalism. The clash between the two 'rights' is also emphasised, in the sense of a zero-sum 'contest'. Certainly, as we have seen, what can be characterised as the extension of 'options', namely the economic growth process, has been accompanied by a shrinking of the place accorded to 'roots' (cultural, territorial and spiritual). However, some trade-offs should certainly be possible. Gellner, indeed, noted that where a minority possesses autonomy, its members, while having access to 'options' through the wider polity, remain more closely attached to their 'roots'. After all, people have strong preferences for the place where they work and live, given half a chance; this is often related to 'roots', at least to remaining where they have been putting down roots and establishing a stable family and social (not say cultural) existence. In obstructing these preferences the utilitarian 'imperative', including notably that of spatial mobility, has much to answer for.

There has been a progressive increase in uprootedness as society has become more 'advanced' in the past half-century, manifested in particular by the break-down of 'natural' solidarities at the small-scale level, starting with the family. How far short we have fallen of, for example, Simone Weil's clarion call, or Tawney's, at the onset of the 'advanced' era (Weil was particularly prescient about the dangers of technocracy and managerialism in public *and* private sectors).[36] Here lies the need, and chance, for minority nationalism, not to assimilate itself to some point on the conventional political spectrum, however contestatory of neo-liberalism, but to adopt an alternative perspective in alignment with other 'entropy-resisting' social and political forces emphasising those rights associated with roots. This requires the maintenance of distinctive and diverse cultural, social and physical arenas and environments (development thus needs to be discriminating, adapted and sensitive to local particularities, in other words in continuity with existing environments). Unconstrained ('entropic') capitalist development ('wealth-creation') is, unfortunately, disruptive and reductionist in these very respects.

The theme of individual choice and rights, so successfully exploited (in one sense) by neo-liberalism, is closely connected to the strengthening of intermediate structures and institutions when it refers to such qualitative yet concrete matters as language, culture, place, tradition, religion, environment and community life. Such rights cannot be secured through self-help or market purchase (or at best only partially and largely adulterated); indeed, individualism reduced to material self-interest and market forces given free rein, as in neo-liberalism, degrades and undermines them. Yet they are additionally important because, as they are largely 'delivered' through institutions and associative action, they invoke a sense of social responsibility and obligation (which the dissociative individualism of the market weakens) and contribute to that personal development of character which is particularly required to sustain a democratic political culture.

Minority nationalism can thus make a fruitful contribution, at least in advanced industrial countries, by contributing to an alternative formula or paradigm to that of the market, or that of the state, as the predominant organising principle of society. Centrifugal forces are inherent in the one, centripetal forces in the other – each tending, when it has over-reached itself (either in too great an alienation or too great a dose of collectivism) to produce a strong reaction in favour of its opposite. These apparently contradictory, lurching swings engendered by the bi-polarised system are certainly not cost free in human and social terms; in particular they rationalise intermediate structures and insti-tutions into the service of market or state, or otherwise reduce and marginalise them if they resist functionalisation. A vacuum is created in society as community and the possibility of rootedness are progressively diminished (hence the cure – whether the turn of collectivism or indivi-dualism – being worse than the disease); while cultural standardisation in the broadest sense is the end on which both converge. In this respect liberal individualism and collectivist statism are but two sides of the same coin, antithetical to a genuinely pluralist structure of society.

Minority nationalism is well placed to play a leading role in a movement seeking to break out of the polarisation and widening gap between the base (the individual) and the superstructure (the state and other macro-societal, increasingly transnational structures), with its inevitable 'hollowing out' of society as intermediate structures are reduced to a narrow functionalism or utilitarianism, if not marginalised altogether. The basic concern of sustaining a minority's rights – political, economic, cultural – is closely associated in practice with the development and strengthening of the range of intermediate structures which define themselves, or can be encouraged to, by reference to the territory in question. But the appeal goes to a wider audience – those for whom the quantitative, material emphasis, whether via the market or state (or a simple mixture of the two), is inadequate if not misguided in its deleterious social, cultural and environmental consequences.

If minority nationalism is only part of the clamour in rich countries for more (presumed, moreover, to be achieved through acquiring self-government status), it has nothing distinctive to offer – simply appearing as an adjunct to the established party system – nor above all anything to contribute to reversing the tendencies examined above. Moreover, material redistribution to a national minority is more a job for a state-wide party, as Urwin argued (citing the case of Labour in Wales).[37] Where minority nationalism *can* blaze a trail is in developing as a political and social movement working through and for intermediate structures in its territory, joining with other forces concerned with enhancing the autonomy, role and community dimension of political, cultural, economic and social organisation at that level.

This needs to involve working for participative structures and developing between them horizontal lines of communication and interdependence (as opposed to the vertical, compartmentalised 'centre-periphery' relations which tend to predominate). Besides rooting the structures much more firmly in the particular territory, such an undertaking is linked to the necessary revalorisation of the notion of the polity, in which the territorial expression of the *res publica* must have predominance over its functional expression by sectoral organisation, even if governmental, and sectional interest (yet in the macro-society and state the remoteness from the territorial base inevitably and strongly emphasises the latter). Difference, identity, autonomy for the individual are in practice crucially linked to their community expression, i.e. they are in the first place public goods dependent on the particular institutional context in which people are able to live their daily lives.

The divisions in society, which Keating (see p.189) calls on minority nationalism to address, should thus be pre-eminently those new ones emerging in 'advanced' or post-industrial states: those which challenge the consensus based on the growth myth[38] which equates progress and improvement in singular fashion with GNP, the production of goods and services (including 'security') and its associated commercialisation bias, and with full-employment for most (if it cannot be for all)[39]; all of which leads to the convergence on a 'massified' type of society in which diversity and variety are trivialised to an individual level and rationalisation, standardisation, deracination and cultural assimilation set the pace. Minority nationalism has a natural home in the opposition to this consensus; there is a value convergence with all those social, cultural, religious and political groups and attitudes which subscribe to an alternative paradigm of quality, variety, diversity and community in human societies and cultures, as well as in the natural world. This includes post-materialists[40], environmentalists and ecologists, conservationists and the organic movement as well as those concerned about humanity's cultural and spiritual inheritance, or about sustaining community structures (economic, social and cultural no less than political), as per an authentically pluralist society. There is the basis for a programmatic concordance which can be expressed in the rights to be made real (and not just formal): to roots, to meaning, to difference without discrimination, to sociability, to place, to ethnic and regional culture, to environmental quality and homeostasis (social and natural), to alternative technology. Commitment to such an undertaking clearly means leaving behind the nation-state model and adoption of a federalist, pluralist, decentralist one, in which the national minority finds its autonomous place in a freer and balanced relationship with the local and especially the higher territorial levels of society and government (including the European Community for those in Western Europe). Existing small states are in any case being increasingly 'opened up' to more structured 'macro' relationships; there is indeed

217

little danger of parochialism being re-asserted through decentralism in today's communication- and information-rich world.

Minority nationalism, looking to the century's end and beyond, needs to have its *raison d'être* in a movement significantly wider than a narrow political nationalism whose ultimate goal is simply statehood; nor should it confound itself with social democracy, even if on some issues it finds itself on the same side against neo-liberalism. This wider movement and the pluralist, federalist option (enriched in a Proudhonion and personalist direction[41]) will serve as a guarantee for those who fear the demons of xenophobia, authoritarianism, not to say repression, lurking in any nationalism, be it ever so 'minority' – as the Northern Irish and Afrikaner cases have so clearly reminded us. In any case, political sovereignty or domination is not a special or privileged key in contemporary conditions to a national minority's social, cultural or economic future (as even the Afrikaners are now finding out, and the Ulster Unionists have largely found out). At least in the west, a fundamentalist focus on statehood will condemn minority nationalism to an increasingly archaic and isolated position, with violence a constant recourse (viz. Corsica, Euskadi, the Northern Irish Nationalists); while adoption of a social democratic perspective can only lead to loss of distinctiveness and indeed integration (viz. the UDB's fate in Brittany). It is becoming clearer that humanity itself, as well as any particular type of society (western or Socialist), needs as a resource the depth and breadth of a diversity of traditions and cultures (not to say environments and eco-systems) in order to confront an uncertain future with a multi-dimensioned, polycentric development pattern – which anyway offers a richer and more balanced quality of life. The crux of the challenge to civilisation looking to the twenty-first century, is to strike a balance between economic imperatives, the state's function, and a pluralist society in which intermediate community structures and local cultures and environments are sustained. Currently and for the forseeable future this means putting the emphasis very much on the latter, to rectify the great existing imbalance in favour of the state-market dualism and their competing quantitative expansionism. In meeting this challenge minority nationalism can have an important role as suggested above, indeed it is naturally suited to it, and is most likely in that way to secure, as far as is practically realisable, the concrete embodiment of the values it fundamentally stands for, the rights of a national minority to what is recognisably its own culture and society, with sufficient leverage, institutionally, over political and economic power to that end.

Notes

1. E. Gellner, *Nations and Nationalism*, London, 1983, pp.47 and 39.

2. ibid., p.47.
3. Uri Ra'anan, *Ethnic Resurgence in Modern Democratic States*, New York, 1979.
4. S. Rokkan and D.W. Urwin, *Economy, Territory, Identity*, London, 1983, p.17.
5. 'La Poussée Régionaliste en Europe Occidental: L'Etat-Nation en Question', *Le Monde Diplomatique*, April 1971.
6. T. Nairn, *The Break-up of Britain*, London, 1977.
7. S. Rokkan and D.W. Urwin, *Politics of Territorial Identity*, London, 1982, p.4.
8. J. Rothschild, *Ethnopolitics*, New York, 1981, p.17.
9. C.H. Williams (ed.), *National Separatism*, Cardiff, 1982.
10. A.H. Birch, 'Minority Nationalist Movements and Theories of Political Integration', *World Politics*, 1978, p.333.
11. J. Cornford (ed.), *Failure of the State*, London, 1975.
12. C.H. Williams, op.cit., p.35.
13. J. Rothschild, op.cit., pp.3–4.
14. M. Hechter, *Internal Colonialism: The Celtic Fringe in British National Development 1536–1966*, London, 1975.
15. A.H. Birch, op.cit.
16. Referred to in C.H. Williams, op.cit., p.25.
17. J.E.S. Hayward and M.M. Watson (eds), *Planning, Politics and Public Policy*, Cambridge 1975, Part IV.
18. S. Rokkan and D.W. Urwin, op.cit., *Economy, Territory and Identity*.
19. A.D. Smith, *Nationalism in the Twentieth Century*, Oxford, 1979, pp.158–9.
20. R. Guthrie and I. McLean, 'Another Part of the Periphery : Reactions to Devolution in an English Development Area', Parliamentary Affairs, 1978, p.193.
21. A.D. Smith, op.cit., pp. 163–4; also 29, 152–3 and 174–5.
22. S. Rokkan and D. Urwin, op. cit. (*Politics of Territorial Identity*), p.433.
23. McIver in C.H. Williams (ed.), op.cit., pp.303–4.
24. A.H. Birch, op.cit., pp.340 and 344.
25. Ibid., p.341.
26. The term invented by R. Dahl and C. Lindblom; see their *Politics, Economics and Welfare*, New York, 1953; also Lindblom's, *Politics and Markets*, New York, 1977.
27. R. Guthrie and I. McLean, op.cit., p.192.
28. Such themes occur in the Conservative, Socialist and Christian Democratic traditions, as well as in the nascent Green movement. See for example: R. Nisbet, *Conservatism*, Milton Keynes, 1987; M.P. Fogarty, *Christian Democracy in Western Europe*, London, 1957; B. Crick, *Socialism*, Milton Keynes, 1987; S. Hampshire and L. Kolakowski (eds), *The Socialist Idea*, London, 1974 (especially ch.4 by C. Taylor); R. Bahro, *From Red to Green*, London, 1984; J. Porritt, *Seeing Green*, Oxford, 1984.
29. This is exemplified in the direction that the philosophy of European Community regional policy has taken in the 1980s: see M. Keating and

B. Jones (eds), *Regions in the European Community*, Oxford, 1985, especially ch.2; also the Second and Third Periodic Reports of the EC Commission on *The Regions of Europe*, Brussels 1984 and 1987.

30. E. Gellner, op.cit.

31. P. Berger, *Pyramids of Sacrifice*, London, 1976, especially ch.6.

32. See M.M. Watson and D.S.C. Humphreys, 'Labour's Approach to Planning: Economics versus Politics', *West European Politics*, 1979, pp.218–36.

33. The already classic exposition of this is: F. Hirsch, *Social Limits to Growth*, London, 1977, especially Parts II and III. A discussion of Hirsch's analysis is undertaken in A. Ellis and K. Kumar (eds), *Dilemmas of Liberal Democracy*, London, 1983.

34. F. Hirsch, op.cit., Part II.

35. S. Rokkan and D.W. Urwin, op.cit. (*Economy, Territory, Identity*), p.115.

36. Simone Weil, *Need for Roots*, London, 1978; and *Oppression and Liberty*, London, 1958. Of R.H. Tawney's works, one sums up beautifully well his constructive approach to what is wrong with the economic system: 'The Conditions of Economic Liberty' in R. Hinden (ed.), *The Radical Tradition*, London, 1964.

37. S. Rokkan and D.W. Urwin, op.cit. (*Politics of Territorial Identity*), p.432.

38. P. Berger, op.cit.

39. A recent challenging examination of the full-employment paradigm is: J. Keane and J. Owens, *After Full Employment*, London, 1986.

40. The term introduced by R. Inglehart in his book, *The Silent Revolution*, Princeton, 1977; a recent article (with J.-R. Rabier) is 'Political Realignment in Advanced Industrial Society', *Government and Opposition*, Autumn, 1986.

41. This is a reference to the writings of the French political thinker, Emmanuel Mounier. Of Proudhon's works, *The Principle of Federation*, Toronto, 1979 (with Introduction by R. Vernon) is the most relevant in this context.

Name index

Subject index

www.ingramcontent.com/pod-product-compliance
Ingram Content Group UK Ltd.
Pitfield, Milton Keynes, MK11 3LW, UK
UKHW041839280225
455677UK00005B/28